FLIP

HOW TO
FIND, FIX, AND SELL
HOUSES FOR PROFIT

FLIP

HOW TO FIND, FIX, AND SELL HOUSES FOR PROFIT

RICK VILLANI AND CLAY DAVIS

McGraw-Hill

New York   Chicago   San Francisco   Lisbon   London   Madrid   Mexico City
Milan   New Delhi   San Juan   Seoul   Singapore   Sydney   Toronto

The McGraw·Hill Companies

3 4 5 6 7 8 9 0 DOC/DOC 0 9 8 7

ISBN-13: 978-0-07-148610-1
ISBN-10: 0-07-148610-0

Contents

Stage One—FIND: How to Find
Houses with Investment Potential

Stage Two—ANALYZE: How to Make an
Offer That Rewards You for Your Risk

Stage Three—BUY: How to Finance, Make an Offer, and Close on an Investment House

Stage Four—FIX: How to Plan and Manage the Construction Process

Stage Five—SELL: How to Prepare and Market an Investment House for Sale

Foreword

What are you looking for? When you picked up this book, you were looking for something. Do you know what it is? Earning extra money? Finding a new career? Starting your own business? Or maybe you're just drawn to the idea of fixing up houses.

I got into real estate when I was twenty-one years old, and I was looking for something too. At first, I thought I just wanted to make some money right out of college. Later, I discovered I also could build a career. Then, within a few years, I realized I could start my own real estate business. And I did.

As I traveled this path, something interesting happened: I found myself making a deeper and more meaningful commitment to real estate. Why? Because I realized that above all else, real estate is a virtually limitless investment opportunity.

What surprised me was how few people actually understood this. It seemed that people gave a tip of the hat to real estate when they said, "The best investment I ever made was buying my home." However, I noticed that they didn't continue to buy and sell real estate. It would seem that the purchase of one's own home was just an accidental investment. The funny thing is that what was true then is still true today: Most people are, at best, accidental investors. That's one of the reasons I decided to write the Millionaire Real Estate Investor series. Not only did I want everyone to recognize that real estate is a wonderful opportunity, I wanted people to take advantage of it.

In the summer of 2004, I started doing the research for my second book, *The Millionaire Real Estate Investor*. As part of that research, my coauthors and I interviewed over 100 millionaire investors from all walks of life and from all over North America. The group we profiled was as diverse as it was successful. I learned a lot from those conversations— more than I could fit into one book—and many of the people I talked to made a strong and lasting impression on me.

Rick and Clay are two of those people. Not only are they investors, they run a company, HomeFixers, that helps hundreds of other investors each year. What they bring to the table is hard-won brass-tacks knowledge from over fifteen years of personal investing as well as riding shotgun on over 1,000 flips with their clients. You'd be hard pressed to find anyone with greater real-world experience in the process of flipping houses.

Rick once remarked that you didn't really get good at fixing and flipping homes until you had three going at the same time. Three, it seems, was more than even the most organized investors could handle effectively without a solid, proven system to guide their actions. When I asked how many they could handle today, Rick and Clay replied that with the system they'd honed over the years, they could handle as many as ten flips at a time. That intrigued me, and I knew I wanted to get to know them better.

We continued to meet, and I discovered that they were not only excellent doers but also dedicated teachers. These were two guys who loved what they were doing and genuinely cared about helping others succeed at fixing and flipping. After getting a good look at their business, I discovered that their knowledge was as vast as their systems were well defined. They knew what they were doing. A little while later, we hatched the idea for them to share their systems and concepts with others. That was when this book, *FLIP*, was born.

I'm excited about this book. Few people know more about fixing up single-family houses for profit than Rick and Clay do. Their insights about analyzing a potential flip property will bring clarity to your decision making. You'll know when to buy and when to walk away. Their offer formula is the most practical and accurate I've seen. Once you understand it, you won't want to buy a property without it. Their step-by-step construction process alone is worth the price of the book. It'll keep you on time and on budget.

Above and beyond Rick and Clay's proven technical expertise, here's what I've come to know about them: They approach their work with integrity and enthusiasm. Their philosophy of real estate investment is shaped by both a desire to make an honest profit and a desire to do work of real worth.

It's a great honor to have Rick and Clay write this book for the Millionaire Real Estate Investor series, a book on a very important subject: how to find, fix, and flip houses for profit. If you choose to follow the map they have laid out for you, I honestly believe you will be taking a personally fulfilling and financially rewarding trip.

Enjoy the ride!

Gary Keller
Author of *The Millionaire Real Estate Agent*
and *The Millionaire Real Estate Investor*

Acknowledgments

First and foremost we want to express our gratitude to Gary Keller and the Keller Williams team for giving us the chance to write this book. We are honored to be a part of the Millionaire Real Estate Investor series and are fortunate to partner with such a professional organization. Thanks, Gary, for the opportunity and for your many contributions to this book.

Jay Papasan at Keller Williams provided tremendous support in orchestrating the project from its inception through to the end. His vision, insight, and expertise were invaluable. We cannot thank him enough for his dedication to *FLIP*.

We are grateful to Dave Jenks for the time he spent reading and editing the manuscript. He is a master of real estate and inspirational writing. We also would like to express our gratitude to others at Keller Williams who helped make *FLIP* a reality, including Jim Talbot, Jefre Outlaw, Olga Uchitel, Suman Jagdish, Dawn Sroka, and Maryanne Jordan.

A huge thank you goes to Chuck Faust for authoring the story line and characters of Samantha, Ed, Mitch, Amy, Bill, and Nancy. Chuck's dedication to understanding how real estate investors think is evident in the high-level of realism of our narratives. Many thanks to Meredith Davis for adding life and personality to the narrative characters. Thanks to Paige Hamilton, who tirelessly edited and reedited, making *FLIP* a better book.

The HomeFixers team was immensely supportive in helping us juggle the tasks of writing a book while running a business. We offer special thanks to Rebekah Kern for her commitment both to HomeFixers and to us. We couldn't have done it without her! We also give thanks to Chris Glass for the keen insight and creativity that helped shape many of the concepts in *FLIP*.

A special thanks to our HomeFixers affiliates Chuck Whiteside, James and Dangela Hill, Andy and Cindy Davies, and Greg and Eursula Clarkson. These guys make their livelihood in real estate investing. Their knowledge and wisdom were immensely valuable in helping us present a comprehensive view of flipping houses.

We would like to thank the craftsmen and trades who have helped build HomeFixers over the years and kept it going while we wrote this book—you are like family to us: Mike Yazalina, John Wrigley, Camille Sales, Jeff Ashmore, Ken Pacha, Matt York, and Jim Tersigni of Carpet Stop; Tobin Carpenter, Rey Cyr, Duane Moore, Marvin Vanicek, Walter Williams, Lita Gordon, Robert Andres, James Dorman, Fernando Hernandez, Brandon Jolly, Marcus Ramirez, Gary Weaver, Terry French, Mike Edwards, Jay Burleson, and the folks at BMC; Don Smith and the crew at Trim Tech; Ken and the staff at Texas Re-Key; Randy and Pete McQuiston at Fiberglass Waterproof Systems; Tiburcio Garcia, Steven Hays, Bob Knox, Jeff Tucker, Jack, and Terri at Custom Quality Marble; the team at Gold Star Cabinets; Rhonda and Kent at Parrish & Co.; and George Celtrick for his hardwood flooring expertise.

Thanks to our supportive customers Avery Carpenter, Ellis San Jose, Marcus Hsia, Kary Aycock, Phill Grove, Shenoah Peck, Rene Lafair, John Harris, Robert Grunnah, Stacy Cunningham, Michael Spickes, David Foster, Justine Smith, and Marilyn Williams. Special thanks to Jay Otto, who generously gave his time, lent his expertise, and shared stories that only a veteran real estate investor of twenty-five-plus years could amass. And thanks to HomeVestors franchise owners Rick and Suzanne Edson, Pete Pesoli, and

John Holman, who have been a huge support to HomeFixers over the years.

We would be remiss if we didn't thank the late Ken D'Angelo, founder of HomeVestors, whose creative genius transformed and legitimized an industry literally from bandit signs to billboards. It was Ken who gave us the initial encouragement to expand our model of "predictable rehabbing" across the nation.

Thanks to Mary Glenn, our editor, and McGraw-Hill for their support. We are grateful to Daina Penikas, who skillfully shepherded *FLIP* from raw manuscript to bound book, and to Seth Morris, who ran point on the marketing.

There are many others who edited, advised, and supported us during this time, including Wendy Papasan, Cameron Tankersley, Cristina Valdes, Dianne Faust, Rudy Gutierrez, Bob Guest, Jim McClarty, Robert McKee, Rick Hair, Damon Jamieson, Karen Lear, Ted Lear, Sherri Williams, Angelique Naylor, Leslie Ray, Dave Merhar, Susan Graham, Bill Temple, Ann Temple, David Temple, Brian Russell, Ed Frank, P.E. and inspectamerica.com, Curt Bilby, Greg Herring, Tod Klubnik, John Hayes, Steve Wells, Kent Presnell, Russ Stolle, Scott Taylor, Joyce Mazero, Rob Lauer, Chris Willis, Jeff Powers, Kenneth Hausmann, Tim Clarkson, Jack and Gayle Little, and Marvin and Sharen Eggleston.

From Rick: I am deeply thankful for Carrie, my wife of twenty-one years and my best friend since high school. She continues to put up with my "great" ideas and my propensity to be consumed with giving them life. Emily, Jack, and Anne, our children, have been a huge support, giving us words of encouragement, water bottles, midnight snacks, and much-needed diversions. I am thankful for my late father Tony Villani, who dedicated his life to real estate, and my mother, Diane Spinosa, who is never far from her sketch pad and graph paper. I thank Larry Spinosa, who is a second father and mentor to me. Thanks to my brother, Tony Villani, and my sister, Susan Presnell, for their constant support. Finally,

I want to give special recognition and thanks to Clay Davis, my business partner and friend. Without his determination, focus, and perseverance, this book would not have been written.

From Clay: First, I thank my wife, Meredith, the love of my life. Her unwavering dedication, love, and support for me are more than I could ever deserve. I offer special thanks to my children, Alayna, Nate, and Benji. Their encouraging words, notes, and prayers were an inspiration on many late nights. Thanks to my parents, Maurice and Peggy Davis, and my brother, Craig Davis, for their encouragement, support, and advice. I thank Rick for making this opportunity possible and putting his confidence in me. His vision and perseverance in the formative years of HomeFixers laid the foundation for *FLIP*.

Finally, we both give thanks to God, from whom all blessings flow.

Rick

Clay

—Rick Villani and Clay Davis

Introduction

WHATEVER HAPPENED TO THE HAUNTED HOUSE?

Close your eyes and think back to when you were a kid. Do you remember that run-down, overgrown house at the far end of the street that you walked by fast? The one that was clearly neglected, possibly not lived in, and certainly unloved. The one that when you asked your folks about it, your dad muttered something about "bulldozing that eyesore" and your mom pointed her finger, warning you to "stay away from there." It was the house where you and your friends rode your bikes to its weedy front yard and dared each other to enter. Double-dared. Triple-dog-dared. No way. For every kid, that was the classic "haunted house."

There was a time when those houses were everywhere. Virtually every neighborhood had one—often vacant and always uncared for—the source of childhood mysteries. But think for a minute: When was the last time you actually saw one?

They're still out there, but it's a lot less common these days to find a dilapidated house in the middle of an otherwise vibrant neighborhood. Why? The "haunted" house has become the "wanted" house. In the early

1990s, real estate investing reached a whole new level. There was a burst of activity driven by independent investors, working on their own, who recognized the opportunity to buy those houses, fix them up, and sell them for a profit. They decided to build their wealth on Main Street instead of Wall Street, and their strategy worked.

Those investors learned the art of flipping a house for a profit, and that is what this book is about. Although today haunted houses—glaringly obvious candidates for flipping—are not as common, the opportunity has absolutely not gone away. There always will be houses that with the right attention, following the right strategy, can create a profitable flip.

Most people are aware of this investment opportunity, and many have even thought about doing it themselves. A lot fewer actually do. Why? It may be that they have the same feeling they had as small kids standing in front of a haunted house—*fear*. They may feel they can't do it. They've never tackled anything like this before. What if it costs more than they planned to fix it up? What if it doesn't sell? What if, in fact, they lose money?

We don't want any fears standing in the way of your taking advantage of this time-tested financial opportunity. Here's what we know. When you understand the FLIP process and formula for buying, rehabbing, and selling houses for a profit, the fear goes away—and excitement takes its place.

EXPERIENCE IS THE BEST TEACHER

At some point in the process of finding, fixing, and flipping houses, all investors are going to encounter at least one problem for which their personal experience hasn't prepared them. Sometimes those problems are as bad as they seem, but most of the time they're not. The key is how well you anticipate the problems, how ready you are to deal with them, and who you have to help you get through them.

That's where this book comes in. We can't find, fix, or sell houses for you, and we certainly can't predict every problem you'll encounter. What we can do is give you a proven formula, a step-by-step process, and real-world advice based on our extensive experience. To that end, we've covered both the practical and the technical aspects of flipping a house. We've also tried to convey the real-life lows and highs of flipping houses, with all the accompanying smells, sights, and sounds.

Some say that experience is the best teacher. You can learn from your own experience or from someone else's. The question is, whose comes first? This book asks you to learn from our experience first. With the experience of over a thousand flips condensed into this book, by the time you finish it, we believe you'll feel like you already have several rehabs under your belt.

WHY WE FLIP OVER THE FLIP

It is our heartfelt intention to provide you with the best guide to buying, fixing, and selling houses. We are passionate about this because we're convinced that flipping houses is one of the best real estate investing strategies available. Consider the six reasons why we flip over the flip.

1. *Flipping generates cash.* Buying, fixing, and selling houses is a quick way to earn money. Done once, a flip creates cash. Done a lot, it creates cash flow. Both put money in your bank account.

2. *Flipping is a short-term venture.* Flipping a house, when done properly, often is accomplished within a few months. This means that if you try it and like it, you can do it again and again. If you decide it's not for you, you're not tied to a long-term commitment. Additionally, you get immediate feedback on your performance, allowing you to learn quickly and build on your growing expertise.

3. *Flipping works in any market.* Why? Because it's about following a process, and that process isn't tied to any specific market or any particular time period. Your success in buying, fixing, and reselling houses comes primarily from finding value (buying a house below retail market value) and creating value (making improvements that increase the selling price beyond their cost). Finding and creating value always works whether your market is cold, lukewarm, or just plain hot.

4. *Flipping can be done part-time.* We know many successful investors who earn tens of thousands of dollars by flipping part-time, and we recommend that everyone start out that way. Then, as you build success and confidence, you'll always have the option of staying part-time or going full-time. Flipping works either way.

5. *Flipping doesn't require a lot of your own money.* In investing, when you find the right opportunity, the money will find you, and that's never been more true than in real estate investing. Lenders know that good real estate deals make good loan opportunities; that is why there are many institutional and private lenders willing to back rehab investors, even first-timers. If you bring them the right deal, they will finance it.

6. *Flipping is available to anyone.* It is an equal opportunity investment choice. Flipping doesn't care who you are, how much you make, where you live, or what you do. If you can find a house worth flipping, you can finance it and thus the opportunity is available to you.

WHY WE WROTE THIS BOOK

What's in this book is the information we would put in the hands of all real estate investors *before* they buy a house. We've been flipping since the early 1990s, and now, in addition to our own investing, we consult with investors across the country as well as the builders who work with them. During this time, it has become clear to us that there is a need for a practical, systematic approach to flipping. There are too many investors out there at risk because they don't follow a step-by-step proven process. In fact, after poring over the available books, we found that very little has been written on how to do it in the most organized and profitable way. Therefore, we developed a finely tuned approach that has saved our clients hundreds of thousands of dollars (and made them even more). Now we want to share that approach with you.

Maybe you're looking for a satisfying activity to complement your day job. Or maybe you are contemplating a change of career and are drawn to the opportunity of real estate investing. Either way, we want you flipping over flipping houses too.

Overview

A Game of Skill

To people who have never studied the game of poker, it can seem like a terribly risky enterprise. After all, huge sums of money are won and lost depending on which cards are dealt. Surely, they think, poker is all about luck or nerve. They call it gambling, and for some people it is. But the truth is, for others it is not.

As David Sklansky writes in his classic work *A Theory of Poker*, "poker is not primarily a game of luck. It is a game of skill." There is a formula for success, and the numbers tell you what to do. All poker professionals will tell you that the vast majority of their work consists of calculating the exact mathematical likelihood that a particular hand will play out in their favor. If the numbers aren't right, they wait. Sometimes they wait for a long time, but when they play a hand, they expect to win. The numbers tell them that they should.

Successful flipping works the same way. You have a formula for success, and if a potential investment doesn't make the grade, you pass. And you keep passing until you find a property where the numbers say it will work. Following systems reduces the risk and improves your chance of success. The best flippers—those who win consistently—have and follow a proven system.

For some, poker is gambling, but for the consistent winners, it's not. For some, flipping is gambling, but for the consistent winners, it's not.

We owe our success to a system we created based on our own experiences and the best practices of successful real estate investors. It will help you recognize the best deals and have the discipline to pass on the bad ones. It will help you protect your profits through the improvement process. And it will help you sell houses for top dollar. In short, our proven model is designed to take the risk out of the game.

How to Flip a House

The core of our system is a five-stage model for how to flip a house, and it's the organizing principle around which this book is constructed. But let's stop for a moment and make sure we're all on the same page. Flipping can mean different things to different people, and so we want to be clear about what we mean.

We define flipping as buying houses under value, fixing them up, and selling them for a profit. Others think it's about buying a property and then immediately turning it for a quick profit. Both work when they are done well. But we'll really zero in on the fix and flip in these pages. We believe that if you can do that, you're better prepared to do both.

Figure 1 provides a brief summary of all five of the stages, along with an explanation of what you'll take away from the corresponding parts of the book.

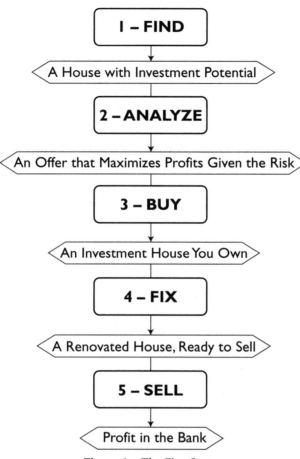

Figure 1 The Five Stages

STAGE 1: FIND

At the beginning of this stage, you'll develop your specific investment criteria for selecting a house, including price range, acceptable condition, and location. At the heart of this stage, you'll create and implement a plan to uncover likely investment properties, which you'll approve or reject by applying your criteria. Most properties won't make the cut, but those which do will move forward to the Analyze stage.

Outcome: A house with investment potential

STAGE 2: ANALYZE

Once you're standing in front of a house that meets your criteria, the real testing begins. You'll need to make decisions about exactly which improvements to make to maximize your profit, create a thorough and accurate improvement budget, and determine what you can sell the house for once it's been fixed up. By crunching these numbers, you'll emerge with a workable offer.

Outcome: An offer that maximizes profits given the risk

STAGE 3: BUY

Beginning with your offer to the seller, this stage represents the last opportunity to abandon a flip. After negotiating an accepted offer, you'll bring in professionals to perform a final examination of the house, including a professional inspector and possibly an appraiser to verify the numbers. If everything checks out, you'll close on the house and move on to the Fix stage.

Outcome: An investment house you own

STAGE 4: FIX

The improvement budget you created in the Analyze stage is the basis for the step-by-step construction plan you'll create in this stage. We can't overstate the importance of the Fix. Your profit depends directly on your ability to implement the plan quickly and thoroughly. Any serious miscalculation has the potential to make your profit diminish or even disappear, and so following a step-by-step improvement process is critical.

Outcome: A renovated house that is ready to sell

STAGE 5: SELL

If you found a good buy, performed the proper analysis (one that includes a realistic selling price), and executed your construction plan successfully, you are set up for success in this final stage. By adding good marketing and some well-chosen finishing touches, you'll be able to maximize the profit from your flip.

Outcome: Profit in the bank

These five stages represent the five different hats you'll wear during a flip. Each represents a major area of focus as well as a skill set you'll learn.

HOW MANY PEOPLE DOES IT TAKE TO FLIP A HOUSE?

As you move through the five stages, you'll quickly discover that there are three resources that you'll need again and again. Actually, they are the timeless resources required for any endeavor: time, talent, and treasure. You may have all three, but chances are that you don't. That's okay. Flipping houses is almost by definition a team effort. If you don't have one of the three, you will always be able to team up with someone who does.

This means you'll have to take a good long look at yourself to make an honest personal assessment. How much time can you devote to flipping? What skills do you bring to the table? Finally, how much money do you have available to invest? This is not some touchy-feely attempt to get in touch with your "inner home flipper." Knowing the answers to those questions is absolutely crucial if you're going to make a profit flipping houses.

Finding, fixing, and eventually selling a rehab property can happen in just a few months from start to finish, but it will require time and attention while the flip is in progress. But it doesn't have to be *your* time. Some prefer to invest their personal time to save money and build "sweat equity" during a rehab. Others prefer to supervise while others perform the work. Clearly defining and understanding the time it will take to rehab a property is critical to your success and will allow you to plan your time accordingly. The same line of thinking applies to talent and treasure as well. If you don't have the talent to do something, you can find someone who does. If you don't have the necessary treasure, you can seek out a partner who is willing to finance your flip.

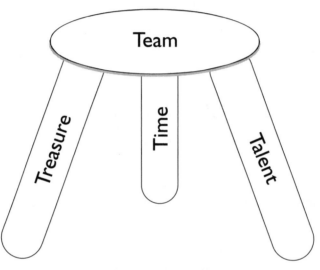

Figure 2   Your Real Estate Investment Platform

Any stable platform requires three supports (Figure 2). Think of time, talent, and treasure as the three legs on which your real estate investment platform is built. And think of the team as the opportunity to pull in additional help when you need it.

THE SCHOOL OF HARD KNOCKS

Now that we've discussed what you need to do (the five-stage model) and the resources you need to get it done (time, talent, and treasure), there's one last gap we want to fill: the gap between theory and practice.

Our five-stage model didn't come from sitting around the office brainstorming. It came from years of personal investing and riding shotgun on over 1,000 flips. Some were wildly successful, and a few were anything but. We have absolute faith in our model, but there's no way a how-to description of the process can substitute for the actual experience, any more than reading a recipe can replace baking a cake.

In addition to the practical, we've gathered what we know about flipping houses into a narrative story called "The Millionaire Real Estate Investors Club" that runs throughout this book. Essentially, *FLIP* is two books in one: the practical and the experiential. You'll find a narrative chapter at the end of each stage that illustrates the emotional side of flipping and describes some real-life situations for which how-to simply doesn't cut it. Essentially everything that happens to the people in these narratives has happened either to our customers or to us.

The characters in the story line represent the types of investor customers we work with every day. First, there's Bill and Nancy, the retired couple ready to start a second career. There's also Samantha, a Fortune 500 professional who is tired of managing a boardroom and eager to try her hand at managing a worksite. Finally, you'll meet Mitch and Amy, a young couple with a knack for home improving who will do a lot of the work themselves. Your guide through the story will be Ed, a veteran flipper who seems to know our model by heart. Each character brings his or her unique mix of time, talent, and treasure (as do all our customers) and faces his or her own challenges along the way.

We believe that by taking these two approaches to teaching our model, we'll have done the best job possible to prepare you for success. Ready? Let's get started.

"You're fired!" Mitch screamed as he slammed the phone down.

It wasn't supposed to be like this. Flipping a house seemed so much easier on those television shows. Of course, on TV they didn't have to deal with Frankie, the contractor who promised to finish the kitchen tile two days ago. Frankie, who picks up the phone only once out of every ten calls. Mitch and his wife, Amy, were running out of time and money. They had to get this house finished soon and sell it quickly.

Mitch grabbed his keys and mumbled something about having to "do it himself" as he stormed out of the house.

He was spending almost two hours a day, every day, driving to and from this place. That was time he could be spending doing something else, *anything* else. His head was throbbing, and he tried to calm down by listening to the radio as he made the long drive to the house.

Mitch reached for the radio. It was 9 p.m.; maybe listening to the Braves could take the edge off.

Tie game, two outs, bottom of the ninth, winning run on second and the cleanup batter at the plate for the Mets.

At times he rued the day they decided to form a real estate investment club with Ed, Samantha, Bill, and Nancy. That was the start of almost four months of frustration for Amy and him. A *millionaire* investment club: What were we thinking?

The Braves closer comes set and delivers strike one.

Ed. The man was a house-flipping guru. He warned against investing in a house that was too far away. Man, I should have listened.

Here's the 0–1 pitch; the batter swings and misses, strike two.

Samantha. Why did everything seem to come so easy for her?

Here comes the 0–2 pitch. It's low and away, ball one.

Bill and Nancy. They were going for a fast, lean fix-up and doing none of the work themselves. Next time, he and Amy would do it more that way, although he had to admit that Amy's and his house looked way better than Bill and Nancy's. But the nicer they made it look, the more it cost. And to keep the project on budget, Mitch found himself doing far more of the actual work than he originally had planned.

The 1–2 pitch. Fouled into the bleachers.

Between his job as a firefighter, the long drive to the property, and all the manual labor he was doing, he was physically and mentally exhausted.

Here's the 1–2 pitch. There's a drive to deep right field; it's to the warning track and gone. That's the game, folks. Mets win.

"Figures." He hit the next station. Daniel Powter's "Had a Bad Day" was playing. He pulled in the empty driveway, parked the car, but left the headlights on to illuminate the front door until he could get it open.

Frankie claimed to have finished about half of the kitchen tile, so if Mitch was lucky, he'd be finished, back home and in bed by 2 a.m. Mitch fumbled with the lock, stepped inside the door, threw the switch and gasped, "Oh no!"

Four Months Earlier

Having risen to the position of marketing director at a Fortune 500 company, Samantha was sharp, precise, and very demanding of herself and others. Despite her success, she just didn't enjoy the job anymore. It was time to try something different.

As the waiter passed out menus, Samantha studied the others at the table. Mitch and Amy were young and enthusiastic. Bill had introduced himself as a retired Marine, and his wife Nancy seemed quiet and supportive. Samantha hadn't quite figured out Ed. He hadn't said much. He looked relaxed and confident—the opposite of everyone else.

"Okay," Samantha said, pulling up her chair. "We have an interesting group here, and I guess it would be a good idea to see why we all want to get into the house-flipping business. How about you, Amy and Mitch? What's your story?"

Mitch glanced at Amy, who nodded for him to go ahead. "After we bought our first home, I found that I actually enjoyed doing a lot of the renovations myself. I'm a Saturday regular at The Home Depot, checking out the latest power tools and buying materials for our next project. Amy and I love watching those home fix-up shows where they transform a room or two, but what we've really gotten into are the ones where they show people fixing up and flipping houses.

"Amy and I figured that we could probably do as good a job as the people on those shows—and they all seem to make pretty good money. I'm a firefighter, and the rotating shifts give me nice chunks of free time. We thought buying and fixing up houses could help us earn some extra money and would be something we could work on together." He smiled at Amy.

"I'm an elementary school art teacher," Amy said, "I've done a little interior design work for friends and family during my free time in the summer. I could see myself starting my own interior design business some day. If Mitch and I can get something like this up and running, it will give me some great design experience."

Samantha liked the couple already. Mitch's interest was genuine, and Amy's excitement about making a job switch was something with which she could identify.

"So now it's your turn, Samantha," Amy prompted. "Why are you interested in flipping houses?"

"Oh, I've spent way too much time on planes," Samantha replied. "I'm tired of traveling. This is something I can do that will let me stay close to home. Bill, Nancy—what brings you two here?"

"Not so fast." Nancy smiled. "You're not going to get off that easy. Tell us about your work. Are you married? Hobbies? C'mon, let's have some details."

Samantha shrugged, "There really isn't much to tell. I've been in the software business for almost 20 years, ever since I got out of college. I'm an avid runner, and no, I've never been married." Samantha shifted in her seat and pointedly turned to Bill and Nancy, "What about the two of you?"

Bill seemed more than ready to start. His voice was deep and low, but more than that, it had a tone that made people want to listen when he spoke. The group at the table looked up from their menus. "When I turned eighteen, I did two things right." Bill counted them off with his fingers. "First, I enlisted in the Marines. And second, before I got shipped off to my first tour in Vietnam, I married my high-school sweetheart." His blue eyes twinkled as he looked over at Nancy, "That was forty years ago last week."

There was general murmur of approval from around the table. Wow, Samantha thought, forty years.

Bill gestured toward Ed. "During my second tour, I served with Ed's father, Mark. He's a good man and a great Marine. After the war, I worked my way up through the ranks to master sergeant and have been in the corps ever since."

"Well, at least until this year," Nancy piped in. "When he retired."

Bill nodded and continued. "We always talked about fixing up houses. Now that I'm retired, we thought it might be fun—and profitable—to give this thing a try. Besides, I'm too young to sit around the house doing nothing."

Nancy looked over at Bill. "I wouldn't know what to do with him; it would drive me crazy."

Bill set his coffee cup down on its saucer. "Anyway, we decided to settle down in this area to be closer to our kids."

"And grandkids," Nancy added.

"Once we got settled in, I gave my old buddy Mark a call and told him about our plans," Bill said. "He suggested that I come to tonight's real estate investment meeting to meet Ed. Nancy and I are glad Samantha suggested that we all have dinner together. Ed, why don't you bring everyone up to speed on yourself?"

Ed set down the menu he had been holding. "Well, there isn't too much to tell," he said, glancing around the table. Everyone was interested to hear his story. "I grew up in construction working summers for my dad."

"Ed's dad is one of the big developers in town," Bill interrupted.

"That's right. After I finished school, it seemed like a good idea to go into the same sort of business—with my own twist, of course. I've been a builder for about fifteen years, and I especially enjoy finding and buying fixer-uppers and then renovating and reselling them. Bill and my dad are lifelong friends. I was glad to be able to offer advice when he told me Bill and Nancy were interested in getting into real estate investing."

Samantha looked at Ed more closely. Ed had seemed different from the others at the meeting because he *was* different: He had experience flipping houses. She couldn't stop herself from asking, "How many houses have you fixed up and sold?"

"At last count, just over a hundred," Ed replied.

"One hundred? Impressive," Samantha said.

The group's attention shifted as the waitress approached their table, "Are you ready to order, or do you need a little more time?" she asked.

"A couple more minutes" said Bill. Turning back to the group, he said, "How about a toast? To us rookies—and even Ed—may we all make a boatload of cash." Glasses clinked all around.

"Yeah," Mitch chimed in. "To the Millionaire Real Estate Investors Club."

"Hey, I like the sound of that," Amy said. There was some laughter. "No, I mean it. Let's be a club. We can get together after the monthly investor meetings like we did tonight to check in with each other and share ideas."

"Great idea. Maybe Ed would come to the meetings too and give us some tips," Amy added.

"Sure, a lot of people helped me get started. It'd be happy to share what I know," Ed said.

"So, it's decided," Bill said. "Ed, what's the first order of business?"

"Well, the question I get asked most often is, 'How do you find those houses?' So that's where we'll start."

Stage One

FIND

How to Find Houses with Investment Potential

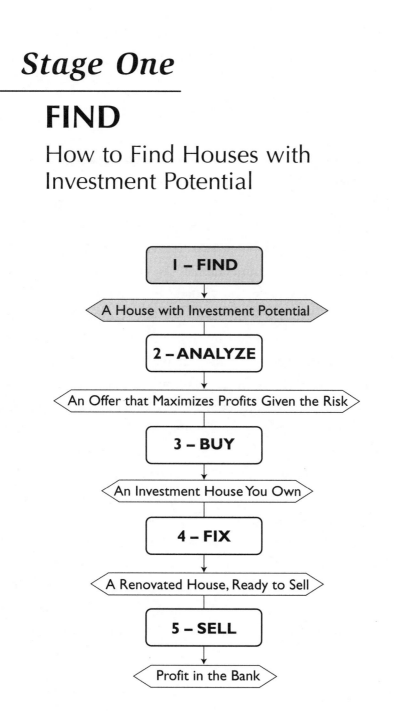

FIND INTRODUCTION

That which we persist in doing becomes easier,
not that the task itself has become easier,
but that our ability to perform it has improved.

—Ralph Waldo Emerson

When we think about finding investment houses, we are reminded of a story about going after big-game fish. Howell Raines, the former executive editor of *The New York Times*, enlisted his close friend Tennant McWilliams to join him on a fishing trip to the Christmas Islands in the South Pacific. They hired a guide and headed offshore in search of big-game fish. The hours passed. As conventional tackle and methods proved fruitless, their initial excitement waned. Just before heading in, their guide suggested that they try the unique approach of trolling an inexpensive billfish fly using a 10-weight fly rod. Amazingly, before long, Raines hooked a large and powerful Pacific blue marlin.

They labored throughout the day, holding on and chasing the fish and patiently waiting for it to exhaust itself. Near the end of a seven-plus-hour struggle (and nearly sinking their wooden skiff), Raines wrote, "Tired as I was, I believed, again, that something wonderful was going to happen. We had waited for it and it was going to happen. We were going to catch this fish. . . . I was going to touch its shoulders, which would be as glossy and deeply colored as a lacquered Chinese box."

When nothing seems to work, what is the motivation to stay out there for "just one more cast"? The joy is in the pursuit; it's the anticipation that at any moment the strike will come. For those of us in real estate investing, the big strike usually comes after months of preparation and hard work. The phone rings. You answer. And the person on the other end of the line says, "I need to sell my house." You are ready to see exactly what kind of fish you have on the line.

The Find stage has three distinct steps. First, you'll identify the neighborhoods that have investment houses. Second, you'll network, advertise, and prospect to generate leads from those target neighborhoods. And third, you'll qualify leads to ensure that they are worth further investigation. In short, we are going to teach you how to fish: where to cast, what bait to use, and how to hook the big one.

Now, before we get into ways to find houses, let's talk about what exactly we're looking for. A good investment house possesses these three elements:

1. The house needs updating and/or repair.
2. It is in an area of town where people want to live.
3. The owner is motivated to sell for under market value.

Chapter 1
Define Your Target

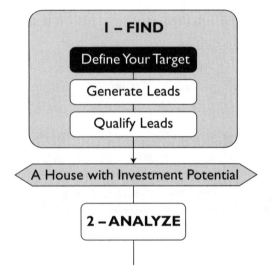

After reading this chapter you will know how to

- Target investment neighborhoods
- Determine what elements make a good target neighborhood
- Select the target neighborhoods that are right for you

Would you buy investment properties in Kathmandu? Unless you live in Nepal, you probably don't have to think too long about your answer. And if someone pressed you for an explanation, it would be easy to come up with some practical reasons why not: It's too far away. It's too difficult to travel there. And what do you know about the Nepalese real estate market, anyway?

When successful real estate investors make decisions about where to search for investment properties, they apply some of the same reasoning you just did in ruling out Kathmandu.

In this chapter you will learn how to use a set of tried and true targeting criteria to determine the target neighborhoods that will give you the best profit potential for flips. In essence, you'll learn how to create a personal house-buying bull's-eye.

Defining target neighborhoods is a two-step process. In the first step, you'll identify the various factors that go into evaluating a neighborhood. We call these factors your *targeting criteria*. Some will be proven *investment* criteria; others will be more *personal* criteria. In the second step, you'll apply the criteria to choose your target neighborhoods (Figure 1-1).

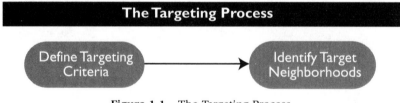

Figure 1-1   The Targeting Process

WHY TARGET?

Targeting neighborhoods helps you focus your resources so that you can find the best possible investment property leads. Those efforts can be time-consuming and costly—all the more reason to identify and target the neighborhoods with the greatest potential for success (Figure 1-2).

The Five Benefits of Defining Target Neighborhoods	
1. Lower Cost Per Qualified Lead	Your money is focused on maximizing high quality leads and minimizing the unwanted ones.
2. Less Time Qualifying Leads	You spend less time filtering and rejecting unwanted leads.
3. Find Houses Quicker	You become an expert in your target neighborhoods enabling quicker assessment of what houses sell for and what they cost to fix up.
4. Buy More Houses	You will have more qualified leads which means more house-buying opportunities.
5. Buy the Most Profitable Houses	You can be choosey about what deals to take because you have more leads to choose from.

Figure 1-2   The Five Benefits of Defining Target Neighborhoods

We can't emphasize enough how important it is to target neighborhoods and become an expert on the properties found in them. Your decision making will be clear, confident, and quick. Even the best investors sometimes make avoidable mistakes when they invest in areas with which they are not familiar.

We've learned this lesson firsthand. We once bought a house that was literally just a few hundred yards outside one of our hot target neighborhoods where we'd done about a dozen rehabs. We were able to get the house at such a low price that we thought we'd have no problem making a good profit. But we didn't do our homework—the house was across a major highway. The rules that governed our target neighborhood simply did not extend to this area. Selling prices were falling and nicely remodeled houses were non-existent. Eleven months later, the house finally sold resulting in a profit of less than $1,000.

What Makes a Good Target Neighborhood?

It's worth pointing out that we're not necessarily talking about "hot" neighborhoods that are increasing in value rapidly. Flipping houses is primarily about buying at a great price and adding value with well-chosen improvements. If you also benefit from the appreciation of the house's value during the time you hold it, that's an added bonus. Just remember that if you rely on appreciation to make your profit, you are acting like a speculator, not an investor. As an investor, when you look for investment potential in different areas, you'll consider a variety of factors. The six most important ones we call The Six Neighborhood Targeting Criteria (Figure 1-3).

The Six Neighborhood Targeting Criteria

1. Proximity of the neighborhood to your work and home.

2. Selling prices of the homes in the neighborhood.

3. Sales activity of the homes in the neighborhood.

4. Ages of the homes in the neighborhood.

5. Appeal and charm of the neighborhood.

6. Safety of the neighborhood.

Figure 1-3 The Six Neighborhood Targeting Criteria

1. Proximity

It is important to keep in mind that during the weeks or months that you're working on an investment house, you'll probably need to be there on a regular basis. Choosing a house in a distant neighborhood will take a toll on your ability to monitor or participate in the rehab. If you have the flexibility and free time to travel across town—or even across the country—by all means, go for it. But if you don't, you should absolutely consider keeping your projects close to home.

2. Selling Price

Flipping an expensive house certainly has the potential to be more profitable than flipping a less expensive one, but it takes more money. You need the capital not only to purchase the home but also to fund the high-end rehab improvements. And these improvements take time, during which you'll have to pay taxes, insurance, interest payments, and other holding costs. There are people who will lend you money to flip a house, but there's a limit to how much you can realistically borrow (we'll cover this in the Buy stage). You don't want to waste time focusing on neighborhoods where the average price is beyond your ability to purchase, hold, and improve a property.

In contrast, the investment challenge in low-end markets lies in being able to buy the property, do the required improvements, and still have a margin of profit that makes it worth the risk. In addition, there tends to be a much smaller pool of interested and qualified buyers for these low-end homes.

One of the biggest factors in maximizing your profits on a flip is how fast the house sells: Every day you hold a house costs you money. Ideally, you want to sell the house in three weeks or less. So everything you do and every decision you make is geared toward the outcome of a quick sale. In general, the more potential buyers there are, the faster a good house will sell. You'll have the largest number of potential buyers if your house is near or just below the median home price in the area (Figure 1-4) and that is a great price point to target.

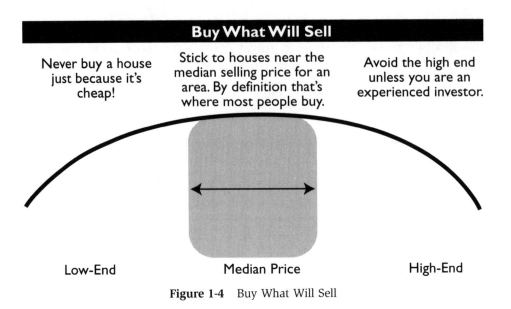

Buy What Will Sell

Never buy a house just because it's cheap!

Stick to houses near the median selling price for an area. By definition that's where most people buy.

Avoid the high end unless you are an experienced investor.

Low-End   Median Price   High-End

Figure 1-4   Buy What Will Sell

3. SALES ACTIVITY

The desirability of a particular area of town can be measured quantitatively by analyzing current housing sales information. Sales activity is a great indicator of a good target neighborhood. Houses just seem to sell faster in some sections of town, while for-sale signs linger in others. In this section, we'll explore the data that will help you understand what makes these neighborhoods attractive to buyers and which can help you determine whether a neighborhood is desirable for real estate investing.

To evaluate current sales activity in a neighborhood thoroughly, you probably will need a real estate agent, who has access to your city's Multiple Listing Service (MLS), to run some reports for you. The MLS is a membership database service developed by and exclusively for licensed real estate brokers and their agents. A good real estate agent will be an invaluable member of your team. In general, real estate agents like working with investors because serious investors buy and sell multiple houses in shorter time frames than most home buyers. Every business loves repeat customers.

The MLS data will provide a detailed picture of what has transpired over the last year or so in terms of market activity in your target neighborhoods. Figure 1-5 shows the nine key areas of information you can ask a real estate agent to investigate about the houses for sale or that have sold in a particular geographic location. When you see sales activity or a lack of it, you will want to understand the cause behind it. These nine areas should provide that insight.

The Nine Key Areas of MLS Information

1. Square footage

2. Price per square foot

3. Property taxes

4. Year built

5. Sales prices

6. Days on market and days to sell

7. Features (bedrooms, bathrooms, living and dining areas, etc.)

8. Amenities (garages, decks, pools, basements, etc.)

9. Neighborhood schools

Figure 1-5 The Nine Key Areas of MLS Information

You want to invest in neighborhoods where a fixed-up house won't sit on the market for months. When you target a geographic area, you'll want to have a good handle on which houses are for sale and why they haven't sold, as well as which ones have sold and why they did. The MLS can provide important underlying data about this sales activity, such as the number of houses on the market and how many are pending for sale and/or have been sold in the last year. In addition, you can see the average number of days these houses were on the market before they sold. In an active neighborhood, houses can routinely sell within a few weeks. In an inactive neighborhood, homes can stay on the market for months.

One particularly interesting bit of data you can gather from the MLS is the selling price per square foot (a 1,000-square-foot house that sold for $100,000 had a sales price of $100 per foot). Why? Selling price per square foot gives you a way to compare the relative value of houses of approximately equal size. For instance, when two houses of similar size are priced very differently, you will want to understand what is causing the difference. This may indicate an investment opportunity.

Specifically, you're looking for neighborhoods with two clusters of house values: a group of homes that sold for a relatively low price per square foot and another group that sold for a higher price per square foot. The first group represents your pool of potential investment properties; the second group indicates that there could be a market for flipping houses (see Figure 1-6).

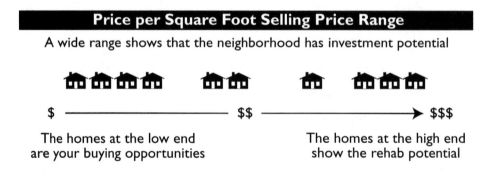

Figure 1-6   Price per Square Foot Selling Price Range

For example, a neighborhood with a group of homes that sold at $100 per square foot and another group that sold at $200 per square foot looks attractive. The range of $100 per square foot means that some 1,000-square-foot houses are selling for $100,000 whereas other houses the same size are selling for twice that price.

A quick word of caution. If there is no group at the high end, you need to consider carefully whether you want to be the first investor to push the limit on price per square foot in the neighborhood. If you find that there aren't many houses with a relatively low price per square foot, you may want to consider whether other investors have been there before you so that now the opportunities are limited.

4. AGE

The age of a house can be a plus or a minus. If a house is too old, the repairs may be too expensive. On the other hand, a house in an older, established neighborhood is likely to have been owned longer, and that can translate to higher owner equity. This makes it easier for the owner to sell for less than market value because he or she has paid off a substantial portion of the mortgage. If a house is too new, there might not be enough opportunity for improvement and the owner may not have built up enough equity to accept a lower offer.

FLIPPING POINT

There is a limit in this consideration of the age of houses. Older is not always better. One can assume that a 20-year-old home is fairly easy to update with paint, fixtures, flooring, appliances, and perhaps a new roof, while a 100-year-old home that needs updating may require that the entire plumbing and electrical systems be brought up to code. If you have ever had to replace the old wiring throughout a historical home, you know how expensive and challenging that can be.

Here are some general rules of thumb to follow when targeting neighborhoods by age for flipping potential:

- The houses should be older (twenty-plus years is best).
- Some of the houses should show signs of aging. This includes dated or distressed paint, siding, fascias, exterior trim, roof, doors, windows, garage doors, driveways, walkways, fencing, and the yard. These are your opportunities to improve.

As you evaluate a neighborhood on the basis of its age, you'll always need to balance the benefit of increased owner equity with the risk of the extensive repairs that often are needed in aging homes.

5. APPEAL

One of the most important investment criteria is the general appeal of the location. In short, you must invest in neighborhoods *where people want to live*. We are talking about finding neighborhoods that are family-friendly; are close to retail, office, and recreational areas; and have schools with good reputations.

Remember, the adage "location, location, location" never loses its truth. The same type of home in a great neighborhood versus one in a less desirable neighborhood always commands a higher price.

You'll want your target neighborhoods to have as many as possible of the factors shown in Figure 1-7.

6. SAFETY

There are two safety issues you will be concerned about: yours and your future buyer's. You should really consider your personal safety when targeting a neighborhood since you may be spending a lot of time there, often at odd hours. When you are working on a house, there may be

The Nine Neighborhood Appeal Factors

1. An established reputation

2. Clean and well-kept yards

3. A low crime rate

4. Good starter homes (smaller, relatively affordable)

5. Close to schools

6. Close to shopping

7. Close to mass transportation

8. Close to business centers

9. Close to parks and recreation

Figure 1-7 The Nine Neighborhood Appeal Factors

times when you don't have proper lighting or locks on the doors (or even windows), so choose neighborhoods where you are comfortable working after dark, especially if you are going to be an active participant in the rehab. Besides, if you don't want to be in the neighborhood after dark, your potential buyers may not either.

IDENTIFYING TARGET NEIGHBORHOODS

There's an old joke about how easy it is to sculpt a horse out of a block of marble: First you get a block of marble, and then you chip away everything that doesn't look like a horse. Think of targeting neighborhoods as starting with a big mass—all the available properties—and then removing all the neighborhoods that don't look like they would have investment houses.

We have created a mapping exercise that we use called the X-it strategy. It's a process of X-ing out potential areas to narrow your investing field to the neighborhoods that meet your targeting criteria.

Before we begin this exercise, you will need the following supplies:

1. A map of the city you'll be investing in

2. A pencil and a highlighter or colored pen

First, open the city map on a table. Then take the colored highlighter or pen and divide the different zip codes, subdivisions, or neighborhoods. Many times, you can find a city map divided by real estate areas in the real estate section of your local paper or on a real estate Web site that serves your area.

Now take your pencil and mark the points where you live and work (or any other place you go to on a regular basis). Then indicate the distance you are willing to travel to handle your investment properties by drawing a boundary around those points. The size of the boundary is up to you. Be sure to consider the traffic during the time you're likely to be traveling.

Next, with your pencil, X out all the neighborhoods that don't fit your proximity range.

Now take a look at each neighborhood within the boundaries and X out the ones that don't fit your other criteria. Is a neighborhood too pricey or too cheap, unsafe, too new, in a bad location? This will take some time and research because you will be applying your targeting criteria to each neighborhood.

The map in Figure 1-8 shows an investor in Austin, Texas, who works downtown and lives in North Austin. Although there are great investment neighborhoods to the east and west, she X-ed out most of them because it's too far to get there. She also marked out four areas within her proximity. Two areas were too pricey, and the other two she excluded because of low sales activity.

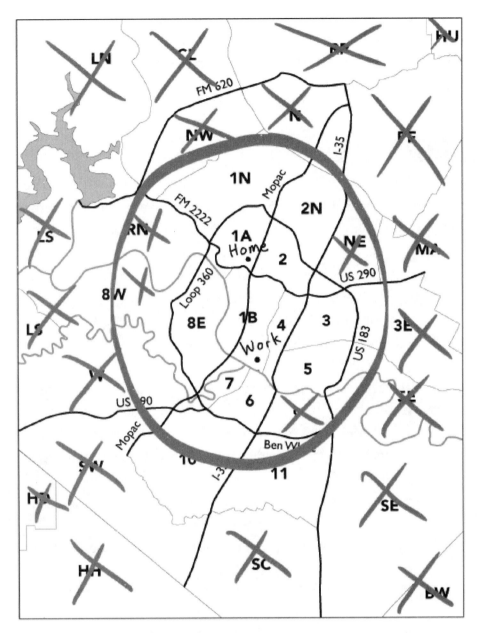

Figure 1-8 Target Neighborhoods in Austin, Texas

After completing the exercise, you should have a clear visual representation of which neighborhoods are ripe for rehabbing. These remaining neighborhoods will be the focus of your lead generating efforts, which are the topic of Chapter 2.

Chapter 2
Generate Leads

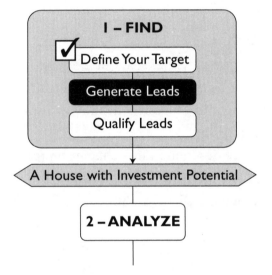

After reading this chapter you will know how to

- Prospect: search for investment houses
- Advertise: attract motivated sellers
- Network: connect with people who can connect you to houses and sellers

You can't invest until you have available properties to evaluate and consider purchasing. Information that helps you find these prospective properties and their owners is called leads. To succeed at flipping you must have leads and, to succeed at a high level, you'll need a lot of leads. The process of generating leads is the irrigation system that keeps your investment potential growing. Without a constant flow of leads coming in, your flipping business can dry up in a flash. We live in Texas, where it's hot and dry four months of the year. Keeping your lawn green can be a challenge. If you don't water it for a couple of weeks, it can take a lot longer than that for the lawn to recover. It's the same with house flipping: A healthy flipping business requires a frequent and consistent influx of leads.

Simply put, a lead is any information that "leads" you to a potential investment property or a potential seller of a house. It can be an address, a personal contact, or a name on a list. Leads create opportunity, and if you make a commitment to generate a healthy volume of leads, your flipping business will flourish.

The techniques we describe in this chapter represent what it takes to create a substantial enough flow of leads to support a fulltime house flipping operation. Obviously, when you're looking for your first flip, you'll focus on just a few of these lead generating activities. Done frequently and consistently, they will yield you the leads necessary to identify your first rehab project. From there, you can ramp up your activities if you choose to grow your flipping business. The choice is yours.

The important thing to remember whether you go big or stay small is the techniques are the same—it's just a matter of adjusting the volume to suit your needs. We group lead generation into three fundamental activities: prospecting, advertising, and networking (Figure 2-1).

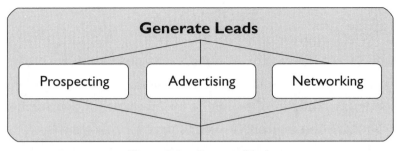

Figure 2-1   Generate Leads

PROSPECTING, ADVERTISING, AND NETWORKING

Meet Joe Clarkson. Until recently Joe lived in one of your target neighborhoods. He is a busy single executive who spends a lot of time on the road. His plans to spend Saturdays working on his house never materialized, and the house slowly deteriorated over the years. Joe landed a new job in another state. With just a few weeks to pack and arrive at his new job, he quickly listed his house and left town without getting to the repairs.

Six months later Joe is still making payments. Those minor repairs became major repairs after a bad storm blew off some siding and knocked several tree limbs into the yard. Joe knows he can't get top dollar with the house in its current condition, so he has pulled the listing and placed an ad in the classifieds describing it as a "handyman special." If that doesn't work, he'll get it fixed up and back on the market some day.

Let's look at how prospecting, advertising, and networking can lead you to Joe's house, which represents a possible flip opportunity for you.

PROSPECTING

Prospecting is the careful examination of neighborhoods, foreclosure lists, and classified ads: anything that can lead you to a potential investment house. It's a matter of searching for investment opportunities.

As you drive through one of your target neighborhoods, you recognize the same thing you've seen on the last couple of streets: signs that a bad storm hit this part of the neighborhood. You stop in front of a particularly bad-looking house. The roof looks pretty worn, and it's not just from last week's storm. There's missing siding and several big broken-off tree limbs in the yard. The lawn looks as if it's been neglected, and multiple flyers are hanging on the front door. You write down the address and note that it looks vacant—a likely investment candidate.

Back at your computer, you look up the owner's address on the tax assessment Web site and write a letter inquiring if the owner is interested in selling. This letter is going to an out-of-state address. The owner, Joe Clarkson, has become a lead as a result of your prospecting efforts.

ADVERTISING

Advertising is getting your message out through signs, direct mail, and other media. The goal is to attract the attention of motivated sellers by letting them know that you have what they need: The ability to buy their houses quickly and without hassles.

To generate awareness, you've been advertising in your target neighborhoods by consistently sending postcards to each resident with the message that you buy houses, can close quickly, and will pay cash. As Joe Clarkson sifts through his forwarded mail in his new city, your postcard catches his attention. He's familiar with these cards by now. In the past he threw them away, but today is different: He needs to sell his vacant house. He picks up the phone to dial your number on the card. Joe Clarkson is now a lead as a direct result of your advertising campaign.

NETWORKING

Networking is developing relationships with people who can lead you to house-buying opportunities. If you network with different groups of people and let them know you are an investor, they'll connect you to potential investment properties and/or homeowners who are ready to sell.

You've established a relationship with a local real estate agent. As you're treating him to lunch, he tells you about one of his clients: Joe Clarkson. He mentions that Joe took a job in another city, listed his house, but never followed up on his suggestions to make repairs. It was listed for six months, but now it's off the market.

The house is apparently in the right condition for investment and is in one of your target neighborhoods. Most important, the owner sounds motivated. The agent gives you Joe's number, and you make contact. This is another lead generated through your network.

Lead Generation Comparison			
	Prospecting	Advertising	Networking
Focus	An interesting house...	An interested seller...	People who help you find interesting houses or interested sellers...
Activity	Searching	Attracting	Connecting
Cost	Low	High	Low

Figure 2-2 Lead Generation Comparison

Each of the three lead generation activities has a specific focus, many strategies, and varied costs. With prospecting, you're personally searching through neighborhoods, public records, lists, classified ads, or even the Multiple Listing Service (MLS) for houses with investment potential. With advertising, you're attracting the attention of sellers through a variety of advertising approaches from direct mail postcards to billboards. With networking, you are connecting with people who can lead you to investment houses and motivated sellers. You can think of the three lead generation activities as searching, attracting, and connecting (Figure 2-2).

Let's take a closer look at how to use these strategies to build your lead generating machine. We'll begin with prospecting.

PROSPECTING: SEARCHING FOR INVESTMENT HOUSES

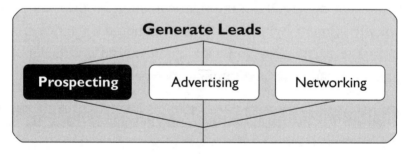

Figure 2-3

The California gold rush reportedly was started by a man named James Marshall in 1848. Apparently he found gold—in flakes and some small nuggets—in the American River during the construction of John Sutter's sawmill. The gold rush caused one of history's largest migrations, and prospecting for gold became a national obsession.

Like prospecting for gold, prospecting for investment houses involves sifting through a lot of what you *don't* want to get to what you do want.

As Norman Vincent Peale said, "Nothing of great value in this life comes easily. The things of highest value sometimes come hard. The gold that has the greatest value lies deepest in the earth." Prospecting can be time-consuming and labor-intensive but often yields great results.

Figure 2-4 shows the four most common places to prospect for potential investment properties.

Four Places to Prospect

1. Your Target Neighborhoods

2. The Multiple Listing Service

3. Classifieds

4. Foreclosures

Figure 2-4   Four Places to Prospect

1. YOUR TARGET NEIGHBORHOODS

One of the tried and true methods of prospecting is combing through your target neighborhoods for vacant houses and then looking up the owners on the tax records and contacting them to see if they're willing to sell. Although this may seem low-tech and monotonous, many investors cite this as one of their top lead producing techniques. Driving also has the side benefit of making you knowledgeable about your target neighborhood as well as comfortable with some of the key research tools of the trade. For all these reasons, driving your target neighborhoods is arguably the best place to start when you are looking for your first flip.

The reason we specify vacant houses is that it increases the odds that you'll get both a motivated seller and an interesting house. "I won't waste my time on anything other than vacant houses, because if it's vacant, I know the seller is motivated," says Andy Davies, our HomeFixers affiliate in Houston.

1. *Hit the streets.* As you drive up and down the streets of your target neighborhoods, your quest is for vacant properties. You're looking for the telltale signs:
   - Piled-up newspapers
   - Lots of mail overflowing from the mailbox
   - Overgrown lawns
   - Boarded-up windows
   - Cluttered entryways
   - Tags on utility meters
   - No receptacles on the curb on trash day
   - No lights on at night
   - General appearance of disrepair

2. *Capture addresses of vacant houses.* Record the addresses in an organized way that works best for you. Most people write them down in a notebook. Others use a clipboard and a customized form. Some speak the information into a recorder, and some take digital pictures of houses. To take a more high-tech approach, you can enter the addresses directly into a personal digital assistant or notebook. Use whatever method encourages you to collect as many addresses as possible.

   Now be aware that the work can get pretty tedious if you try to cover a lot of ground in a single day. You may find it best to break it up into shorter trips throughout each week. Another way to break the monotony is to write down addresses when you see "For Sale by Owner" (FSBO) signs and call them while you're driving. Many FSBOs sit on the market, and the owner may be willing to sell at a discount. Writing down "For Rent" signs and calling them can also be productive: Many landlords are tired of dealing with tenants and vacancies.

   One of the tougher parts of prospecting is finding the owners of vacant houses, and so when you're out driving, you might consider talking to the neighbors when you spot a particularly promising property. The more information you can collect, the better your detective work will go later on. The neighbors may know the name and contact information of the owner, or they may know someone else who needs to sell or where other vacant houses are located.

3. *Look up the property owner and contact information.* Now that you've collected your vacant-house addresses, the detective work begins: finding the owners' names and contact information so that you can get in touch with them to see if they are willing to sell.

   You usually can find out who the owners are and where they live by searching the tax rolls. Many municipalities list property tax records online, allowing you to search by address or owner name. If you can't find online records, contact the local tax assessor's office and ask how you can access these public records. Tax rolls usually don't list phone numbers; you'll have to call information or use an Internet phone directory to search online.

   If you can't find the owner (maybe the address listed on the property rolls is incorrect or the telephone has been disconnected), you can try to track down the owner through a business that conducts "skip traces." Again, an Internet search for the keywords "skip trace" will give you plenty of possibilities.

4. *Make contact.* Once you've found the owners and their addresses, send them a postcard or letter to see if they want to sell the house. Your message should be polite and to the point. Figure 2-5 shows an example of a postcard.

Driving through neighborhoods is a numbers game. Our investors say that they buy about two to three houses for every thousand postcards they send out. The average number of vacant houses they say they can collect in an hour is somewhere between ten and twenty. Thus, driving eight hours a week will yield about 350 to 700 addresses per month. If

---

Do You Need to Sell Your House?

We Pay Cash and Close Quickly!

Dear [Property Owner],

    We would like to buy your house at [Property Address].

    If you are interested in selling, please call my office at (555) 456-7890. We'll send you a written offer the next day.

    I would appreciate a call one way or another so I'll know you received this card.

Thank you,

[Your Name]

[Your Company Name]

Figure 2-5   Sample Postcard

you have a goal of doing an investment house a month, this method alone can get you there. So do the math and create a plan that fits your goals and available time.

FLIPPING POINT

A lot of investors who don't have time to spend driving around prefer to hire people to do the scouting for them. Investors sometimes refer to these scouts as "bird dogs." They tell them what to look for and where. They usually pay a couple of dollars per address, or more if the scout provides the owner's contact information.

2. THE MLS

The MLS is a massive source of investment leads. However, it is also a source that is being searched by other investors who may be looking for the same types of properties as you are. The MLS is a constantly changing database as houses come on and off the market and as their status and price change. To be successful, you need to (1) check the MLS frequently and be able to react immediately or (2) mine the data in creative ways that your competitors may not have thought of. Although some of the information found on the MLS is publicly available through other sources, the tools to sort it and the richer data are available only to licensed real estate agents. Agents who understand the value they can bring to investors can help you prospect the MLS.

Here are some of the customized reports your agent can provide for you:

- *Property value report.* This is a report on your target neighborhood, sorted by price per square foot, that allows you to identify properties for sale that could be undervalued. For example, if your target neighborhood has an average cost per square foot of $150, the houses selling for less than $100 merit a closer look.

- *Expired/canceled listing report.* This report shows the houses in your target neighborhoods where listing periods have expired or the owners, for whatever reason, decided to take the house off the market before it sold. In some cases, the owner may be highly motivated to sell after having listed the property for a period of time or if the house has a problem that the owner is unwilling to fix. In either case, this may be an investment opportunity.

- *Days on market report.* This is a report that shows how long houses have been on the market. The listing time period is measured by "days on market" (DOM). Houses that have been on the market for significantly longer than the average may represent the same opportunity as the expired or canceled listings. They may have a motivated seller or a problem that requires an investor to fix.

- *Keyword report.* You can have your agent create a report that is based on keywords to show homes that fit your investing criteria. It is as if there were a secret language in property descriptions with code words that can signify potential investment properties.

Here's a list of common words to search for, but don't use them all at the same time or the list will be too long. Try a few at a time to find out which ones yield the best results in your market.

- "Handyman special"
- "Needs work/updating/TLC"
- "Repair allowance"
- "Assumable"
- "Undervalue"
- "Deal"
- "As is"
- "Motivated seller"
- "VLB" (vacant on lock box)
- "Estate sale"

One of the keys to finding an investment property through the MLS is to find it before other investors do. If your agent's MLS database has an e-mail alert option to notify you of new and modified listings in your target neighborhoods, ask to be set up with a daily alert. This daily e-mail is a great way to keep your finger on the pulse of your target neighborhoods. As with a daily weather report, you'll get a sense of the highs or lows, whether a storm is brewing, and where.

3. THE CLASSIFIEDS

The classifieds are a great place to find houses for sale that are not listed in the MLS. Many newspapers post their classified ads on the Internet, so you can view them online or pick up the newspaper and look through it the old-fashioned way. You'll be looking in the "Houses for Sale" section, which includes investment ads, FSBO ads, and agent listings. Most papers break out real estate ads by neighborhood, and that helps narrow down the search according to your target. As with the list mentioned above, look for the same kinds of clues that may indicate a potential investment property (Figure 2-6).

Clues to Rehab Properties in Real Estate Ads

- "Handyman special"
- "Vacant"
- "Motivated seller"
- "Must-sell"
- "As-is"
- "Needs work"
- "Fixer-upper"
- "Estate sale"
- "Needs updating"
- "Great neighborhood"
- "Charming"

Figure 2-6 Clues to Rehab Properties in Real Estate Ads

Also look in the "Houses for Rent" section because landlords may be motivated sellers. Some are accidental landlords, possibly because they inherited a property and may be leasing it out temporarily. Or perhaps the owners moved out of their home, leased it out, and haven't gotten around to selling it yet. Some landlords find themselves tiring of dealing with renters or their rental property needs extensive repairs. The scenarios are diverse, but the point is that if there's a property for rent in your target neighborhood, do a drive-by and see if it fits your criteria.

One of the most popular Web sites that uses a classified ad approach is www.craigslist.org. With new classified ad sites cropping up, Craigslist is not your only option, but it has been very successful and a perfect model for other sites. Try entering "For Sale by Owner (<u>Your City</u>)" on a popular search engine and see what pops up.

4. FORECLOSURES

You've probably heard it said that someone bought a property "on the courthouse steps." What exactly does that mean, and how does it work? We all know that everyday catastrophes happen and mortgages don't get paid. Whether it is a death, divorce, medical crisis, or job loss, someone somewhere suddenly finds that he is unable to pay his mortgage. Although it's sad for a homeowner to lose his home, lenders also bear some of the burden. Depending on where the house is in the foreclosure process, an investor may be able to save the homeowner from foreclosure or, if it's too late for that, relieve the bank of its debt burden.

Once a house has started the foreclosure process, there is a motivated owner or lender who needs to sell the house quickly. Competition can drive up the price, so keep in mind that not all foreclosures make good investments. Also, foreclosure laws vary from state to state. It is important to educate yourself before going in headfirst. You may want to talk to a real estate attorney and the city and county authorities who regulate foreclosures in your area.

There are three different phases that a foreclosure can go through that present an investment opportunity: preforeclosure, public auction, and real estate owned (Figure 2-7).

1. Preforeclosure

Borrowers who are in default are usually given a grace period (preforeclosure period) of a month to a year (depending on the state) to pay off the loan to avoid going into full foreclosure. During the preforeclosure period, investors have two ways to purchase a property: directly from the seller and indirectly from the lender.

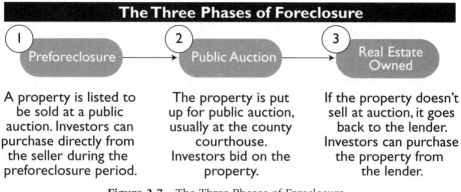

The Three Phases of Foreclosure

1 Preforeclosure → 2 Public Auction → 3 Real Estate Owned

A property is listed to be sold at a public auction. Investors can purchase directly from the seller during the preforeclosure period.

The property is put up for public auction, usually at the county courthouse. Investors bid on the property.

If the property doesn't sell at auction, it goes back to the lender. Investors can purchase the property from the lender.

Figure 2-7   The Three Phases of Foreclosure

This period is when the homeowner absolutely has the most motivation to sell. But to make a deal work, the investor needs to be able to buy the house at a price that

1. Pays off the debt
2. Allows the investor to profit from the deal
3. Possibly gives the seller some walking money

If the debt on the house is greater than or too close to the value, you may have to go directly to the lender to negotiate.

Lenders sometimes will allow the sale of a property to another party (such as a real estate investor) for less than what is owed to avoid the costs associated with the foreclosure process. This is called a short sale. The investor has to negotiate directly with the lender to reach a final price. In a short sale, most lenders will not allow the homeowner to walk

FLIPPING POINT

Local taxing authorities distribute preforeclosure lists on a regular basis, usually monthly. There are also numerous Web sites that offer preforeclosure lists, but be warned that these sites often charge for lists that are freely available and publicly posted in the newspaper, at the courthouse, or on a civic Web site.

away from the deal with any cash. Why? The lender already is losing money by selling the property for less than what is owed.

Figure 2-8 lists other sources of foreclosures and auctions.

Other Sources of Foreclosures and Auctions

- U.S. Department of Housing and Urban Development (HUD)
- Veterans Administration (VA)
- Federal Housing Authority (FHA)
- Federal National Mortgage Insurance Association (Fannie Mae)
- Federal Home Loan Mortgage Corporation (Freddie Mac)
- Internal Revenue Service (check your local IRS office)
- Property Tax Sales (check your local taxing authority)

Figure 2-8   Other Sources of Foreclosures and Auctions

2. Public Auction

Once the preforeclosure grace period has elapsed, a defaulted property is listed to be sold at an auction where the public can bid on the property. Auctions often are held at the local county courthouse (the "courthouse steps"). Look for auction dates and times posted in the same locations that have preforeclosure listings.

This phase of the foreclosure process involves the highest risk with not necessarily the greatest reward. You need to be able to pay in cash on the spot without a formal inspection of the property. In some cases, the homeowner may be able to repurchase the property within a certain period (right of redemption). Another risk comes from being in a live bidding situation. You must know your top price and have the discipline to walk away. We suggest that you just sit back and watch during your first auction experience. If you scoped out properties that you thought you could bid on, pay close attention to how those auctions turn out. The goal is to understand how things work before you dive in.

3. Real Estate Owned

If a property doesn't sell at auction, it goes back to the lender, where it is pooled with other real estate owned (REO) properties. Lenders want to get these properties off the books quickly (in most cases within 90 days) even if it means taking a loss. It's important to keep in mind that lenders are in the business of lending money, not owning real estate. In short, the lender is now a motivated seller and these properties are priced to sell fast, not for profit.

Finding REO properties takes some effort. First, call the major lending institutions in your area to see if they maintain an inventory of REO properties. If they do, find out who is responsible for disposing of REOs. It may be someone in an REO department, if they have one, or a local attorney or real estate agent who works with the lender. Once you've tracked them down, ask if they will share a current list of REO properties with you.

In this section, we have covered the main prospecting strategies, but your prospecting possibilities are limited only by your creativity. No matter which strategy you choose, prospecting involves a careful search for potential investment properties. It takes time and effort, but it almost always produces results. Next, we'll explore a completely different approach to lead generation: attracting sellers to you.

ADVERTISING: ATTRACTING MOTIVATED SELLERS

Advertising can be a very effective way to generate leads. Advertising catches the attention of interested sellers by letting them know that you have exactly what they need: the ability to buy a house quickly and without hassles.

Although it typically is more expensive than prospecting, advertising has one great advantage: *It keeps working even when you're not.* Most of the effort in advertising is front-loaded. Once the initial hard work is

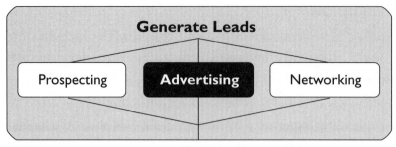

Figure 2-9

done, you only need to refine and maintain your efforts, freeing you to focus on other areas of your house-flipping business.

With prospecting, you narrow your focus to likely candidates before investing in communicating with them (e.g., identifying three vacant houses in a neighborhood of one thousand and then calling or sending notes to those owners). However, with advertising, you communicate your message to a larger group of people to attract the attention of the few who can benefit from your message (e.g., blanketing a neighborhood with a thousand cards with the hope of finding three house-buying opportunities).

Advertising is a two-step process. First, decide what you are going to say. Second, deliver the message to your target audience (Figure 2-10).

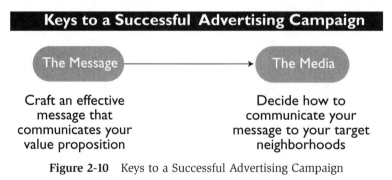

Figure 2-10   Keys to a Successful Advertising Campaign

CRAFTING YOUR MESSAGE

Can you name the product or company that these popular slogans are advertising?

- Melts in your mouth, not in your hand.
- Tastes great, less filling.
- Takes a licking and keeps on ticking.
- Let your fingers do the walking.
- When your package absolutely, positively, has to get there overnight.

If you guessed M&Ms, Miller Lite, Timex, Yellow Pages, and FedEx, congratulations. Each of these timeless messages has a clearly defined unique selling proposition (USP). A great USP very clearly answers the question of why you should do business with the advertiser.

The first step to crafting your message is to understand exactly what you're offering potential sellers. In other words, what is your product? In most cases, in flipping houses, your product is *fast cash and no hassles.*

Your ideal customer is someone who lives in your target neighborhood, needs cash quickly, and is willing to sacrifice some of the value in her house to get it. Your customer is usually someone who must act quickly and is very motivated to get out from under her mortgage payments.

Based on what your product is and who your customers are, you need to come up with a message that demonstrates that you can solve your customers' problems. Focus on the benefits to the customers, such as:

- Your ability to close fast with cash *enables them to sell quickly*
- Your ability to close fast with cash *allows them to stop making payments*
- Your ability to close fast with cash *gets them out of debt*
- Your ability to close fast with cash *helps them avoid foreclosure*

Come up with a message that will set you apart from the other investors in the area: Think clever, short, and memorable. You may even want to consider blending in elements of the target neighborhood, so that potential sellers understand you are specifically interested in and knowledgeable about their area.

Your message should motivate sellers to stop what they are doing and contact you. In advertising lingo, this is the *call to action.* Figure 2-11 shows some examples.

- "Avoid foreclosure. Cash for your home. Call Now."

- "Need to sell soon? I can help."

- "Sell your house now. No hassles. Fast cash."

- "Problem-fixer. House-fixer. I buy homes."

- "Get out from under your roof TODAY"

- "Keep [neighborhood] beautiful. Sell me your home."

- "Buried in debt? I buy [neighborhood] houses hassle-free."

- "Looking for [neighborhood] homes to buy today."

Figure 2-11 Message Examples

You get the idea. These aren't necessarily ADDY award winners, but don't be too quick to throw them under the bus. Successful investors use similar, straightforward messages every day with great results. If you want to, feel free to come up with something more fun and original.

FLIPPING POINT

Your message is directed to a wide audience. Unless you craft that message carefully, you're likely to get a lot of calls from sellers who won't have a good reason to sell their houses at a low enough price for you to buy them, fix them up, and sell them for a profit. HomeVestors, a national franchise company for investors, solved this problem with its "We Buy Ugly Houses" billboards. The beauty of this message is that it both explains what they do (buy houses) and qualifies the kinds of customers they can help (those with "ugly" or problem houses). You need to do the same thing with your advertising—be specific about what you are looking for.

GET THE WORD OUT

Once you've crafted a great message, it's time to get the word out to your target neighborhoods. Advertising mediums range from a business card stapled to a bulletin board to sixty-second fully produced television spots. The point is that you don't have to spend a fortune to have an effective campaign, though you certainly can do that. You're trying to attract a select group of people in a select group of neighborhoods, so choose your advertising mediums accordingly. Let's explore the six most popular ones (Figure 2-12).

The Six Most Popular Advertising Mediums

1. Direct Mail

2. Business Cards

3. Signs

4. Print Advertising

5. The Internet

6. Radio and Television

Figure 2-12   The Six Most Popular Advertising Mediums

Whatever medium you choose, remember that this is your opportunity to create an image for you and your business. Although, you may still be looking for your first property, a "branded" look is worth pursing because it puts you in position to build a positive, consistent, professional image that people will respect and remember. The continual use of a color scheme and style will help create the familiarity and confidence that a brand inspires.

1. Direct Mail

If you use only one advertising method, make it direct mail. Direct mail is a tried and true technique that consists of sending letters, postcards, or flyers to all the houses in your target neighborhoods. The type of mailing doesn't matter, but make sure it looks professional, includes your message, stands out, and has a clear call to action—a way for them to easily contact you.

Address lists are readily available from a variety of sources on the Internet. A search for "residential mailing lists" will give you more than enough options to cover your target neighborhoods. Then it's simply a matter of getting your message printed on whatever medium you choose and heading to the post office. Don't expect the phone to ring off the hook after the first mailing. As scores of investors will attest, it's consistent mailings over time with the right message that get the best results.

2. Business Cards

A simple and effective way to advertise yourself and what you do is through your business card. You may want to include a brief message on the card or just your name, your contact information, and what you do: John Doe, Rehab Specialist, 123/456-7890. Of course, include a mailing address, phone number, fax number, e-mail address, and Web site address if you have one.

Your business card is a reflection of how serious you are as an investor. We recommend that you spend a few dollars getting high-quality business cards made at a professional printer rather than using your home computer and printer.

Your business card is your calling card and should be left everywhere you roam. Post it at the convenience store, Laundromat, and gas station. Take out an ad in your neighborhood newsletter, using your business card as the advertisement. Hand it out to neighbors and include it with any letters you send out to prospective sellers. Spread the word about who you are and what you're looking for.

3. Signs

Signs can be made relatively inexpensively and displayed almost anywhere. Nevertheless, check local city ordinances before posting to make sure your signs don't get you into trouble. You have a variety of options for how to get your message out through signs. Figure 2-13 illustrates the main four.

Four Types of Advertising Signs	
1. Yard Signs	Signs posted in the yards of your current flip projects
2. "Bandit" Signs	Signs posted in high-traffic areas (make sure they are posted legally)
3. Billboards	Can be pricey, but some investors find the return rate very high
4. Car Magnets	Printed signs that are magnetized to stick to your car door

Figure 2-13 Four Types of Advertising Signs

Most towns have local sign shops where you can get professionally made signs. As with business cards, we recommend spending a few extra dollars to create a professional, quality look.

4. Print Advertising

Real estate investors have a wealth of options to promote their businesses in print advertisements. Some investors run ads in the real estate, business, or classified section of the newspaper. Other print vehicles for investor ads include free local publications such as PennySavers and various free real estate publications that usually are stocked in convenience stores, gas stations, and grocery stores.

Many neighborhood homeowners associations (HOAs) publish a monthly newsletter, and sometimes they run a classified section that includes FSBO properties. You can benefit both ways by getting on the mailing list for your target neighborhood's HOA.

If you don't have access to a freelance graphic designer, many publications will design your advertisement for a fee.

5. The Internet

The Internet is filled with online classified ad sites that generate revenue through advertising. It's hard to gauge the effectiveness of these types of ads unless you try them out, but the costs should be relatively low. In addition, most major cities have city-oriented and real-estate-oriented Web sites that accept advertising.

Check to see if your target neighborhood HOAs have Web sites that accept advertising. Some neighborhoods have online blogs, bulletin boards, or e-mail newsletters. These are good opportunities not only to post an ad but also to be an active member of the neighborhood community.

6. Radio and Television

Producing a thirty- or sixty-second commercial can be done for two mediums: radio and television. Radio is less expensive than television. If you don't have the voice for radio, you can hire someone to read your ad. Rates vary by metropolitan areas, but radio spots are relatively affordable, especially on news-only formats. Keep your copy short and to the point. Listen to currently running ads to get ideas on how to craft yours. Every radio station has advertising representatives, so call and talk to someone there to get the rates and to ask for help if you need it.

There are two kinds of television advertising. One involves a video shoot, music, and maybe actors, and the other involves just words and pictures. If you want to keep costs down, stick with the words-and-pictures ads. Again, you can contact your local television station's advertising representative to get prices and ask for help in creating your advertisement.

As you grow your rehab business, you may find other, more creative ways to get your name and message out there. Figure 2-14 shows some other advertising ideas to consider.

Other Advertising Ideas

- T-shirts or other apparel

- Door hangers

- Exhibiting at local home shows

- Sponsoring a Little League or other team

- Flyers in direct mail packets such as Valpak or Money Mailer

- Company newsletters

Figure 2-14   Other Advertising Ideas

YOUR MEDIA PLAN

Your media plan defines the details of where and how often you're going to advertise. To maximize your advertising dollars, you need to balance a couple of variables: reach and frequency (Figure 2-15).

Reach and Frequency

Reach	How many people are in the target audience of an advertisement?
Frequency	How often is an individual in your target audience exposed to an advertisement?

Figure 2-15   Reach and Frequency

Reach is how many people are exposed to your advertisements. For example, handing one person your business card is the smallest possible reach; buying a television ad during the Super Bowl would be the largest possible reach. You want to choose the media that will reach your target neighborhoods best. For example, if you target a few select neighborhoods, postcards to those neighborhoods are a very effective strategy. In contrast, if your neighborhoods are spread throughout a city, a billboard or radio spot may be a better option.

Frequency is the number of times an individual is exposed to your advertisements. Success in advertising comes from gaining mindshare in your target audience. One postcard is quickly forgotten, but a postcard a month is much more likely to create a lasting impression on your audience.

When putting together your media plan, you'll have to make decisions on reach versus frequency. For example, it costs the same to send one postcard to five similar-sized neighborhoods as it does to send five postcards to one neighborhood. In the first case your reach is five times as large, whereas in the second the frequency is five times greater. In balancing the two, there's a minimum standard of frequency, depending on the medium. At the very least, touch them twice—once is almost never enough. Based on your resources, you may have to narrow your reach to hit and exceed that minimum standard (Figure 2-16).

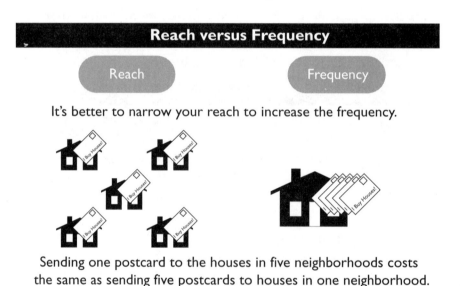

Reach versus Frequency

Reach   Frequency

It's better to narrow your reach to increase the frequency.

Sending one postcard to the houses in five neighborhoods costs the same as sending five postcards to houses in one neighborhood.

Figure 2-16   Reach versus Frequency

Keep track of which ads work best and from what source. When people call from an ad, find out where they saw it so that you can fine-tune your efforts in the future. As you measure the results of your advertising campaign, you'll make adjustments to your media plan. For example, you may remove an unproductive neighborhood from your target area so that you can focus your resources on the neighborhoods that are generating leads.

However, never stop advertising to productive neighborhoods just because you think you've got mindshare. Someone once asked the chewing gum magnate William Wrigley why he continued to advertise when his product completely dominated the market. "Simple," he replied. "Sales is a train, and advertising is the engine. Cut off the engine and the train will slowly come to a halt."

NETWORKING: THE PEOPLE WHO CONNECT YOU WITH HOUSES OR SELLERS

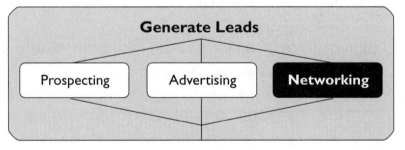

Figure 2-17

When the Academy Award–nominated actor Harrison Ford moved to Hollywood in 1964 at the age of twenty-two to become an actor, he first worked at Columbia Pictures (where he subsequently was fired) and then at Universal Studios where he did bit television spots. But it was his side job that launched his career. To support his wife and two sons between acting jobs, he became a self-taught carpenter. Eventually, Ford found himself building cabinets in director George Lucas's home. Lucas enlisted Ford to read lines for actors who were being cast in Lucas's upcoming film. He read his lines so well that Ford was cast as Han Solo in the *Star Wars* films and blasted into stardom.

This story illustrates the fact that success often comes not from what you do or even how well you do it but from who you know. As Harrison Ford could attest "knowing" someone doesn't have to mean "friends for life." It can simply be an acquaintance with whom you have shared your goals. The people you know make up your *network*: your circle of friends, business associates, and peers.

BUILDING YOUR NETWORK

In his best-selling book *The Millionaire Real Estate Investor*, Gary Keller writes that the core of your lead generation network is composed of people whose professions put them in direct contact with either sellers or houses. Figure 2-18 shows some examples of people who can become part of your core lead generation network.

Networking is building relationships with people who have access to houses and sellers and who will pass these leads on to you. However, it's not just about you. Successful networking involves mutually beneficial relationships. Help the people in your network with business leads, a finder's fee, or even a piece of the action. If nothing else, a simple thank-you note or small gift is always appreciated. Your reputation is paramount here. Be sure to return phone calls and messages promptly. Be ready to act quickly and be generous and gracious in your responses.

One of the best places to begin networking is real estate investment clubs. These organizations have sprung up in cities all across North America. The club meetings (usually held every month) are often filled to capacity with investors, lenders, builders, and everyone else associated with real estate investing. If you're just starting out, these clubs are an excellent way to begin building your network. And don't forget to tell

1. Other Investors
2. Realtors
3. Appraisers
4. Lenders
5. Inspectors
6. Lawyers
7. Accountants
8. Contractors
9. Courthouse Clerks
10. Builders
11. Developers
12. Neighborhood Residents

Figure 2-18 The People in Your Network

your friends, family and neighbors that you're now an investor and on the lookout for deals. You may be surprised how effective it can be to simply reconnect with the people you already know and share with them that you're interested in flipping houses.

Networking opportunities can come out of the strangest circumstances. One such opportunity came about when the guy at the pet store reversed the numbers on the dog tag of Rick's pet golden retriever "Abby." He engraved 4136 instead of 4163. That was the same week that Abby got out and took an unsupervised tour through the neighborhood. The first place Rick looked was 4136 thinking someone might have found her and brought her to the address on the tag. An elderly woman came to the door with a paint roller in her hand. Seeing the very tall ladder, high vaulted ceilings and drop cloths, it was obvious that the job was more than she should be doing alone. Curiosity got the best of Rick and he inquired. She explained that she and her husband were forced to relocate immediately—he had already flown up to Minnesota and she was left to sell the house and join him as soon as she could. The result? An unexpected networking opportunity with one of Rick's neighbors and a house that was purchased below market value. The woman was able to leave the rollers and drop cloths and join her husband within a couple of weeks. And Abby? She turned up the same day in another neighbor's yard.

CULTIVATING YOUR NETWORK

We recommend some kind of contact management system to keep track of your network. The people in that network can be broken down into four categories: resources, allied resources, advocates, and core advocates. Each category is based on the likelihood that these people will send you leads (Figure 2-19). As you meet people and drop them into your lead generation network, everyone starts out as a resource: someone who *might* send you leads. Over time, you'll discover the ones who will and focus your networking activities on them.

Categories of Your Network	
Resources	People who might send you leads.
Allied Resources	People who can and will send you leads.
Advocates	People who will absolutely send you leads.
Core Advocates	People who are in a great position to send you leads and will.

Figure 2-19 Categories of Your Network

Source: From *The Millionaire Real Estate Investor* by Gary Keller

You'll want to keep track of the last time you made contact, how many leads you received, and which leads became a house purchase. The people in your network can change categories quickly. With one phone call, a resource can jump to being an advocate. Be aware of who's making your investment lead machine hum and treat those people accordingly: Stay in regular contact with them and show your gratitude.

Keller recommends creating an "all properties bulletin" (APB) that lists exactly what type of property you are looking for and where you are looking. Share these criteria by contacting the people in your network on the basis of the way you categorize them. The more likely they are to send you leads, the more often you should contact them. Figure 2-20 shows a rough script to make sure you cover the key points of the conversation.

Your Networking Script	
Introduce Yourself	Tell them who you are and why you are calling
Share Target	Tell them what type of house you are looking for and in what neighborhoods
Ask For Help	Give them your phone number if they ever hear about a property that fits your needs and if they know of anyone else who can help you find properties
Be Thankful	Say "thank you," offer to help them, and follow up with a note or e-mail

Figure 2-20   Your Networking Script

Source: From *The Millionaire Real Estate Investor* by Gary Keller

As in prospecting, getting solid leads from your network is a numbers game. The bigger your network is and the more systematically you contact the people in it, the more leads you'll get. Don't get discouraged and stop connecting; sooner or later, someone in your network is going to run across a property that is exactly what you are looking for.

In this chapter we have covered the three main activities of lead generation. Prospecting is searching for properties by searching through lots of what you don't want to get to what you do want: the streets of your target neighborhoods, listings, ads, and so forth. Advertising attracts sellers to you with a carefully crafted message that reaches your target neighborhoods. Networking involves contacting people to tell them about your business, what you do, and how they can help. One of the most important things to remember is not to let your lead-generating efforts wax and wane when you get involved in a rehab or you may find yourself waiting months for the next flip.

After years of working with real estate investors, we get the majority of our leads by networking. If you are just starting out and have limited resources, prospecting is a great place to start while you build your network. For many people, advertising becomes a viable strategy as their investment businesses grow and more resources become available.

Once those leads start coming in, you will need to be able to filter the good leads from the bad. We call this process qualifying leads, and it is the topic of Chapter 3.

POINTS TO REMEMBER

Lead generating is the irrigation system that keeps your investment business growing. Effective lead generation is composed of three activities: prospecting, advertising, and networking.

1. *Prospecting* involves the physical search for potential investment, using a variety of prospect-hunting tools, from driving around your target neighborhoods looking for properties to asking your real estate agent to run MLS reports and foreclosure listings, scanning the classifieds, researching public records on the Internet, and making contact with homeowners to see if they are interested in selling their property.

2. *Advertising* is the process of attracting motivated sellers to you by getting the message out to your target audience that you are buying houses for quick cash. Your message should contain your unique selling proposition as well as a call to action. Your advertising plan can include a multitargeted approach such as direct mail, signs, and print ads in local publications.

3. *Networking* is connecting to people who can lead you to potential sellers and potential investment properties. Your network is probably the most important element in your lead-generating operation and involves building relationships with people you come into contact with every day and/or people you know who may be able to help you find out about properties in your target neighborhood.

For your first flip, focus on prospecting by driving around your target neighborhoods and networking with your local real estate investment club. These are inexpensive yet proven ways to jump-start your lead generating for investment properties.

Chapter 3
Qualify Leads

After reading this chapter you will know how to

- Qualify a house
- Qualify a seller
- Go through the process of qualifying a lead

In August 2006, members of the International Astronomic Union voted to revise the definition of a planet. Suddenly there were only eight planets in our solar system. Pluto no longer qualified. The diminutive Pluto did not meet all four of the newly established criteria for defining a planet, one of which was based on size.

Although there was vigorous debate, in the end the scientists overwhelmingly voted for the change. Referring to the vote, Professor Iwan Williams said, "I have a slight tear in my eye today, yes; but at the end of the day we have to describe the solar system as it really is, not as we would like it to be."

It's important to approach qualifying real estate investment leads with the objectivity of a scientist, to see a lead for what it is, not what you want it to be. A *qualified* lead is a lead that is worth further investigation. Two components must exist for a lead to be worth your time and effort:

1. A house that meets your specific buying criteria
2. A seller who is willing to sell below retail market value

If a lead doesn't have both components, it's not a qualified lead. Discard it and move on to the next one.

When your lead generation efforts ramp up, the qualifying process will be done primarily through a conversation with the homeowner, usually over the phone. If you hop in the car to check out every lead before qualifying it, you'll find yourself wasting a lot of time. We'll present a checklist at the end of this chapter that walks you through the qualifying process.

FLIPPING POINT

Just because a house doesn't meet your personal criteria or a seller won't meet your specific price, that doesn't mean that the lead won't work for another investor. If you think it has potential, pass it on to someone in your network.

QUALIFY THE HOUSE

In qualifying a house, your goal is to determine whether the house fits the three parts of your fundamental buying criteria. First, the house should be in one of your target neighborhoods. Second, the repairs needed on the house must not exceed what you're willing or able to take on. Third, the house can't be a Neighborhood Misfit or, in other words, so "unique" or "strikingly distinctive" that mainstream buyers will be turned off. Test every lead against these criteria to determine if the house is a good investment opportunity for you (Figure 3-1).

The Three Fundamental House-Buying Criteria
1. In Your Target Neighborhood?
2. In Satisfactory Condition?
3. Not a Neighborhood Misfit?

Figure 3-1   The Three Fundamental House-Buying Criteria

1. IN YOUR TARGET NEIGHBORHOOD

First and foremost, verify that the house is in one of your target neighborhoods. Although you are focusing your lead generation efforts on your target neighborhoods, leads generated through advertising and networking can come from anywhere. If you don't already know the answer, your first question to the homeowner should be, "What is the address of the house?" If the street name isn't familiar, ask the owner to hold on while you check to see if it is in one of your target neighborhoods. If it is not, simply say, "While I appreciate your taking the time to call me, I'm sorry, I just don't invest in that part of town. Would it be a problem if I passed along your information to some other investors I know who might be able to help you out?"

2. In Satisfactory Condition

Next, you want to get a rough idea of the condition of the house to see if you are willing to accept the risks involved in owning and improving it. Ask a few leading questions to uncover any major issues the house may have (Figure 3-2). The satisfactory condition level is up to you. For example, you may welcome extensive remodeling work but want to avoid major structural and environmental issues. The homeowner won't always know the answers, but if they do, it can save you the time and expense it takes to discover these issues on your own.

Qualifying for Condition: Major Issues

1. Fire damage?

2. Lead paint?

3. Water damage?

4. Major foundation problems?

5. Collapsed roof?

6. Asbestos?

7. Major termite damage?

8. Aluminum wiring?

Figure 3-2   Qualifying for Condition: Major Issues

3. Not a Neighborhood Misfit

One of the keys to maximizing your profit in flipping houses is selling a house quickly once it's been fixed up and is back on the market. Make sure that aspects of the house that you *cannot change* (or that are impractical to change) do not deviate too far from the neighborhood norm. For example, 1960s modern architecture with a flat roof and no front windows is a misfit in a neighborhood full of colonial two-stories. (There's a reason it looks so attractive on paper compared to the rest of the neighborhood.) Figure 2-3 shows some other attributes that make a house a misfit.

Neighborhood Misfits: Aspects You Can't Change

1. Unusual Architecture—roof pitch and elevation

2. Lot Irregularity—too small, too steep, odd shape

3. Layout—low ceilings, one bathroom or tiny kitchen without space to remodel

4. House Size—much too small or much too large

5. Street—unusually busy, parking issues due to nearby school or office

6. Neighbors—unsightly or oversized houses, commercial buildings

7. Infrastructure—power lines, retention ponds, railroad tracks, highway noise

8. Scene of a Crime—a crime or suicide can turn off buyers

Figure 3-3   Neighborhood Misfits: Aspects You Can't Change

Most of the buyers in a neighborhood are looking for a house that meets the neighborhood norm. You may do a terrific job fixing up a house, but if it's a misfit, you may have difficulty selling it because there will be fewer interested buyers.

FLIPPING POINT

Misfits *can* make excellent investment opportunities, but you need to be able to accept the challenges you will face when you put it back on the market: a lower selling price for the neighborhood and a potentially longer time to sell.

If the house meets your buying criteria, you have the first half of a qualified lead: a qualified house. Next, it's time to qualify the seller.

QUALIFY THE SELLER

The second step in qualifying a lead is to qualify the seller. Your goal is to find out if the homeowner is willing and able to sell for less than the *retail market value*. The retail market value is the price a typical home buyer would pay for the house. Two conditions must exist for a home-owner to consider selling for less: The homeowner must have the means and the motivation to sell.

First, the owner must have the *means* to sell the house below retail market value and still pay off the mortgage and any other debt related to the house. In our experience, there are only three ways this happens (see Figure 3-4):

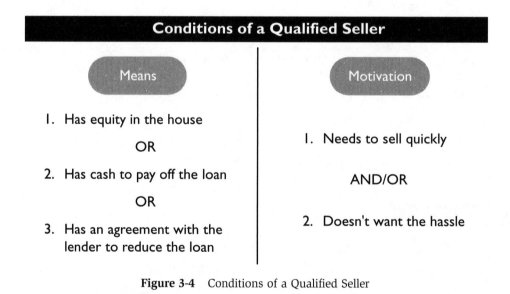

Figure 3-4   Conditions of a Qualified Seller

1. The homeowner has equity in the house. Equity is the difference between what the homeowner owes and what he could get from selling it.
2. The homeowner has the cash necessary to pay off any shortfall in the loan.
3. The lender has agreed not to be paid in full when the house sells (usually in the foreclosure process).

The second condition that allows a homeowner to sell for below retail market value is her *motivation* to sell. Someone willing to sell below retail market value needs to sell quickly, doesn't want the hassles of selling, or both.

One of the investors we work with tells the remarkable story of a motivated seller. To paraphrase, the call went like this:

Seller: I saw your postcard and need to sell my house today.

Investor: Wow! Why do you need to sell so fast?

Seller: You'll never believe this, but my boyfriend just won the lottery, and I'm flying out tomorrow to be with him. And I'm not coming back. I've already quit my job and need to sell my house now.

Investor: What's your address? I'll be right there.

As it turned out, she had an attractive house and readily accepted his discounted price. Unfortunately, the chances of your finding a seller with such a positive motivation are about the same as those of winning the lottery yourself.

A number of other factors can cause a seller to be motivated, such as life events, financial hardships, the inability or unwillingness to make repairs, and vacancy (Figure 3-5). Your ability to buy a house quickly can help people avoid or get out from under these difficult situations.

Factors That Make a Seller Motivated

Life Events
- Relocating to another city for a job
- Physically unable to maintain the property
- Divorcing and needs to sell

Financial Hardship
- Can't afford existing house payments
- Already moved and now facing two mortgage payments

Must Sell As Is
- Can't afford to fix the house and must sell it as is
- Is too busy to fix the house and wants to sell it as is

Vacancy
- Doesn't want to remotely manage the repairs
- Unable to rent it

Figure 3-5   Factors That Make a Seller Motivated

If you determine that the seller has both the means and the motivation to sell the house at less than retail value, you have a qualified seller. In the next section, we'll walk you through a checklist that gives you some questions that you can ask to qualify a lead.

THE QUALIFYING CONVERSATION

The following introductory script and checklist guide you through the questions you should ask to qualify the house as well as the seller. We've grouped the questions by the information they are designed to uncover. You may want to make a list that orders and phrases the questions in a way you like. Keep it handy so that you have it ready when a lead comes in.

We're giving you this script and checklist because we want you to be systematic and effective in qualifying potential leads. The point is that these aren't casual conversations; they're purposeful and friendly investigations. You don't want to waste your time and you don't want to waste their time—the only way to do that is to follow a system. There are four objectives with your qualifying checklist:

1. To convince the seller that you may be a solution to her problem
2. To determine if this is a house that meets your buying criteria
3. To discover if the seller has the motivation and means to meet your price
4. To turn up any other opportunities for you or your network

GETTING THE QUALIFYING CONVERSATION STARTED

Script Option 1 (When the Seller Contacts You)

Investor: Hello. It's a great day at [your investment company]. How can I help you?

Homeowner: *I'm thinking about selling my home.*

Investor: Great. Would you mind telling me how you heard about me?

Homeowner: *I got one of your postcards.*

Investor: Where is your house?

Homeowner: *123 Bird Street. So you buy homes?*

Investor: Well, I'm an investor and am certainly interested in houses in that area. If it's not a problem, I'd like to take just a few minutes of your time to ask a few questions about your property and why you are thinking about selling. I want to make the best use of your time, and these questions will help me understand whether we need to set up an appointment for me to come see your house.

Script Option 2 (When You Contact the Seller)

Investor: Hi. My name is [name]. I'm calling because I am interested in your house at [address].

Homeowner: *How can I help you?*

Investor: Well, I've noticed [you're trying to sell your own house *or* your house has been on the market for a long time *or* your house is facing foreclosure *or* your house has been vacant for some time *or* you have a house that you've been trying to rent] and I think I might be able to help you out.

Homeowner: *How?*

Investor: Well, I'm an investor and am interested in buying your house. Have you ever thought about selling?

Homeowner: *Yes* or *no.*

Investor: [If *YES*] Great. If it's not a problem, I'll just take a couple of minutes of your time to ask you a few questions about your property and why you are thinking about selling. I want to make the best use of your time, and these questions will help me understand whether we need to set up an appointment for me to come see your house.

Investor: [If *NO*] Would you mind my asking why you're not interested in selling your property? [Explore their objections to selling, and if there is not a win-win solution you can provide, thank them for their time.]

QUALIFYING QUESTIONS ABOUT THE HOUSE

In Satisfactory Condition?

1. When was your house built?
2. What condition is the house in?

3. How much do you think it will cost to fix it up?
4. Have you ever filed an insurance claim?
5. Are there any cracks in the foundation?
6. Has your house ever been in a fire?
7. Have you ever had any water leaks or damage (posing potential mold issues)?
8. Does your house have asbestos siding or tiles?
9. Have you ever had any termite problems?
10. Is the roof in good condition, or has it ever leaked?
11. Do you know if the house has aluminum wiring?

A Neighborhood Misfit?

12. What do you really like about the house?
13. What really bothers you about the house?
14. What's the square footage?
15. What makes your house unique? How does your house compare with the other houses in the neighborhood?
16. If money was no object, what would you do to the house?
17. How many bedrooms and bathrooms?
18. What is the kitchen like?
19. How does your lot compare with others in the neighborhood?
20. Is it near railroad tracks? Power lines? A drainage ditch? Anything unusual?
21. Does the lot border anything other than houses, such as a commercial building or school?

If a lead comes in as a phone call, you won't have the luxury of researching the house beforehand. Have your Web resources such as a mapping service and the tax rolls bookmarked so that you can research the property quickly while you talk to the seller.

Whether they call you or you call them, you want to know as much about the property as possible from information sources you absolutely

Get as much information as you can before you call a lead. This will help you focus on the questions you need answered to qualify the house. And if you find a reason to disqualify the house before you contact the seller, you can save yourself the call.

trust, such as the Multiple Listing Service (MLS) and tax rolls. This also will help you limit the conversation to the questions you don't already have answers to. The information you gather during the call can really help you later in the process when you are analyzing the house or negotiating the deal.

QUALIFYING QUESTIONS ABOUT THE HOMEOWNER

Do They Have the Means?

1. How long have you owned the house?
2. Do you remember what you paid for the house?
3. Do you have an asking price in mind?
4. Is there a mortgage? Do you know the balance?
5. Are you the sole owner of the property?
6. Are you aware of any liens or judgments against the property?

Do They Have the Motivation?

7. Why are you interested in selling the house?
8. How quickly do you want to sell?
9. Is anyone living in the house?
10. Are the house payments up to date?

WRAPPING UP THE QUALIFYING CONVERSATION

Script Option 1 (If the Lead Qualifies)

Investor: This sounds like something I would be interested in. Would it be inconvenient for me to stop by this evening/afternoon/morning at [suggest a specific time]?

Script Option 2 (If the Lead Doesn't Qualify)

Investor: Well, thanks for your time, but unfortunately, I don't think this property would work for me. Would you mind if I shared your information with some of the other investors I know who may be able to help you out?

Let's say you've asked the right questions and the answers give you a sense that you have a qualified house and a qualified seller. It's time to evaluate the house thoroughly to determine its potential investment value. In the Analyze stage, you will gather the information and perform the analysis necessary to make a smart offer on the house.

You qualify a lead to determine if it's worth the time and expense involved in doing a thorough analysis. The qualifying process has two steps: qualifying the house and qualifying the seller.

Here are some things to remember:

1. Qualifying the house is a matter of applying your three buying criteria:
   - Verify that the house is in one of your target neighborhoods.
   - Determine whether you are willing to take on a house in its condition.
   - Verify that the house is not a neighborhood misfit that would be hard to sell once it is fixed up.

2. Qualifying the seller requires that two conditions be met:
   - The seller has the means to pay off the mortgage through equity, cash, or an agreement with the lender to forgive the shortfall.
   - The seller has the motivation to sell the house below market value: the seller needs quick cash or the seller doesn't want the hassle of selling the house.

Mitch and Amy

It had been two months since Mitch and Amy decided to concentrate on finding houses by using the prospecting methods Ed had talked about at their meeting. Prospecting was the best method for their situation. Mitch had plenty of time between shifts at the fire station, and they didn't have a lot of money to spend on advertising. Besides, Mitch wasn't keen on networking.

Mitch spent several hours a week driving through their selected neighborhoods and looking for vacant houses, but hadn't turned up any real investment possibilities. Things were not developing as quickly as they had hoped. Amy was doing online research, tracking down owners, and sending letters after school. So far, the calls had been few and far between and none had gone anywhere.

"When are we going to find a house?" Amy asked one night as they sat on the couch. "It's been two months, and nothing."

"I know," Mitch agreed. He shifted so that Amy could rub his back. All that driving was making him sore. "I'm beginning to have some doubts too."

"Really?"

Mitch sighed. "I know Ed said we just needed to be persistent and it would work out, but we haven't even come close. Maybe this just isn't for us."

Amy stopped rubbing, resting her hands on his back. "I've been thinking the same thing."

"Let's make a deadline," Mitch offered, turning to face her. "If we don't get a house in the next two months, we'll reconsider the whole thing."

"Sounds like a plan," Amy said. "I'll mark it on the calendar."

Just a week later, Mitch had a breakthrough. On several of his trips through Greenbriar Estates, he had noticed an older man walking his dog, often carrying an armful of sun-yellowed newspapers. Finally, his curiosity got the better of him, and he stopped the car and approached the man.

"Excuse me, sir," he said with a smile. "I noticed you carrying those newspapers. Mind if I ask why?"

The man gave him the once-over and pointed to Mitch's fire station T-shirt.

"You a firefighter?" the man asked.

"Yes, sir," Mitch replied. "I sure am."

"My brother was a firefighter before he retired." The man extended his hand. "My name is Ben. Now, how can I help you?"

"I was just curious about those newspapers you're always carrying."

Ben shrugged. "I've lived here since they opened up this neighborhood. I think it's a great place to live. But when folks move out, sometimes the papers tend to pile up and become an eyesore. So I pick 'em up and throw 'em away."

Mitch had not thought of that. It helped explain why he wasn't spotting very many vacant houses in this neighborhood. Ben the newspaper snatcher.

Ben continued. "It's such a shame. People nowadays don't seem to take as much pride in their neighborhoods as they used to. I think you can tell a good neighborhood by how many neat yards it has." He pointed across the street. "That one is right next to my house, and it's been empty for months. Been mowing the grass since the renters moved out."

Mitch had not thought of that either—looks like there's more to spotting a good prospect than piled up newspapers and an overgrown lawn. "That's nice of you. Do you happen to know who owns it? I'm interested in buying and fixing up houses in this neighborhood," Mitch told him.

"Sure do," Ben said.

Mitch copied down the owners' names from Ben along with the addresses of three other vacant houses in Greenbriar Estates.

Later, when Mitch told Amy about Ben, she suggested that he talk to more people in the neighborhood. He also started to call the phone numbers on the "For Sale by Owner" and "House for Rent" signs to see whether they were worth pursuing. Even though he'd initially been resistant to the idea, Mitch was beginning to see the value of getting to know people in his target area. Maybe he'd even like networking.

Bill and Nancy

Bill took the first sip of his freshly brewed coffee and sighed contentedly: "Ah, life is good." In just a few minutes, he would be meeting someone who might provide a good lead on his first house to flip. He savored the warmth of the cup, the rich aromas, and the sounds of people placing their orders. This was his favorite diner.

He enjoyed being with other people; it really energized him. When Ed had suggested networking as a strategy for finding houses, Bill had gotten excited. He was a natural networker, and it took barely any effort.

Ed had introduced him to Tom, a go-getter in his early thirties who had flipped more than fifty houses the previous year. Tom was "the man" in the southern metro area. Bill hoped to imitate his success in the north; that was why he had arranged his first meeting with Tom almost two months earlier.

Bill made an impression on Tom from the start. The first time they met, he offered to pay Tom for his advice (besides paying for lunch). The offer was genuine. He knew he was taking some of Tom's valuable time. Tom graciously declined the offer, but after the meeting, Bill recalled that Tom worked with the local Big Brothers chapter. He sent a $100 donation to the charity in Tom's name.

A couple of weeks later, Tom had gotten a group of investors together to build a house for a needy family. Bill showed up at the worksite with coffee for everyone and said, "Just tell me what you need, and I will get it done." Tom put the former drill sergeant to work and later claimed that the project was done in half the time as a result of Bill's efforts.

Ever since he and Nancy had decided to find a house to flip, Bill had been having lunches with Tom and about a dozen other people, including real estate agents, contractors, lenders, a lawyer, and someone from each of the neighborhood associations in his area.

Nancy had been a big help in organizing a database with the names and phone numbers of all the people in his network. They used it to track the times Bill called or met with people. They also added notes from his meetings. Nancy had helped him set up reminders in his calendar to call his contacts. He didn't mind talking on the phone, but he much preferred meeting in person.

Tom stirred another creamer into his mug of coffee and said, "Bill, I have a line on a good house to flip. It's too far away for me, but it happens to be very close to you."

Bill smiled. Yes, life is good, he thought.

Samantha

Samantha was halfway through the Sunday crossword and still hadn't finished her first cup of coffee when the phone rang. Typically, she would have resented the interruption, but this was a call on her new business phone.

After a slow start, her advertising campaign was beginning to show results, just as Ed had said it would. She hadn't found the right house yet, but she knew it was a numbers game: The more leads she got, the better the chance that she'd find one that worked.

"This is Samantha."

"Um, hi. I got one of those bright green postcards you've been sending out. I'm looking to sell my house." The person at the other end of the line sounded a little nervous.

"Great, could you give me the address?" she said as she headed down the hall to her computer.

Her computer screen jumped to life as she moved the mouse. Samantha quickly made a note that he had called because of her postcards. She was keeping track of which of her advertising strategies were proving effective.

"It's 2784 Seneca Drive." The street name sounded familiar, and she did a quick Internet search to find out whether it was in one of her target neighborhoods. If it wasn't, she would get the caller off the phone quickly and politely.

"I love that area," she said to the caller once she had confirmed that it was in her target neighborhood. Referring to the qualifying script Ed had helped her create, she started asking a series of questions to qualify the seller and the property quickly.

"What is your name?"

"Andy Harrison."

"Well, Andy, I'm certainly interested in houses in that area. If it's not a problem, I'd like to take just a few minutes to ask you some questions about your property and why you are thinking about selling. I want to make the best use of your time, and these questions will help me understand whether we need to set up an appointment to see your house."

"Sure, no problem," Andy responded.

Samantha recalled her conversation with Ed about the two requirements for a qualified seller: the means and the motivation. First, does the seller have enough money in the house or in the bank to sell it below market value? Second, does the seller have a reason to sell it below market value instead of trying to sell it through the conventional channels?

"All right, how long have you owned the house?"

"Eleven years."

While they were talking, Samantha pulled up the county tax assessment Web site and did a search on the property. She quickly found the square footage and the current appraised value.

"And what is your asking price?"

"I was really hoping to get about $150,000." But Andy didn't sound very sure, and he paused. Samantha bit her tongue and reminded herself not to say anything. Ed had told her to listen and not give the seller any feedback after asking this question.

After a short silence, Andy said, "Oh, I don't know, maybe even $140,000. I really just want to get this over with."

Samantha moved on. "What do you owe on the house?"

There was a pause. "Frankly, I don't think that is any of your business." He seemed perturbed. "Maybe my calling was a mistake."

That changed quickly, Samantha thought. She wondered what had brought that on when things seemed to be going so smoothly. "Andy, I hope I didn't offend you."

"No." Andy sounded exasperated. "It's just that you're the third person I've called, and it seems like everyone is trying to rip me off."

"Well, Andy, I can't speak for anyone else, but I would not try to rip you off. You have a house that you would like to sell quickly, and I need to find out certain information to see if this is a worthwhile investment for me. My sincere hope is that we can eventually reach a deal that will be mutually beneficial."

"Why do you need to know how much equity I have in my house?"

Well, at least he hasn't hung up yet, Samantha thought. She always trusted her instincts, and although it was early in the call, she had a hunch that this could turn out to be a good deal. It was worth hanging in there. "I agree this is a personal financial question, but frankly, it helps me determine if this will work out for both of us. The long and the short of it is that I need to make money, but I also want to see you walk away satisfied that you were treated fairly. This has to be a win-win, and that's the only way I do business. Andy, you would not regret working with me."

Silence. Andy seemed to be thinking it over. "Sixty thousand," was all he said.

Samantha breathed a sigh of relief. "Okay, do you mind if I ask you some more questions?"

"Go ahead," Andy said.

It looked like Andy would be able to pay off the mortgage and still be able to end up with some cash in his pocket. On that positive note, Samantha decided to switch gears. Did he have enough motivation to sell for lower than market value?

"Andy, why are you selling the house?" She held her breath, hoping the question wouldn't offend him.

"Well, I got transferred to Memphis. I tried selling it myself. I sold it to some people and agreed to let them move in before closing. What a mistake. We never closed and it took some time to get them out."

"I'm sorry to hear that. Have you already bought a place in Memphis?" Samantha asked.

"Yes, and I'm not too thrilled about paying two mortgages."

Andy obviously had a big motivation to sell. "I hear you," Samantha responded sympathetically. "Is the house vacant?"

"Yes, it is. We've already moved to Memphis, and I'm down for the weekend to take care of the lawn, get some things fixed, you know."

In spite of herself, Samantha was getting a little excited. Her instincts may have been correct; this call had some potential. Now it was time to see if the house qualified. She made sure her voice sounded casual and matter-of-fact.

"How old is the house?"

"It's twenty-one years old. I think it was one of the first ones built when the area was developed."

"Andy, you mentioned that you were fixing a few things. What kind of condition is the house in?"

Andy hesitated a moment. "Nothing all that major. I was never that handy to begin with and then those people really didn't take care of the place while they were there. So there's probably some stuff that needs to be fixed."

Not much information there, but there could be some red flags. She fired off a series of questions. "Have you ever filed a claim on your insurance?" No. "Any cracks in the foundation?" No. "Water damage?" No, not that he knew of. She continued until she had as good a picture of the house as she could get from Andy.

This was the most promising call she'd had in the month or so she'd been advertising. "Okay, Andy, I know you're only in town for a short time. Could I come by this afternoon?"

"I'm kinda tied up this afternoon. I'll leave a key under the mat and you can call me if you have any questions."

"Great, that works for me." Samantha couldn't wait to check out the house and run the numbers. Maybe this would be the one. She dialed Ed's number to see if he could meet her at the house.

Mitch and Amy

Mitch rolled his head to loosen the muscles in his neck as he walked in the front door. He was getting a little tired of all the driving. Another four-hour stint "driving for dollars," as he had heard it described at an investment club meeting, had yielded a couple more leads, but they still had not found their first house.

He was surprised that the house was dark; Amy was usually home by now. Two steps into the foyer he saw that two candles were on the dining room table and that it was set for two.

"Would you like to join me for dinner?" Amy asked with a grin.

"What's the occasion?"

Amy handed him a glass. "A toast," she said. "To us, and," she said, pausing for effect, "our first house."

"What?" Mitch didn't know what to think.

Amy set down her glass and leaned forward, "Mitch, I think we might have our first house. Do you remember when you told me about Ben the newspaper snatcher? Well, we sent a letter to the owner. She called me today, and I talked with her for about half an hour. Everything's falling into place. She said the house in Greenbriar wasn't for sale, but she did have another house she wanted to sell. I think it's the one for us."

"Really? What do you know about it?"

Amy flashed a deliberate smile. "I called Monica right after I got off the phone and asked her to pull some comps for us." Monica was the real estate agent who had been prospecting for them.

"And what did she say?"

"She got back to me about an hour ago and said that it should sell for $125,000 once it was all fixed up. Mitch, the owner seems like she wants to get her money out of the house, and it's in no shape to be put on the market but not a complete disaster." Amy paused again for effect. "She said she'd let it go for around $75,000."

Mitch quickly ran the numbers in his head. "That sounds like it might really work."

"Uh, Mitch, there's one more thing." Amy hesitated. "The house is not exactly nearby."

Stage Two

ANALYZE

How to Make an Offer That Rewards You for Your Risk

ANALYZE Introduction

> *Take calculated risks. That is*
> *quite different from being rash.*

—General George S. Patton, Jr.

Once you've generated a lead and verified its potential as an investment property, it's time to take a closer look. Take a moment to pat yourself on the back. Finding investment properties is tough work, but your consistency and perseverance have paid off. Many would-be investors never get serious about the business of searching and therefore never find a house worth investigating. You've passed the first test. Feel free to savor the moment, but not for too long. Now the real work begins. It's time to see if we have found a keeper.

In our opinion, the Analyze stage is the most important part of the investment process. This is where careful investors make their money and risk takers often lose theirs. This part of the book is devoted to teaching you how to make smart offers, specifically, how to perform the analysis and count the costs to determine your *maximum offer*: the absolute most you can pay for a property and still realize a solid profit. Knowing your maximum offer gives you the ability to stay objective during the buying process. You will be able to present your offer with confidence, keep your emotions in check, and walk away from an unprofitable or risky deal without regrets.

Experience shows that in the real estate investment game you often have to move quickly. This can create a real tension between thoroughly analyzing a property and making a timely offer. We follow a proven process that helps us be as thorough as possible while still reacting quickly to house-buying opportunities. The more times you do this analysis, the faster you will become without sacrificing accuracy.

THE MAXIMUM OFFER FORMULA

To come up with the maximum offer, we use a four-part formula:

1. Start with the *eventual selling price* (ESP) of the house (often referred to as the after-repair value).

2. Subtract the *improvement costs*: a comprehensive and accurate estimate of the total expenses you will incur in doing the improvements.

3. Subtract the *quiet costs*. These are the often overlooked expenses associated with buying, holding, and selling a house.

4. Subtract an amount that represents the *minimum profit* you should receive in light of the risks.

The remaining amount is your *maximum offer* (Figure 1).

The FLIP Maximum Offer Formula
Eventual Selling Price
− Improvement Costs
− Quiet Costs
− Minimum Profit
= Maximum Offer

Figure 1   The FLIP Maximum Offer Formula

FLIPPING POINT

There are a lot of quick offer formulas out there today, but the measure of a good formula is not just how quick it is but how accurate it is. By including your quiet costs and accounting for risk, the FLIP formula will help you make the right offer fast without overcomplicating things. With the FLIP formula, your offer sometimes will be higher than a quick offer calculation, allowing you to buy more houses. At other times your offer will be much less, helping you steer clear of riskier deals. The key is to make the right decision, not necessarily a quick decision.

We divide the Analyze stage into five steps. In the first, you'll discover exactly what improvements you'll make to the house. With this as a guide, the remaining steps address each part of the offer formula in order, starting with the eventual selling price and ending with your minimum required profit.

To help us follow the steps of the Analyze stage in a clear and practical way, we'll be using an example house that we're considering as an investment. Let's begin by establishing a few details:

- It's located at 1202 Fence Post Trail in the Western Hills subdivision.
- It's a four-bedroom, two-and-a-half-bathroom house with 2,000 square feet that was built in 1987.
- The homeowner is asking $179,000 for the house, but he's motivated to sell quickly. During your conversation with him while qualifying the lead, you felt that the seller might accept closer to $150,000 if you could close quickly with cash.
- You'll use $20,000 of your own money and borrow the rest of the money needed to buy the house, pay the quiet costs, and pay for the improvements. Your lender requires 3 points (3 percent of the loan up front) and a 13 percent annual interest rate. Remember, this is a short-term loan from a private lender, so the costs and interest rate will be substantially higher than for a long-term mortgage loan.

With that example in mind, let's begin with one of the most important skills needed in flipping houses: the ability to determine the right improvements to make to a house to maximize your profit.

Chapter 4
Identify Improvements

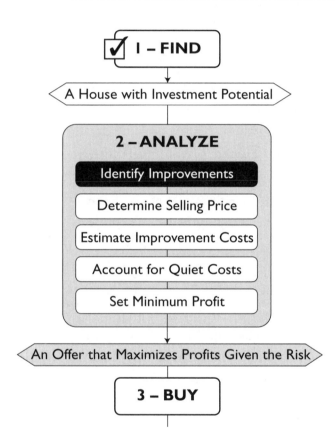

After reading this chapter you will know how to

- Identify the fixes you must make
- Identify the design choices you should make
- Identify the undiscovered potential you could bring out

Rick will never forget the walkthrough of his first prospective investment house:

It was in an unsavory part of town, and the stares I was getting from the guys drinking beer next door suggested that I wasn't welcome in the neighborhood. The owner of the property couldn't get off work to let me in, but he told me that I could remove the plywood nailed over the side door and let myself in. Great, now they're going to think I'm breaking in, I told myself. I smiled, held up a crowbar, and said, "I've got the key." They laughed. I removed the plywood and stepped inside, where I suddenly was struck with a revolting stench. The jitters I had about the neighbors quickly gave way to nausea and the dread of what might be inside the house. So that's what the guys were laughing at, I thought. The place was being used as an outhouse.

I dashed back outside and took a deep breath. I was overwhelmed with the magnitude of this project. Where should I start? What did I have to do? Was it even worth it? Then I was struck with a simple but powerful idea. It was just three words and I scribbled them down. Then I took another deep breath and went in to take notes until I had to go back outside for fresh air. I repeated the process until I had filled several sheets on my legal pad. Even to this day, those three words affect how HomeFixers assesses dozens of houses each month.

The three words that Rick wrote were *must*, *should*, and *could*.

DECIDING WHAT TO DO

Each month HomeFixers helps dozens of real estate investors from all over the country make improvement decisions that will maximize their profits. There are hundreds and maybe even thousands of improvements that can be made to any house. How do you decide what to do? Maybe more important, what should you not do? Building on Rick's walkthrough from years ago, we've found that as you walk through a house, the best way to make improvement decisions is by asking these three questions: What *must* I do? What *should* I do? and What *could* I do? See Figure 4-1.

The Three Walkthrough Questions

1. What must I do?   What are the problems that need to be fixed?

2. What should I do?   What is the proper level of finish out?

3. What could I do?   What is the untapped potential?

Figure 4-1   The Three Walkthrough Questions

THE MUST-DO'S

As you step into a house the first time and look around, it is easy to become overwhelmed just like Rick was. In our experience, the best place to begin is with the most obvious improvements: the problems. Walk through a house one room at a time, looking at the appliances, fixtures, and systems, and ask yourself, "Is it functioning? Does it work?" Does the roof keep water out, and do the doors open and close? If the utilities are on, does water flow, do the drains work without leaking, do the lights turn on, does the air blow cool? You're determining what's dead or alive: what works and what doesn't. If it does work, how much life is left in it? What's its condition? Are the doors broken, are the windows broken, do the fans rattle, are the appliances on their last legs? The must-do's are a no-brainer: They're nonnegotiable; you have to do them. You will do them cost-effectively, but there is no choice about doing them—you must.

To make it easier to capture the data as you walk through a house, we've put together a checklist of common must-do's (Figure 4-2). This will help you avoid making the mistake of overlooking an important problem. The list is based on the way HomeFixers does home assessments for its investor clients and is organized by the same categories we use when analyzing a rehab project. Visit flipthebook.com for the most up-to-date and printable versions.

The Must-Do's: Problems You Must Take Care Of

Safety and Security
❏ Windows don't close
❏ Windows don't lock
❏ Exterior doors don't close
❏ Exterior doors don't lock
❏ The house is not secure

Cleaning and Disposal
❏ Junk in yard
❏ Trash and debris inside house
❏ Germs and grime on surfaces
❏ Pet odors

Structural and Drainage
❏ Foundation is unstable or not level
❏ Floor joists are damaged, crooked, or unstable
❏ Rafters are damaged, crooked, or unstable
❏ Window and door headers are damaged, crooked, or unstable
❏ Roof is sagging, bulging, sway-backed, or unsupported

❏ Walls are crooked and/or bulging
❏ Foundation shows signs of settlement
❏ Chimney, porches, patio, or stairs are pulling away from the house
❏ Inadequate drainage
❏ Soil is not properly graded to keep water away from the home
❏ Water seepage in the crawl space and/or basement
❏ Wet or damp basement
❏ Buckled floors or mildewy odor in basement
❏ French drains are needed or are not functioning as intended
❏ Gutters and/or downspouts are needed or are in need of repair or replacement

Pest Control
❏ Signs of active termites
❏ Fleas, roaches, spiders, wasps, hornets

Figure 4-2

The Must-Do's: Problems You Must Take Care Of

❑ Bees

❑ Indications of rodents

Roof

❑ Roof leaks

❑ Shingles are old, damaged, worn, or missing

❑ Flashings are in need of replacement

❑ Improper flashing

❑ Rolled roof is wrinkled and/or damaged

❑ Water standing on roof

❑ More than two layers of shingles on roof

❑ Vents need to be replaced

❑ Decking is rotted and/or sagging

❑ Pipe protrusions need to be painted

❑ Nails need to be caulked

Exterior Rough Carpentry
(siding, fascia, soffit, exterior doors, exterior trim, garage door, porch, deck, columns, railings, privacy fence)

❑ Loose and rotted siding

❑ Wood rot along bottom of siding

❑ Siding in contact with soil

❑ Fascia boards rotted

❑ Soffit board and eaves have rotten wood

❑ Wood rot at front porch column

and/or railing

❑ Wood rot at bottom of garage door posts

❑ Water damage on lower panels of garage door

❑ Door threshold is rotten

❑ Doors are missing proper weather stripping

❑ Deck, railings, and stairs in need of repair

❑ Wood privacy fence damaged or missing pickets

Interior Rough Carpentry

❑ Mushy subfloor

❑ Rotted or termite-eaten studs

❑ The floor, wall, or roof framing sags, bulges, or has deflections

Windows

❑ Broken window glass

❑ Window screens missing or damaged

❑ Windows won't open or shut

❑ Seal broken in double-pane glass (fogged)

❑ Missing locks

❑ Windows missing proper caulking

Fireplace

❑ Fireplace/chimney has excessive creosote buildup

❑ Bricks/mortar in need of repair

Figure 4-2 *(continued)*

The Must-Do's: Problems You Must Take Care Of

HVAC

❏ Furnace not functioning or at the end of its useful life

❏ Wall heater not functioning or at the end of its useful life

❏ HVAC system needed

❏ Condenser not functioning or at the end of its useful life

❏ Ducts are decaying and need to be replaced

❏ HVAC filter dirty; system in need of service

❏ Condensate line needs to be extended

❏ Exhaust fan units don't vent to the exterior

❏ Exhaust fans rattle

❏ Air vents are rusty and mildewed

❏ Thermostat needs to be replaced

Plumbing

❏ Hot water heater not up to current code (height, flue, temperature and pressure (T&P) valve, overflow, combustion air intake)

❏ Walk-in shower (leaking shower pan)

❏ Toilet leaks, runs, doesn't flush, loose

❏ Bathtub is chipped, stained, cracked (needs to be replaced or refinished)

❏ Bathtub/shower handles leak

❏ Sinks badly stained, scratched, chipped, or broken

❏ Faucets drip or leak

❏ Hot and cold water faucets reversed

❏ Drains are slow or leaky

❏ Gas space heaters and wall heaters present

❏ Washing machine connections are badly corroded or leaking

❏ Ice maker box leaking

❏ Outside faucets leak and/or need vacuum breakers to prevent backflow

❏ Old galvanized iron water supply lines are present

❏ Connected pipes have incompatible materials

❏ Main drain lines leak

❏ Water supply lines leak

❏ Vent lines not present

❏ Sewer lines leak

Electrical

❏ Ground fault interrupt circuit (GFCI) needed in kitchen, bathrooms, utility room, outside, unfinished basements, and garage

❏ Smoke detectors needed

❏ Electrical service insufficient

❏ Old fuse system

Figure 4-2

Stage Two: ANALYZE

The Must-Do's: Problems You Must Take Care Of

❏ Old knob and tube wiring present

❏ Ungrounded outlets

❏ Hot and neutral wires are reversed (use outlet tester)

❏ Aluminum wiring present (typically mid-1960s to early 1970s)

❏ Damaged or missing outlets

❏ Damaged or missing switches

❏ Exposed wiring

Masonry and Concrete Work

❏ Masonry is crumbling

❏ Stone, brick, or stucco siding in need of repair

❏ Brick in fireplace in need of repair

❏ Concrete underpinning cracked, missing, or in need of repair

❏ Sidewalks, driveway, patio cracked or in need of repair

Insulation

❏ Inadequate insulation in attic or walls

Walls

❏ Missing drywall/plaster

❏ Cracks in drywall/plaster

❏ Holes in drywall/plaster (behind doors from doorknobs, etc.)

❏ Loose drywall seams and corner bead

❏ Missing texture

❏ Wallpaper is worn and/or peeling

❏ Paneling is scratched or has holes

Cabinetry

❏ Missing cabinet doors and drawers

❏ Cabinet floor (bottom) under sink is rotted and needs to be replaced

❏ Cabinets are rotted, worn, scratched, sagging

Interior Doors and Trim

❏ Doors are damaged

❏ Doors are misaligned

❏ Window sill is water-damaged

❏ Baseboard is missing or damaged

❏ Doorjamb is cracked or damaged

❏ Space between the guardrails at the stairway is too wide

Paint

❏ Paint is peeling

❏ Water stains on sheetrock ceilings

❏ Interior in need of paint

❏ Exterior needs caulk and paint

Countertops

❏ Countertops are scratched and worn

Tile and Vinyl

❏ Tile countertop is damaged

❏ Tile around bathtub/shower is missing or damaged

❏ Tile needs to be caulked

❏ Tile needs to be regrouted

❏ Tile floor is missing or damaged

❏ Vinyl is peeling

Figure 4-2 *(continued)*

The Must-Do's: Problems You Must Take Care Of

❑ Holes in vinyl

Hardwood Floors

❑ Boards are termite-damaged or rotted

❑ Floors are badly stained

Hardware and Accessories

❑ Doorknobs and deadbolts not functioning; doorstops missing

❑ Bathroom towel bars and paper holder missing

❑ Mirrors damaged

❑ Shower door missing or broken

Appliances

❑ Range not functioning or at the end of its useful life

❑ Dishwasher not functioning or at the end of its useful life

❑ Wall oven not functioning or at the end of its useful life

❑ Cooktop not functioning or at the end of its useful life

❑ Vent hood not functioning or at the end of its useful life

❑ Microwave not functioning or at the end of its useful life

❑ Refrigerator not functioning or at the end of its useful life

❑ Garbage disposal not functioning or at the end of its useful life

❑ Trash compactor not functioning or at the end of its useful life

❑ Ice maker not functioning or at the end of its useful life

Carpet

❑ Carpet in need of replacement (stained, worn, burn marks, holes)

Landscaping

❑ Trees are overgrown and too close to the roof; shrubs need to be trimmed

Figure 4-2 The Must-Do's: Problems You Must Take Care Of

At first this may seem like a daunting list, and you may have skimmed over it. The fact of the matter is that it takes a lot of time to do a thorough home assessment. This is where you really make your money (or avoid losing it), so every minute is a worthwhile investment.

Plan on spending about three to four hours if it's your first couple of times. If you can't spend a lot of time at the house (if people live there, there are renters, etc.), take a lot of digital pictures, which we do every time. Other things to bring with you besides a digital camera are a clipboard, legal pad and pen (or a handheld voice recorder), outlet tester, voltage tester, insect repellent, flashlight, tape measure, gloves, hat, antibacterial wipes, and in some cases a crowbar.

By the way, as professional rehabbers, we walk through a house in an even more systematic and planned way. We have a software program that has a 500-point questionnaire designed to capture all of the must-do's, should-do's, and could-do's. Because we do such a large volume of home assessments, we use a tablet personal computer as we go through a house to capture hundreds of data points quickly.

For the last five years, we've been compiling data from over a thousand home assessments and lessons learned from hundreds of rehab construction projects. From this, we have built a unique proprietary tool: the HomeFixers Cost Assessment Report. It's an in-depth feasibility study that details what to do to a house to maximize profits. If you have a HomeFixers affiliate in your city (check homefixers.com), you can order a HomeFixers Cost Assessment Report.

A common question we get when we talk to people about analyzing houses is, "Can I buy the HomeFixers Cost Assessment Software?" The answer is yes. If you're interested, the details are outlined on flipthebook.com. Although you can invest in either of these services, you don't have to. We are sharing what we've learned in this book so that you can do it on your own if you choose.

THE SHOULD-DO'S

If you do only what you must do, at a minimum you'll have a clean and functional house. But you'll be leaving profit on the table if you ignore what you *should do* on the basis of what the market expects for the neighborhood. The should-do's speak to the finishing touches that affect the look and the feel of the house and make it more attractive. The standard examples are flooring, countertops, trim, tile, lighting, and paint.

We love beautiful houses. If money were no object, we would choose high-end finishes for every house we fix up: hardwood floors, granite countertops, recessed lighting, and so on. But our end game is maximum profit, not the most beautiful house. To maximize your profit, you should choose design finishes that buyers expect in your market, no better and no worse.

FLIPPING POINT

If you don't select design finishes that are on a par with what's expected for the neighborhood, you run the risk of overimproving or underimproving a house. Either way, you can reduce your profit drastically.

You might ask, "How do I know what buyers expect? How can I know for sure what I should do?" The answer is simple. You'll have your own personal construction and design consultant with you every step of the way. Meet neighborhood norm. No, we're not talking about some guy named Norm who hangs out on his front porch all day talking to the neighbors, although such a person may be an excellent source of information about the neighborhood. The neighborhood norm is what is normal for the neighborhood. More specifically, the neighborhood norm is the typical condition, features, and amenities of the houses that are selling in the neighborhood where your prospective investment property is located. What's typical for the neighborhood tells you what you should do to improve your potential investment property.

Based on the work you did in selecting your target neighborhoods, you already have a feel for what the norms are. What you now want to do is fill in the blanks. To do this, get into as many houses as you can: open houses, pending listings, new construction, remodels, estate sales, garage sales, and anything else that can (legally) get you into nearby houses. If you're working with a real estate agent to buy an investment house, she or he can get you into the active and pending listings. The goal is to determine what kind of look, feel, and finish-out is the norm.

Once you've looked at a number of houses, you'll realize that the design possibilities and features are almost endless. We've taken a lot of the guesswork out of comparing houses on the basis of design by identifying four distinct finish-out levels. This enables you to walk quickly through a house and immediately classify the four design levels as Basic, Standard, Designer, or Custom.

1. BASIC

Basic design is functional, with no frills. If something needs to be replaced, it's replaced with the least expensive materials available. The house looks neat and clean but plain. *Repair* is the operative word. Replace only if necessary because of safety, function, and condition but not design. Just think: A penny saved is a penny earned.

2. STANDARD

Standard design is nice but inexpensive. If something needs to be replaced, choose materials that match the rest of the house. But as with basic, never replace for the sake of design aesthetics. The house looks pleasant, like the finish-out of an average median-income two-bedroom suburban apartment. Form follows function.

3. Designer

A designer house is notable in respect to its design and finishes. You may replace functional systems and features solely for the sake of improved design. Everything is in new or "like new" condition. The house looks beautiful and up to date and probably will create an impression.

4. Custom

A custom house is built to impress, from the height of the ceilings to the species of hardwood used in the floors. You may replace functional and even up-to-date systems and features with even higher-end brands. Systems represent the latest technological advancements and are in perfect working order. The structure and finish-out are architecturally and creatively designed and appointed. Think: My home is my palace.

If you look around, you'll notice that these four design levels show up in a lot of other areas. Toyota offers four sedans: Corolla (basic), Camry (standard), Avalon (designer), and its luxury brand, Lexus (custom).

Closer to home (pun intended), you'll see this in the brands and materials you select for your project. Just look at how General Electric positions its line of kitchen appliances: Hotpoint (basic), GE (standard), Profile (designer), and Monogram (custom). As with GE's four lines, our design categories have a little spillover between groups, but it's apparent that there are four very distinct levels of finish-out (Figure 4-3).

Four Design and Finish Levels

	Basic	Standard	Designer	Custom
Front door	Metal Six-panel	Metal fan lite	Stock wood	Custom wood with glass
Side or back door	Slab (flat, no panel)	Six-panel	Full-lite nine-lite	Custom wood with glass
Windows	Repair existing window	Aluminum	Vinyl	Wood
Siding	Repair (patch) siding	Vertical plywood siding (T1–11)	Hardiplank, possibly with some stone, brick, or stucco	Combination of several materials: Stone and stucco possibly with some Hardi, cedar, or metal
Texture	Spatter	Drag	Orange peel (remove any popcorn ceiling texture)	None or trowel
Kitchen cabinets	Stock white or oak	Stock oak (choice of stains)	Stock maple or cherry with a few glass doors	Custom species with a number of custom glass doors
Bathroom cabinets	Stock 24- or 30-inch vanity	Stock 30-inch vanity	Stock 36+-inch vanity with cultured marble top	Custom vanity cabinet with granite top

(continued)

Figure 4-3

Four Design and Finish Levels

	Basic	Standard	Designer	Custom
Interior doors	Slab (flat, no panel)	Six-panel	Special-order hollow core	Special-order solid core
Baseboards	Repair or replace sections with existing type	3 inches or less high	4 inches or more high, paint grade	5 inches or more high, possibly stain-grade
Window trim	Sill and apron	Sill and apron	Sill, apron, and possibly window trim on first floor windows	All windows are completely cased and trimmed
Crown molding	No	No	Sparingly	Everywhere
Openings between rooms	Drywall	Drywall	Some cased openings in key places	Every opening is cased
Wall paint	Off-white	Off-white	A designer color	Color or faux finish
Ceiling paint	Same color as walls	Same color as walls	Shade of white	Designer choice
Accent paint	None	None	One or two walls	Several paint color changes for different rooms
Trim paint	Same color as walls	A shade of white	Usually a shade of white	Designer color or stained

Figure 4-3

114

Four Design and Finish Levels

	Basic	Standard	Designer	Custom
Millwork paint (cabinets, mantle, etc.)	A shade of white	Same as trim paint	Usually an off-white	Designer color or stained
Siding paint	Match existing paint to prevent multiple coats	Safe color	Designer color	Designer color
Exterior trim paint	Same paint as siding	Same paint as siding	Same paint as siding or a shade of white or a designer color	Designer color
Front door paint	A color that goes with the siding and trim	A color that goes with the siding and trim	Designer color or stained	Stained
Countertop	Inexpensive plastic laminate	Moderately priced plastic laminate	Designer laminate, Silestone, basic granite	Custom granite (beveled bull nose, honed)
Backsplash	4-inch plastic laminate strip	Plastic laminate or one row of tile	Ceramic or inexpensive quarry tile	Custom quarry tile, glass tile, handmade or hand-painted tile
Tub surrounds	Basic white 4 x 4's	Basic 4 x 4's	Subway or other tile pattern	Quarry tile (mosaic or other pattern)

(continued)

Figure 4-3

115

Four Design and Finish Levels

	Basic	Standard	Designer	Custom
Shower surrounds	Basic white 4 x 4's	Basic 4 x 4's	Subway or other tile pattern	Quarry tile (mosaic or other pattern)
Flooring for kitchen	Vinyl	Basic ceramic tile 12 inches x 12 inches	High-end ceramic tile or quarry tile	Slate, travertine, or hardwoods
Flooring for bathroom	Vinyl	Vinyl or basic ceramic tile 12 inches x 12 inches	High-end ceramic tile or quarry tile	Slate, travertine, or hardwoods
Flooring for utility room	Vinyl	Vinyl or basic ceramic tile 12 inches x 12 inches	High-end ceramic tile or quarry tile	Travertine or similar
Flooring for front entryway	Vinyl	Basic ceramic tile 12 inches x 12 inches	High-end ceramic tile or quarry tile	Slate, travertine, or hardwoods
Kitchen sink	6-inch stainless	7-inch stainless	9-inch overmount or undermount stainless	Farmhouse or other custom sink
Kitchen faucet	Chrome basic	Includes sprayer	Sprayer pulls from faucet	Custom one-lever

Figure 4-3

Four Design and Finish Levels

	Basic	Standard	Designer	Custom
Bathroom sink	Integrated plastic (imitation cultured marble)	Integrated plastic (imitation cultured marble)	Integrated cultured marble or porcelain drop-in	Undermount
Bathroom faucets	Two-handle basic	One- or two-handle basic	One-handle satin nickel	Custom (e.g., oil-rubbed bronze)
Surface mount lights	White globe (some pull string)	White mushroom-type	Satin nickel mushroom or similar (not too expensive)	Special order (e.g., oil-rubbed bronze with custom glass)
Special lighting	None	None	Some recessed lights in kitchen, breakfast, and family room; some pendants	Recessed lights throughout (usually low-voltage halogen), under-cabinet lights, pendant lights
Ceiling fans	None	Cheap, white with light kit	Satin nickel with light kit	Special order with no light kit
Appliances	Hotpoint (usually white)	GE (usually white or black)	GE Profile (usually stainless)	GE Monogram or special (Viking, Sub Zero, etc.)
Carpet	Plush	Berber	Frieze	Wool

(continued)

Figure 4-3

Four Design and Finish Levels

	Basic	Standard	Designer	Custom
Doorknobs	Inexpensive brass	Inexpensive satin nickel look	Brushed nickel look	Distressed pewter or oil-rubbed bronze
Cabinet knobs and pulls	None	None	Brushed nickel	Special order (e.g., distressed pewter)
Towel bar	Budget metal	Chrome	Brushed nickel or similar	Special order (e.g., oil-rubbed bronze)
Bathroom mirror	Cut and installed by a glass company	Cut and installed by a glass company	Framed (stock)	Special order (framed)
Landscaping	Cut grass	Cut grass, mulch gardens	Cut grass, install shrubs, plants, flowers, plant grass, mulch beds	Cut grass, install shrubs, plants, flowers, plant grass, mulch beds, install small trees, crushed granite, or stone walkways

Figure 4-3 Four Design and Finish Levels

These design levels will change over time, and you may want to customize them. Again, visit flipthebook.com if you'd like to download an updated version.

As you visit houses in your target area to determine the neighborhood norm, keep a list that shows the addresses you've visited and what you "discovered" about the design level of each house (basic, standard, designer, or custom). You can determine the neighborhood norm from the design level that occurs most often on your list, but you'll probably develop an intuition about the appropriate design level for the neighborhood once you've visited a couple of houses.

Let's look at how the design level comparison turned out for our example house on Fence Post Trail. The house is in the Western Hills subdivision, and so we took a close look at ten other houses in that neighborhood (Figure 4-4). As you can see, the market is clearly telling us that we should choose a designer-level finish.

Western Hills Design Level Comparisons

1.	1239 Mustang Run	Designer
2.	1198 Corral Cove	Standard
3.	1293 Wagon Trail	Standard
4.	1087 Prairie Dog Lane	Designer
5.	1072 Fence Post Trail	Designer
6.	1229 Round Up Bend	Designer
7.	1169 Wagon Trail	Designer
8.	1140 Mustang Run	Basic
9.	1210 Saddle Path	Designer
10.	1120 Corral Cove	Designer

Figure 4-4 Western Hills Design Level Comparisons

One final caveat about the should-do's: There can be a domino effect when it comes to replacing materials, fixtures, and appliances. Unless you plan for it, your experience might go something like this:

> *Wow, I can't believe what a difference installing new cabinet doors made. But those countertops sure look dingy now. I guess I'll have to replace them now.*
>
> *I'll bet a nice tile backsplash would be just the thing to set off those new cabinets and countertops.*
>
> *Hmm. I thought we were going to save this old kitchen sink, but now it kind of sticks out.*
>
> *Well, I can't get just any faucet for the new sink—that one with the pull-out sprayer will work great. Whoa. This is getting expensive.*
>
> *Do I have to replace the appliances now?*

You get the idea. What started as a minor update turned into a major remodel once you saw how nice the new cabinet doors looked. There is a natural "synergy" to the design choices you make in a house. Some design improvements can inadvertently create the need for other design improvements even when there is nothing functionally wrong. Although your fully renovated kitchen might add a lot of value to the house, our

FLIPPING POINT

For over twenty years, *Remodeling* magazine's annual Cost vs. Value Report has reported consistently that there are few, if any, single improvements you can make to a house that can net more than the cost of making them. Simply put, a $1,500 deck won't add $2,000 (and probably not even $1,500) to your asking price without other complementary improvements. The bottom line: If you want to see the value of a house go up beyond the investment you have made to improve it, you've got to improve synergistically. The sum of the improved parts is greater and helps make the house jump in value.

point here is to make sure you plan for those improvements and account for them in determining your maximum offer.

THE COULD-DO'S

The third way of identifying which improvements to make to a house is to ask: What *could* I do to maximize my profit? These are the extra things that make a house a better place to live. At HomeFixers we've identified five important areas of increased opportunity to maximize profits (Figure 4-5).

Five Opportunities to Extract Untapped Potential	
1. Amenities	Sprinkler systems, pantry cabinets, extra sinks, garage-door openers—the little things that make a house easier to live in
2. Openings	Widening room openings and/or removing walls between the kitchen and living areas
3. Conversions	Turning a garage, basement, attic, porch, or covered patio into heated and cooled living space
4. Additions	Adding additional bedrooms, bathrooms, bonus rooms, or even an entire second story
5. Layout Changes	Major remodeling that involves changing the entire layout of the house

Figure 4-5 Five Opportunities to Extract Untapped Potential

Amenities, open floor plans, conversions, additions, and layout changes all have the potential to increase your profit. But just as with the design choices, you need to make decisions that are appropriate for the neighborhood. Here's an in-depth look at each of these five opportunities for maximizing profits ranked by its level of cost and complexity:

1. *Amenities*. Comfort and convenience improvements that make a house easier to live in; they make it more suitable to a person's needs:

   - Adding a second sink to a bathroom vanity (a great idea for a two-bathroom house where the children have to share one bathroom).
   - Adding a pantry cabinet or pantry closet to a kitchen that doesn't have one.
   - Adding a kitchen island to increase countertop space, storage, or for an additional seating (eating) area.
   - Replacing a pedestal sink in the master bath with a vanity cabinet to increase storage.
   - Expanding or adding a closet to a room or hallway. Closet space was ranked among the top three most desirable amenities in a dream home in a study of 1,000 homeowners nationwide conducted by the market research company GfK Roper Reports. Additionally, a den can be considered a bedroom if you add a closet, increasing potential resale value.
   - Installing an over-the-range microwave to free up counter space in a small kitchen.
   - Converting a bathtub into a walk-in shower.
   - Installing a sprinkler system.
   - Installing an electric garage-door opener.
   - Installing a home security system.
   - Installing dimmer switches in key areas like the kitchen or dining room.
   - Installing extra data, voice, or cable jacks.
   - Installing accent lighting or task lighting (under cabinets, etc.).
   - Installing additional lighting in dark rooms.

2. *Openings*. Widening doorways, building a kitchen pass-through, or removing walls, furdowns, kitchen fluorescent light boxes, and

dropped ceilings—all can give a home a more updated look, visually adding more space and/or light.

3. *Conversions.* Converting a space that already has a roof and/or foundation into heated and cooled space is an efficient way to add square feet without the high cost of a full-fledged addition. This could be a room for special activities (media room, game room, sewing room, exercise room) or added convenience (extra bathroom, breakfast room, laundry room, mud room, family room). Other examples would be finishing a basement, attic, or front or back porch; enclosing a patio; and converting a garage or a portion of the garage into a work area.

4. *Additions.* Adding square footage (adding both a foundation and a roof) is a good strategy in neighborhoods where the average selling price per square foot is at least twice the building cost per square foot.

5. *Layout changes.* You can consider redesigning within the existing heated and cooled space to enhance navigation, flow, organization, entertaining, and so on. For example, you could create an enlarged master bathroom, move the kitchen, or combine two small bedrooms to make a master bedroom. The fundamental problem with layout changes is that you incur the cost of making the changes without the benefit of increasing the square footage.

We want to emphasize that these are all opportunities to increase your profit, but with those opportunities comes increased risk. If you do only the must-do's and the should-do's, you have the best chance of getting a good profit with the least amount of risk. The could-do's represent another level of profit opportunities that are done with caution and when the neighborhood norm indicates there is an opportunity.

As you go through houses in your target neighborhood, make notes about their layout and structure to help you determine whether your investment house could benefit from could-do improvements.

Let's look at what the market is telling us about the additional areas of opportunity for 1202 Fence Post Trail (Figure 4-6).

	Finish Level	Amenities	Openings	Conversions	Additions	Layout Changes
Address						
1. 1239 Mustang Run	Designer	Sprinkler System	✓			
2. 1198 Corral Cove	Standard		✓			
3. 1293 Wagon Trail	Standard	Sprinkler System			Master bed/bath	
4. 1087 Prairie Dog Lane	Designer	Sprinkler System	✓	Garage		
5. 1072 Fence Post Trail	Designer	Sprinkler System	✓			
6. 1229 Round Up Bend	Designer	Sprinkler System	✓			
7. 1169 Wagon Trail	Designer	Sprinkler System	✓	Back Porch		
8. 1140 Mustang Run	Basic					
9. 1210 Saddle Path	Designer	Sprinkler System	✓			
10. 1120 Corral Cove	Designer	Sprinkler System	✓			Room over garage became master

Western Hills Design and Remodeling Comparisons

Figure 4-6   Western Hills Design and Remodeling Comparisons

The market is telling us that there is a clear opportunity for increasing profit by adding a sprinkler system (our house is one of the few that doesn't have one). Additionally, eight of the ten houses we saw have open floor plans (ours is pretty compartmentalized but could be changed easily). Thus, our vision for the house at 1202 Fence Post Trail is designer-level finishes with an open floor plan and the addition of a sprinkler system (Figure 4-7).

1202 Fence Post Trail Vision

Should	Finish Level	Designer	
Could	Extra Opportunity	Amenities	Sprinkler System
Could	Extra Opportunity	Openings	Open Floor Plan

Figure 4-7   1202 Fence Post Trail Vision

Armed with our vision of what to do to the house, we are ready to move on to the first part of the FLIP Maximum Offer Formula: determining the eventual selling price.

could work for your property: Amenities, Openings, Conversions, Additions, and Layout Changes.

Now you know what improvements you will be planning if you buy the house. This is a major step in the analysis process. Do it thoroughly. You'll be glad you did.

Chapter 5
Determine Selling Price

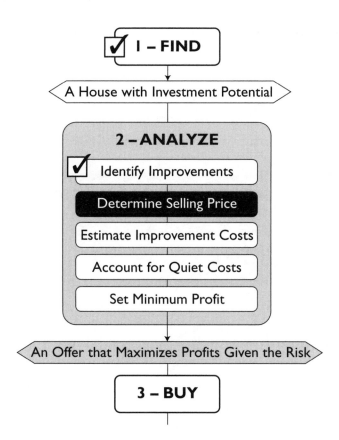

After reading this chapter you will know how to

- Estimate the selling price by referencing comparable houses
- Adjust the selling price on the basis of market trends
- Finalize the selling price with the help of experts

Every year on February 2, thousands of people descend on the small town of Punxsutawney in eastern Pennsylvania to see Punxsutawney Phil, the "weather-predicting" groundhog. Legend has it that if the hibernating animal sees his shadow as he emerges from his burrow that morning, winter will last another six weeks. If he doesn't see it, spring will come early.

Unfortunately, real estate investors don't have a Punxsutawney Phil to help with their predictions of selling prices, but there's not a shadow of a doubt that when armed with the right tools investors can predict future selling prices with remarkably high accuracy. We call that future selling price the *eventual selling price* (ESP). It's the price for which a house will sell quickly after it has been fixed up. Determining the ESP is the first and most influential of the four components in the FLIP Maximum Offer Formula for a prospective investment property (Figure 5-1).

FLIP Maximum Offer Formula
Eventual Selling Price
− Improvement Costs
− Quiet Costs
− Minimum Profit
= Maximum Offer

Figure 5-1 FLIP Maximum Offer Formula

The natural excitement of finding a good prospect can cause you to be overly optimistic and overestimate the selling price when you should be dispassionately neutral. One of our customers and a veteran real estate investor, Jay Otto, has been buying, fixing up, and selling about a dozen houses a year since the early 1980s. Jay's attitude is that of a reluctant buyer: "I look for every conceivable reason not to buy a property, and when I finally, absolutely have to, I'll buy it—but only after the house has forced me to buy it." Jay admits that his conservative approach causes him to miss some opportunities. However, he'd prefer to miss a few good opportunities if that helps him avoid the bad ones. When determining the ESP for your flip, we would encourage you to adopt Jay's attitude and remove any wishful thinking from the equation.

Like determining what to do to a house, coming up with an accurate selling price requires reading and interpreting the market. We're going to show you a four-step process for coming up with an ESP (Figure 5-2). (We think it's a little more accurate than a weather-predicting rodent.)

Four-Step Process for Determining the ESP

1. Pull the comps

2. Drive the comps

3. Read the market

4. Check with experts

Figure 5-2   Four-Step Process for Determining the ESP

STEP ONE: PULL THE COMPS

Most of us know that the Multiple Listing Service (MLS) is a great place to look for houses for sale. But the power of the MLS as a database of historical sales data becomes especially evident when one is determining the eventual selling price of a house. We'll start the process of determining the ESP by mining the MLS to come up with a rough selling price.

Ask your real estate agent to create a comparative market analysis (CMA) report for houses that have sold recently in the same neighborhood as your prospective investment house. You want similar houses, but you also want a decent set of results, so don't get too specific in the search. We suggest that you use the following five search parameters:

1. *Recently sold.* You should get six or more months' worth of sales data to get a large number of comps (at least ten). However, the ideal would be to use comparable houses that have sold within the last three months.

2. *Nearby.* Compare your prospective investment house only to houses in the same neighborhood.

3. *Size.* The comparable houses should be roughly the same size. You won't get meaningful data by comparing a 1,500-square-foot house with a 5,000-square-foot house. We suggest ± 500 square feet as a range for the search. The closer the better.

4. *Age.* In general, houses built around the same time in the same neighborhood tend to have the same architecture, condition, and basic features. We suggest ± 10 years for the search. Again, the closer in age, the better the comp.

5. *Layout.* The comparable houses should have about the same number of bedrooms and bathrooms as the prospective investment house. We suggest ± 1 for both bedrooms and bathrooms.

FLIPPING POINT

If your CMA report results in too few houses, you can relax the parameters to include houses with a greater range of square footage, age, and layout. But be wary of including any comps that have selling dates older than six months. Home values in a neighborhood can change dramatically in a few months. If you still can't get a good number of results, you need to question whether the house is truly in a desirable neighborhood.

Let's continue to use 1202 Fence Post Trail as an example. Recall that it's a 2,000-square-foot house built in 1987 with four bedrooms and two and a half bathrooms. Your agent will pull the appropriate comps (Figure 5-3).

CMA Search Parameters for 1202 Fence Post Trail

1. Recently Sold   Within the last three months

2. Nearby   In the Western Hills Subdivision

3. Similar Size   1,500–2,500 square feet

4. Similar Layout   3 to 5 bedrooms, 1.5 to 3.5 bathrooms

5. Similar Age   Built from 1977 to 1997

Figure 5-3   CMA Search Parameters for 1202 Fence Post Trail

You can get a rough estimate of the ESP directly from the results of the CMA. The report for the Fence Post Trail example shows that eleven houses met our search parameters (Figure 5-4). The average price per square foot of all eleven comps is $138. From that, we calculate a rough selling price by multiplying the square footage of the prospective investment house by $138 to get $276,000 ($138 × 2,000 square feet = $276,000).

Comparative Market Analysis for the Western Hills Subdivision

	Address	Price Sold	Square Feet	Price Per SQ FT	Beds	Baths	Stories	Year Built
1.	1300 Mustang Run	$255,360	2,250	$113	4	2	2	1983
2.	1684 Prairie Dog Lane	$285,000	2,266	$126	4	2.5	2	1983
3.	1900 Round Up Bend	$322,950	2,484	$130	4	2.5	2	1988
4.	1435 Wagon Trail	$271,320	2,016	$135	4	2	1	1982
5.	1400 Trails End Circle	$244,900	1,786	$137	4	2	1	1984
6.	1439 Wagon Trail	$244,900	1,786	$137	3	2	1	1985
7.	1905 Round Up Bend	$343,000	2,417	$142	3	2	1	1986
8.	1189 Rodeo Drive	$289,900	1,997	$145	4	2	1	1984
9.	1400 Saddle Path	$299,000	2,057	$145	4	3	1	1989
10.	1164 Rodeo Drive	$285,000	1,939	$147	3	2	1	1981
11.	1515 Coral Cove	$356,393	2,247	$159	4	2	2	1980
	AVERAGE	$290,702	2,113	$138	4	2	1	1984
	1202 Fence Post Trail		2,000		4	2.5	2	1987

Figure 5-4   Comparative Market Analysis for the Western Hills Subdivision

THE NEIGHBORHOOD MODEL

In addition to indicating a rough selling price, CMA reports provide a kind of "model home" by looking at the averages of comparable houses. The typical house selling in the neighborhood has 2,113 square feet, four bedrooms (actually 3.73, but we're rounding), two bathrooms, one story and was built in 1984 (Figure 5-5).

The "Model" House in Western Hills	
Square Feet	2,113
Bedrooms	4
Bathrooms	2
# of Stories	1
Age	1984

Figure 5-5   The "Model" House in Western Hills

Comparing 1202 Fence Post Trail with the model house, we see that the Fence Post Trail house has more bathrooms and is newer than the model house. But it's also a bit smaller and has two stories, whereas the neighborhood model house has one. All things considered, the house on Fence Post Trail looks good compared with the houses selling in the neighborhood (Figure 5-6).

What does that mean? It means that the prospective investment house is in the middle of the road for the comps: There's no reason to believe (yet) that we could get any more or any less than $276,000. If a prospective investment house turns out to be better or worse than the model house, you need to adjust the rough ESP appropriately. We wish there were an absolute, fail-safe formula for how much to adjust the selling price, but there isn't. That's why there are three more steps you must go through in determining the ESP.

Fence Post Trail versus the Model House in Western Hills			
	The Model House	Fence Post Trail	Comparison
Square Feet	2,113	2,000	Worse
Bedrooms	4	4	Same
Bathrooms	2	2.5	Better
# of Stories	1	2	Worse
Age	1984	1987	Better
OVERALL			Same

Figure 5-6   Fence Post Trail versus the Model House in Western Hills

STEP TWO: DRIVE THE COMPS

We now have a rough selling price for the house and an idea of what kinds of houses are selling in the neighborhood. But the MLS data do not provide a complete picture. The next step is to fill in details about the comps by driving to each of them to gather some eyewitness data. The more details we have about the comparable houses, the more accurate the estimate of the ESP will be. We're trying to see how an investment house in its final, fixed-up condition would compare to the houses we used for our comps. We compare houses by using five visual inspection factors (Figure 5-7).

Because we are comparing our house to ten or more other houses, we use a numerical rating system to help keep track of how our house compares to the neighborhood. We keep the rating system simple so that we'll be inclined to use it over and over. Based on the five criteria (condition, curb, view, street, and proximity), we make a single judgment call: If we think the investment house overall would be "better" than the comp, we give our property +1 point. If we feel it would be worse, we give it −1 point. If we believe it's the same, we give it 0 points (Figure 5-8).

The Five Visual Inspection Factors

1.	Condition	The roof, siding, garage doors, windows, porches, driveway, walkways
2.	Curb Appeal	The architecture, trees, lawn, landscaping, lot size, and grade
3.	View	Water, city skyline, mountains, any eyesores
4.	Street	Cul-de-sac, major street, major intersection, pride of ownership evident
5.	Proximity to Infrastructure	Commercial businesses, factories, undesirable establishments, rail road tracks, highways, power lines, parking lots, bus stops

Figure 5-7   The Five Visual Inspection Factors

Next, we add up all the individual scores to get a total score. In the example, 1202 Fence Post Trail is visually worse (–2 pts.) than the average comps. What does that mean? It means that based on the visual inspection, we think there is something about the comps that would give them an overall greater appeal than the house on Fence Post Trail in its fixed-up condition. Some of the comps have bigger trees and a better view, but the biggest thing revealed by the visual inspection is that 1202 Fence Post Trail is one of only a few two-story stucco Tudor-style houses in a neighborhood of mostly single-story ranch houses. We'll have to reduce the rough selling price to account for the difficulty of selling a Tudor-style house in the Western Hills Subdivision.

FLIPPING POINT

When you are comparing any comp to your prospective investment property, remember that you are comparing it to your property as if your property were in its fixed-up condition, ready to be put back on the market for sale.

Visual Inspection Report for Western Hills Subdivision	
Address	Comparison
1. 1300 Mustang Run	Better (+1)
2. 1684 Prairie Dog Lane	Worse (−1)
3. 1900 Round Up Bend	Worse (−1)
4. 1435 Wagon Trail	Same (0)
5. 1400 Trails End Circle	Worse (−1)
6. 1439 Wagon Trail	Same (0)
7. 1905 Round Up Bend	Same (0)
8. 1289 Rodeo Drive	Worse (−1)
9. 1400 Saddle Path	Better (+1)
10. 1264 Rodeo Drive	Better (+1)
11. 1515 Coral Cove	Worse (−1)
TOTAL	Worse (−2)

Figure 5-8   Visual Inspection Report for Western Hills Subdivision

STEP THREE: READ THE MARKET

What is the market environment today, and what will it look like when you're getting ready to sell your house? What's the six-month forecast? Beyond the comparable neighborhood data, the overall market environment is an important factor in predicting the selling price. We look at four indicators that will raise or lower our expectations about the selling price of a house:

1. *Mortgage rate trends.* Are mortgage rates in the area heading up or down over the next six months? Higher mortgage rates put downward pressure on home prices. It takes only a small change in those rates to affect what buyers are able to afford.

2. *Seasonal buying cycle.* Home sales (and therefore home prices) usually take a dip during the winter months but pick up in the

summer. Will the month in which you list your house be favorable or unfavorable in terms of the seasonal buying cycle?

3. *Time on market.* Your real estate agent can check inventory levels as well as average days on the market to determine how quickly houses are selling in your neighborhood.

4. *Developments.* Is there something that will cause more people to want to live in a neighborhood where you are considering a prospective investment property? Major employers, schools, stores, churches, parks, pools, recreation facilities, and entertainment venues can have an impact on the number of people coming to or leaving a neighborhood. It's also a good idea to see what's happening just outside the neighborhood. If a new subdivision will be opening up down the road, you may experience a fall in selling prices in your neighborhood. Pay attention to the business and city sections of the local paper and check out the Chamber of Commerce to follow local market trends.

For Fence Post Trail, our analysis of market trends revealed that experts are predicting a rise in interest rates. We also noticed that many of the comps were sold during the peak of the seasonal buying cycle. We'll take both of those trends into consideration when we decide on the ESP for 1202 Fence Post Trail. In this case, it looks like we'll need to somewhat reduce our eventual selling price below the comps.

Step Four: Check With Experts

Local housing experts are very valuable members of your network. Their expertise and specific knowledge can save you thousands of dollars. From time to time, we consult three types of experts who can give us reliable advice on the ESP of a house. We're not suggesting that you need to talk with all three types of experts every time, but it never hurts to get a qualified second opinion.

1. *Neighborhood specialist real estate agents.* These agents specialize in selling houses in a certain neighborhood. Often, it seems that they have more listings in a neighborhood than do all other agents combined. These specialists are in your target neighborhoods almost every day and have a wealth of knowledge at their fingertips.

2. *Appraisers.* A professional appraiser is an expert at estimating the value of a house. However, you may not want to pay $300 to $500 for an appraisal of a property for which you might not even make an offer. If you have a relationship with an appraiser, see if he or she will do a verbal appraisal for a substantially reduced fee. Be sure the appraiser realizes you're looking for the selling price of the house in its fixed-up condition.

3. *Neighborhood residents.* Some residents have more knowledge about a neighborhood than many professionals do. While checking out the comps, take the time to get out of your car and talk to some of the locals.

The more respectful you are of the time you ask of your experts, the more likely they are to help you the next time you call. We recommend that you come up with an eventual selling price before going to your experts. Then go to them for confirmation or to help you refine the price. If you ask them to do all the work for you, make sure you are willing to pay a fair price for their help.

Back to the Fence Post Trail example. We went to our neighborhood specialist to discuss the ESP and found out an interesting bit of news. She told us that in two weeks bulldozers were going to start clearing the land for the phase II development of Western Hills. This means that in the next eight to twelve months many new houses will be on the market in the same neighborhood. This information will certainly have a negative bearing on the ESP for the Fence Post Trail house.

FINALIZE YOUR ESP

We're now ready to come up with the ESP for 1202 Fence Post Trail. Our rough selling price based on the comps was $276,000. During the visual inspection we discovered that none of the recently sold houses was a two-story Tudor-style house like our prospective investment house. The market trend analysis revealed that our house will be selling in a less favorable environment for mortgage interest rates and seasonal buying patterns. Finally, we found out that a lot of new homes are about to be built in the neighborhood. None of those factors makes us want to abandon the flip, but we've decided that $250,000 is a more realistic ESP for the house. We now have the first part of the offer formula (Figure 5-9).

1202 Fence Post Trail: Maximum Offer Formula	
Eventual Selling Price	$250,000
− Improvement Costs	
− Quiet Costs	
− Minimum Profit	
= Maximum Offer	

Figure 5-9   1202 Fence Post Trail: Maximum Offer Formula

In Chapter 6, we'll come up with an estimate for how much the repairs and improvements are going to cost.

Determining the eventual selling price of a flipped house is the first and most influential of the four components (the other three are improvement costs, quiet costs, and minimum profit) in determining the maximum offer to a seller. There are three steps for arriving at an eventual selling price:

1. Run a comparative market analysis to see what similar houses are going for in the target neighborhood. You should look at similarities in size, age, and layout and proximity to the investment house.

2. Look closely at market trends that affect house sales. Will your investment house be ready to sell during the slower holiday season or the fast-paced summer? Are there economic developments occurring nearby that can have a positive impact on house sales in that area? Finally, take into consideration how long houses are taking to sell (days on the market).

3. Check with local experts to see if your numbers are in the ballpark. These specialists can include real estate agents, appraisers, and even neighbors who are knowledgeable about the price of housing in their neighborhood.

Chapter 6

Estimate Improvement Costs

After reading this chapter you will know how to

- Recognize the dangers of missing or miscalculating improvement costs
- Balance thoroughness, accuracy, and speed in estimating
- Estimate improvement costs by hiring a professional, by yourself or using a rule of thumb

In Chapter 5, we observed that the natural feelings of optimism that surround finding a promising new investment property can work against you, causing you to overestimate the eventual selling price to rationalize buying a house. Those feelings of optimism also can work against you when you are estimating the improvement costs, but this time they'll be coaxing you into underestimating. They whisper: "It just needs paint and carpet, and that's not very expensive." "You can get a dishwasher on sale for $200." "You can do a lot of this work yourself." Resist the temptation.

Our objective in this chapter is to give you an effective, level-headed method for determining the improvement costs for a flip. Estimating the improvement cost is the second part of our four-part FLIP formula for making a smart offer (Figure 6-1).

FLIP Maximum Offer Formula	
	Eventual Selling Price
−	Improvement Costs
−	Quiet Costs
−	Minimum Profit
=	Maximum Offer

Figure 6-1   FLIP Maximum Offer Formula

The mistake we've seen most frequently among real estate investors is underestimating the improvement costs. They miss some of the improvements (not comprehensive enough) and miscalculate the cost of other improvements (not accurate enough). A small miss or miscalculation can snowball into a big hit on your profits. Added together, these little mistakes can lead to an even bigger one—no profit at all.

To illustrate, let's say we forgot to include a new dishwasher in our estimate. During our must-should-could walkthrough, we noted that we needed to update the kitchen. However, when we costed out the improvements, the dishwasher was left out. That was an honest mistake since the house never had one.

That's $300 for the dishwasher, hose kit, sales tax, and installation. Because there wasn't a previous dishwasher, we had to create a 24-inch-wide space in the cabinets ($75), add a switch and wiring ($100), and do some minor plumbing ($50). Total cost to add the dishwasher, $525? Not exactly. The extra costs don't stop there because we already had installed countertops and a tile floor. We chipped the countertop and cracked the grout in the tile floor to create the space and install the dishwasher, adding an extra $175. Now we're at $700 and haven't even accounted for any extra holding costs during the delay (Figure 6-2).

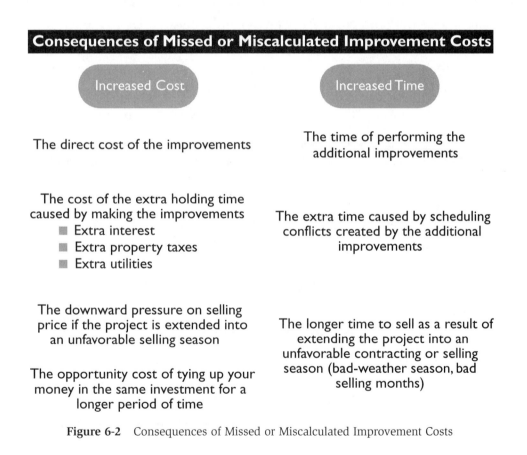

Consequences of Missed or Miscalculated Improvement Costs

Increased Cost

The direct cost of the improvements

The cost of the extra holding time caused by making the improvements
- Extra interest
- Extra property taxes
- Extra utilities

The downward pressure on selling price if the project is extended into an unfavorable selling season

The opportunity cost of tying up your money in the same investment for a longer period of time

Increased Time

The time of performing the additional improvements

The extra time caused by scheduling conflicts created by the additional improvements

The longer time to sell as a result of extending the project into an unfavorable contracting or selling season (bad-weather season, bad selling months)

Figure 6-2   Consequences of Missed or Miscalculated Improvement Costs

With the cascading effect on the work still left to be done, almost two extra weeks was added to the project, and we ended up paying an extra $600 (about $300 a week) in interest, property taxes, utilities, and so on. Thus, the $300 dishwasher grew to a cost of $1,300. Multiply that by ten "little" misses and you can see that just a few miscalculations can eat up most, if not all, of your profit.

Estimating improvement costs requires that you balance the two variables of thoroughness and accuracy while incorporating a third factor: speed. It's one thing to misjudge the cost of a new dishwasher by $30, but as we've seen, if you forget that you need a new dishwasher, you could cost yourself $1,300. That's why being thorough is so important. Accuracy runs a close second: If you don't get the costs exactly right, you can still erode your profit with lots of little misses. Thoroughness and accuracy are critical skills of an experienced estimator, and both can be compromised by the need for speed. Once you've found a promising investment property, you'll want to make an offer as soon as possible, because in the competitive arena of house flipping, time is of the essence.

Three Ways to Estimate Improvement Costs			
	Thoroughness	Accuracy	Speed
1. Hire a Professional	Excellent	Good	Good
2. Do It Yourself	Good	Good	Poor
3. Use Rules of Thumb	Poor	Fair	Excellent

Figure 6-3   Three Ways to Estimate Improvement Costs

There are three main ways to estimate the improvement costs for a flip, and each one involves trade-offs when it comes to thoroughness, accuracy, and speed (Figure 6-3).

1. *Hire a professional.* A general contractor can give you a professional cost assessment. An experienced contractor has completed

so many projects that when it comes to estimating, he or she rarely misses anything of importance.

2. *Do the estimating yourself.* Cost out all the individual material and labor costs. This is a good option as long as you've done your homework ahead of time, but it can be slow going until you've built up some experience.

3. *Use rules of thumb.* These rough guidelines get you in the ballpark. Using a rule of thumb is a great way to get a quick rough estimate. It may not be comprehensive, but it can be accurate enough to put an offer in until you come back and validate the numbers.

You can decide which option works best for you, but we can't emphasize enough that the third option is done for speed to make a quick offer. (Just remember to include a contingency clause in your offer contract to protect you in case the property has unexpected surprises and your rough estimate is off. We cover this clause in the Buy stage.) Although you certainly can make an offer by using a rule-of-thumb estimate, never go forward with buying a house by using *only* that estimate. Always hire a professional or do a comprehensive cost estimate yourself between the time the contract is accepted and when you close on the house.

Whichever method you choose, your starting point in estimating improvement costs is the improvement plan you created during the must-should-could walkthrough. You'll be turning that improvement plan into a detailed scope of work with all the labor and materials costs.

HIRING A GENERAL CONTRACTOR

Especially for your first couple of flips, some of the best advice we can give you is to hire an experienced general contractor to manage the construction. A nice benefit of hiring a general contractor is that he or she will do the cost estimating for you. In an ideal situation, your general contractor will accompany you on your must-should-could walkthrough and point out many of the things about the house that must be addressed as well as work with you to come up with the things that should and could be done in light of what's going on in the neighborhood. The general contractor will take your improvement plan and turn it into a scope of work, budget, and timetable.

FLIPPING POINT

Choose a general contractor who is comfortable working with real estate investors and has completed a number of rehab projects in which the whole property got a face-lift (not just a kitchen or bathroom). It is important that your general contractor understands that the goal is to maximize profit. Upgrades and extras should be suggested only because they are likely to increase your profit, not because they just increase the house's value (a subtle but important distinction).

Even if you've decided to manage the work yourself, it is possible to hire a general contractor to give you a detailed estimate. This may cost upwards of $500. (Since the contractor is not going to do the work, you want to provide enough incentive so that you can get a comprehensive, accurate, and quick response), but it's $500 well spent if it ensures detailed, accurate, and timely advice that will save or make you money because it leads to your making a better offer. Most general contractors are experienced cost estimators, but it takes about half a day to do a comprehensive cost estimate, including the time spent at the property. You may be able to establish a relationship with a general contractor who will give you a discount after you've hired him or her a couple of times. At HomeFixers, our cost assessments are very detailed and many of our customers use them as a blueprint for future flips. What we're saying here is that for estimating purposes, you may need the help of a professional for your first couple of times, until you get the hang of it.

DOING THE COST ESTIMATING YOURSELF

People often struggle with getting a reliable improvement cost estimate on their own. Here are a few reasons why it can be so challenging:

- There are hundreds of construction tasks that need to be priced.
- There are dozens of different trade categories (which means going to multiple sources to get cost information).
- Costing out most construction tasks means estimating two costs. Not only do you have to know the material costs, you have to know how much contractors will charge to install the materials.
- Material costs can change quickly because of economic, geographic, seasonal, and catastrophic factors (hurricanes, floods, etc.).
- Labor costs can swing wildly as a result of competition, seasonal demand, and, frankly, for no rhyme or reason.
- Some tasks require specialists to give estimates (foundations, structural, septic, well, chimney, pool, etc.) that have to be scheduled and usually cost some money.

Do you still want to give it a try yourself? Some people might ask, "Do you have rocks in your head?" Actually, Rick is one of those "rocks in the head" people and is proud of it. He managed his first rehab project and his second and his third and his fourth. In fact, Rick's rehabs were going so well that other investors began asking him to consider managing their projects. He liked fixing up houses, but he also liked real estate investing. When he finally decided to do both, HomeFixers was born. Let's take a closer look at how we created our original cost-estimating system and break it down so that you can use the same system to estimate your improvement costs.

CAMP HOME DEPOT

We quickly realized that one of the big keys to being a successful rehabber is to become a crackerjack estimator. Professional contractors can rattle off the cost of five gallons of paint, a square of shingles, and a palette of tile because that's their day job, all day, everyday. We knew we had to be that good in a hurry.

Basic training for us started at Home Depot, but any big home improvement center will do the trick. Rick spent thirteen hours the first day, eight hours the second day, and another eight hours the third day combing the aisles. What was he doing? Copying all the stock-keeping unit (SKU) numbers, costs, and descriptions for every item that conceivably could be found in a rehab project. In the end, we had a massive cost list for every product broken down by category and the room of the house in which it was likely to be found. Figure 6-4 is an excerpt from our original spreadsheet. With a little more tweaking, we came up with the first version of the cost-estimating software we use today.

It became apparent that if we wanted a fast, thorough, and accurate estimate of improvement costs, it was vital to be prepared ahead of time: before we ever set eyes on a prospective investment house. We had to invest the time up front and know the cost of the most common repairs, rather than chase down the costs in the short time between getting an offer accepted and closing on a property. You'll have to make that same commitment, if you plan to do your own cost estimates.

					HomeFixers Cost List				
QTY	Price Each	Extension	Plus Sales Tax	Category	Subcategory	SKU	Room	Source Name	Description
1	$164	$164	$177.12	Doors	Exterior Door	828-367	Exterior	Hardware Store	9-LITE - 36IN - LH - Exterior
1	$219	$219	$236.52	Plumbing	Bathtub	167-347	Bathroom	Hardware Store	AMERICAST RIGHT HAND TUB-WHITE
1	$139	$139	$150.12	Cabinets	Bathroom Cabinets	245-490	Bathroom	Hardware Store	Bathroom Vanity Base Cabinet W/Sink - Oak - 30IN W X18IN D
1	$56.49	$56.49	$61.01	Doors	Interior Door	601-063	Entire House	Hardware Store	6-PANL - 30IN - RH - Interior - Prehung (JLQ8)
1	$22.50	$22.50	$22.50	Carpentry Labor Cost	Finished Carpentry Labor	Labor Cost	Entire House	Marvin	Install prehung doors throughout the entire house (PER DOOR)
35	$0.39	$13.65	$14.74	Carpentry	Finished Carpentry Materials	707-066	Entire House	Hardware Store	Trim/Base - Primed - 11/16IN X 2-1/4IN (PER FT)
35	$0.29	$10.15	$10.15	Carpentry Labor Cost	Finished Carpentry Labor	Labor Cost	Entire House	Marvin	Install trim around all doors (PER LINEAR FT)
1	$11.63	$11.63	$12.56	Electrical	Light Fixtures, Bulbs, Etc.	284-904	Bedrooms	Hardware Store	Bedroom Light Fixture - 9.25IN - Mushroom - Ribbed Glass - Polished Brass - 2 60W Light Bulbs
1	$1.37	$1.37	$1.48	Electrical	Light Fixtures, Bulbs, Etc.	186-039	Entire House	Hardware Store	Light Bulbs - Soft White - 60W - 4-Pack - Philips DuraMax
1	$5.93	$5.93	$6.40	Electrical	Smoke Detector	182-262	Entire House	Hardware Store	Smoke Detector - Fire Sentry
1	$119	$119	$128.52	Plumbing	Kitchen Sink - Sink	170-097	Kitchen	Hardware Store	33X22X8.25 SINK SIGNATURE DBL BOWL - STAINLESS STEEL
1	$66	$66	$71.28	Plumbing	Kitchen Sink - Faucet	817-865	Kitchen	Hardware Store	PRICE PFISTER FAUCET - 1 HDL KIT W/SPRY CH3H GENESIS
1	$59.95	$59.95	$64.75	Plumbing	Kitchen Sink - Disposal	119-667	Kitchen	Hardware Store	1/2 HP BADGER 5 DISPOSER JLQ6
1	$3.98	$3.98	$4.30	Plumbing	Kitchen Sink - Basket Strainer	767-770	Kitchen	Hardware Store	PVC SWTHRT BSKT STRNR-ASSEMBL JLQ2
1	$11.99	$11.99	$12.95	Doors	Doorknobs	614-130	Entire House	Hardware Store	Kwikset - Bed & Bath - Doorknob - Polished Brass - Shelby (USE FOR BATHROOMS, MASTER BEDROOM AND ENTRY TO GARAGE)
1	$8.91	$8.91	$9.62	Hardware	Bathroom Fixtures	137-011	Bathroom	Hardware Store	Toilet paper holder
1	$299	$299	$322.92	Appliances	Range	339-118 or 355-386	Kitchen	Hardware Store	Electric Range - Hot Point - White
1	$197	$197	$212.76	Appliances	Microwave/ Vent Hood	115-032 or 113-047	Kitchen	Hardware Store	Microhood - Hot Point - White
1	$9.98	$9.98	$10.78	Landscaping	Shrubs	221-620	Exterior	Hardware Store	LIGUSTRUM WAXLEAF 3G

Figure 6-4   HomeFixers Cost List

We want to emphasize this point: To be a successful rehabber is to be a skilled estimator, and to become a skilled estimator is to become a student of construction costs. If you are armed with a tool such as the spreadsheet shown in Figure 6-4 and are committed to continuing education (with frequent study sessions at Lowe's, Home Depot, Sears, Best

Buy, etc.), you will be on the path to being a skilled improvement cost estimator.

To help you get started, we looked at all of our estimates and pulled out the 101 most common tasks that we've seen in our jobs (see the Appendix for this list or go to flipthebook.com to download the list in spreadsheet format). You'll still have to do the homework to add the costs or you could consider using the software that we use to estimate all of our rehab projects. The software we created has all of the tasks and material and labor costs organized by each contracting category. The appendix list alone will be a foundational guide to your own improvement cost estimating. If you use it, you will be way ahead of those who try to "wing it" and figure it out on the go.

GOING INTO LABOR

Labor costs are more difficult to determine than are materials costs because there can be such a wide swing in what contractors charge. We've found that the best way to estimate labor costs is to get away from paying by the hour and set a fixed price for as many construction tasks as possible. That results in a fair way of paying contractors that lets you predetermine the price and ensure consistency each time you do an estimate.

For example, we did some homework and found that the average experienced trim carpenter in Austin, Texas, was happy making $30 per hour. We went to the job site and timed our trim carpenter, Marvin, as he did various tasks. As an example, we found that Marvin could install a prehung door in about thirty minutes. We made allowances for tool setup and breakdown, unforeseen surprises, emergency trips to the hardware store, and the like, and came up with forty-five minutes to hang an interior prehung door. Forty-five minutes multiplied by $30 per hour yielded a fixed labor cost of $22.50.

Marvin came out a winner because he knew he could hang two doors an hour if he was efficient with his time, thus making $45 ($22.50 multiplied by 2) instead of $30 per hour. We came out a winner because we had a happy, motivated carpenter, but most important, we now had an accurate fixed labor cost that could be used again and again for all the future jobs we would estimate.

Over time we compiled a large list of field-tested fixed costs for all of our labor tasks. This had the side benefit of making it easier to attract and interview new trades. We knew we had an attractive pay plan that rewarded productivity, but we also began to become experts in knowing how long things take. All we had to do when interviewing a new trim carpenter was ask questions such as "How long does it typically take you to hang an interior prehung door?" and wait for the answer. If he wasn't sure or wasn't specific, we would tell him what our research showed. More often than not, he was agreeable to our suggested rate.

At HomeFixers, we had the advantage of having a lot of projects going on that provided a great test kitchen for gathering labor costs. Until you have several houses' worth of data under your tool belt, we suggest that you use one of the big remodeling cost books such as *Marshall & Swift's Home Repair and Remodel Cost Guide*. This is a comprehensive resource that includes cost tables with localized costs for cities throughout the United States.

With a little patience and a some research, you can do exactly what we did. On the one hand, we created a big list of materials costs. And on the other, we created a big list of field-tested labor costs. All we had to do was marry them into a total cost for each task. To pull from the above examples, we looked up the cost of a six-panel interior prehung door ($61.01 with sales tax) and married it to the fixed labor cost of $22.50 to get a total cost of $83.51. We realized that a prehung interior door needs about 35 linear feet of trim ($24.89 in materials and labor.) Finally, we added $25 for a door knob and door stop to arrive at a total default cost of $133.40 (rounded up to $135.00). Now every time we walk through a basic or standard house and determine that it needs a new bedroom door, we know it's going to be $135. You can see how useful this would be if you did it for all the most common construction tasks investors face. You also can see that waiting to do this until you have a prospective investment house on the radar is not going to work.

FLIPPING POINT

Here's a great tip for getting quick pricing for a number of tasks: Turn to "turnkeys." These are the specialized tradespeople who will give you a price for both the materials and the labor. A turnkey is like a mini general contractor with his own area of expertise. They're specialists at doing one thing and can give you a fast, accurate, and consistent price for doing many of the things in a rehab project. We call them for window glass and mirrors, new roofs, cabinetry, laminate and granite countertops, cultured marble vanity tops, paint, tile, garage doors, carpet, light fixtures, and appliances. The downside to turnkeys is that they're usually not the least expensive option. But in our experience, paying for predictability is usually worth it. We'll go in depth on turnkey trades in the Fix stage.

THE 5 PERCENT CONTINGENCY

If you use a general contractor to estimate your improvement costs, the contractor undoubtedly will add some kind of contingency for unforeseen construction costs. Whether it's for vandalism, construction site theft, or hidden nasties that you couldn't have known about until you stripped off the drywall (leaks, termites, bees, odors that are hard to get rid of, etc.), we suggest that you do what the pros do: incorporate a 5 percent contingency. For example, if you had budgeted for $10,000 in construction costs, you would add another $500 for your contingency.

USE RULES OF THUMB

When it absolutely, positively has to get done overnight, use rules of thumb.

It dawned on us a couple of years ago that a great way to compare houses and categorize the work we do from one job to another is to compare them on the basis of improvement cost per square foot (total improvement cost divided by the total square feet of the house).

Consider two houses that both need $30,000 in improvements. The mistake one might make is to assume that the two projects are similar since the improvement costs are the same. However, one house is 5,000 square feet and the other is 1,000 square feet. That means that the 5,000-square-foot house has $6 per square foot in improvement costs and the other has $30 per square foot. These are two completely different projects (Figure 6-5).

Improvement Complexity Comparison			
Cost	Square Feet	Cost/SQ FT	Improvements
$30,000	5,000	$6	The basics such as paint, carpet, new fixtures
$30,000	1,000	$30	The basics plus roof, cabinets, countertops, tile and rough work like framing, plumbing, HVAC, electrical, sheetrock

Figure 6-5   Improvement Complexity Comparison

In our experience, spending $6 per square foot on a rehab translates to doing the very basics, such as paint, carpet, and some new fixtures. Conversely, $30 per square foot is a much more complex job. Besides doing all the basics, your improvements could include a lot of rough work, such as framing, plumbing, HVAC, and electrical and sheetrock repairs.

The proper way to compare jobs is by improvement cost per square foot. One $6-per-square-foot job is essentially the same as any other $6-per-square-foot job, and a $30-per-square-foot job most likely will be like any other $30-per-square-foot job. This understanding led to our rule-of-thumb method for estimating improvement costs. The first step is to assign the construction job to one of four broad cost-per-square-foot categories that we define as make-habs, rehabs, remodels, and restructures:

1. *Make-hab* (around $5 per square foot). A make-hab construction project entails about the least amount of work you could do to a house but still call it an improvement project. For us, it means "make habitable" which falls somewhere between just cleaning the place up and a rehab—thus our term "make-hab." It includes cleanout (getting rid of all the junk and grime), paint, carpet, and final cleaning.

2. *Rehab* (around $15 per square foot). A rehab is the most common kind of construction job investors undertake. These are mostly cosmetic improvements with minimal permitting and inspections, if any. Rehabs address all the must-dos to ensure that a house is in good working order and would pass a home inspection: broken windows, wood rot, a leaky roof, and repairing the major systems (HVAC, electrical, and plumbing). The should-do design choices also are completed in keeping with the neighborhood norm: paint, carpet, fixtures (replace lights, fans, sinks, faucets, and toilets as appropriate), hardware and accessories (replace doorknobs, doorstops, and bathroom accessories), countertops, backsplash, appliances (if possible, keep the old appliances), tile, doors, garage doors (only if absolutely necessary), cabinetry (refurbishing the existing cabinets unless that's not possible), some trim (usually a windowsill or some baseboards), landscaping, and a spit-and-polish cleaning.

3. *Remodel* (around $25 per square foot). Remodels involve everything in a rehab project and then some. The key word in remod-

els is *replacing*. These are jobs in which you're replacing a lot of sheetrock; replacing bathtubs, tile, and walk-in showers; and replacing the cabinetry, doors, and trim. Remodels also involve widening any openings.

4. *Restructure* (around $40 per square foot). Restructuring is everything in the first three categories plus making major layout changes (moving or adding a bathroom, increasing the size of the kitchen, building an addition, etc.).

Next, assign the finish level (basic, standard, or designer; custom is never a rule of thumb) that you selected in your improvement plan. Then, using the grid in Figure 6-6, you can quickly get the cost-per-square-foot rule of thumb for your construction project.

The FLIP Rule-of-Thumb Guidelines			
	Basic	Standard	Designer
1. Make-Hab	$3	$5	$7
2. Rehab	$12	$15	$18
3. Remodel	$20	$25	$30
4. Restructure	$35	$40	$45

(Improvement Costs Per Square Foot)

Figure 6-6   The FLIP Rule-of-Thumb Guidelines

For example, with a standard rehab on a house with 1,000 square feet, your rule-of-thumb cost of improvements would be $15,000 (1,000 square feet multiplied by $15 per square foot). The dollar amounts may change, depending on how you define the finish levels for your target market, but you can adjust them on the basis of the objectives for the project.

The numbers in this grid are rough, but they come from our analysis of real investment projects. To illustrate this, Figure 6-7 shows what the first $21 per square foot looks like in a standard finish-out–level investment house in our market: Austin, Texas.

	Trade Category	Cost/ SQ FT	% of Total	Description
	Improvement Costs Per Square Foot for a Standard Finish-Out			
1	Cleanout	$0.75	4%	Light demolition, includes one 40-yard dumpster
2	Broken Window Glass	$0.15	1%	Replace glass only
3	Rough Carpentry	$0.60	3%	Repairs only—includes replacing some rotted studs and subfloor inside and some rotted fascia
4	Roof	$1.95	9%	20-year tear off and re-shingle for a one-story
5	HVAC New System	$2.80	13%	New ducts, new inside and outside unit, vents and thermostat
6	HVAC Thermostat and Grills Only	$0.25	1%	Programmable thermostat and new air vents
7	Service Panel Upgrade	$0.80	4%	Service Panel Upgrade
8	New Bathtubs	$0.40	2%	New Bathtubs
9	Drywall	$0.70	3%	Equivalent to sheetrocking about 18% of the house
10	Cabinetry	$2.00	10%	Standard stock oak—includes installation
11	Doors	$0.45	2%	Includes a basic prehung metal front door plus two interior prehung doors and trim
12	Trim	$0.25	1%	Includes replacing some baseboards, window sills, window aprons, and some repairs
13	Garage Door	$0.60	3%	Standard aluminum, no windows
14	Interior Paint	$1.50	7%	Interior two-color paint job
15	Exterior Paint	$1.00	5%	Exterior two-color paint job
16	Countertops	$0.30	2%	Plastic laminate like Formica or Wilsonart
17	Tile Tub Surrounds	$0.50	2%	Standard 4" x 4" tile plus installation
18	Electrical Fixtures	$0.80	4%	Includes installing new GFCI outlets; replacing some broken outlets, switches and jacks; new faceplates; new standard lights; fans; smoke detectors plus installation
19	Plumbing Fixtures	$0.50	2%	Includes standard kitchen sink, faucet, bathroom faucets, toilets, toilet seats and installation cost
20	Plumbing Hot Water Heater	$0.45	2%	40-gallon hot water heater
21	Flooring	$2.14	10%	20% tile at $4/SF and 80% carpet at 1.55/SF)
22	Hardware and Accessories	$0.40	2%	Includes doorknobs, doorstops, towel bars, paper holders, bathroom mirrors, house numbers
23	Appliances	$1.00	5%	Standard: stove, dishwasher, microwave, disposal and installation cost
24	Interim and Final Cleanings	$0.20	1%	Sweep, dust, tub, windows, countertops, floors
25	Landscaping	$0.45	2%	Landscaping: shrubs, flowers, mulch
	TOTAL	$20.94	100%	

Figure 6-7   Improvement Costs per Square Foot for a Standard Finish-Out

These are the most common tasks in the rehab category, but it's rare to have to do *all of them* on the *same* rehab. Thus, for a standard rehab in our rule-of-thumb guidelines, we estimate $15 per square foot, which includes most but not all of these common tasks. We filled in the rest of the numbers in the grid in the same way.

Again, it is important to remember that this method of calculating the improvement price per square foot is intended to give you a ballpark figure fast. You must always confirm these numbers with a comprehensive, accurate cost estimate before closing on a house.

You now know the three ways to estimate the improvements costs for a house. Before we move on to calculating the quiet costs for a flip, let's quickly revisit our 1202 Fence Post Trail example. To focus more time on our lead generation efforts, we decided to have a general contractor do the work for us. His estimate came back at $40,000, or $20 per square foot, for this designer rehab (Figure 6-8).

1202 Fence Post Trail: Improvement Costs	
Eventual Selling Price	$250,000
− Improvement Costs	$40,000
− Quiet Costs	
− Minimum Profit	
= Maximum Offer	

Figure 6-8 1202 Fence Post Trail: Improvement Costs

We'll revisit this example in Chapter 7, where we determine the quiet costs.

POINTS TO REMEMBER

If there is one area where investors make the most mistakes, it is estimating the cost of repairs and improvements. These costs often are miscalculated or missed completely, robbing the investor of some or all of the profit. Not only can miscalculations eat up profit, they can cause a cascading effect that can interrupt your schedule severely, costing you even more money in holding and quiet costs. Taking the time to understand and master estimating, even before you have a real investment property to analyze, will put you ahead of the game.

Estimating costs requires a delicate balance of thoroughness, speed, and accuracy. There are three ways to achieve a quick and accurate accounting of these costs:

1. hire a professional to evaluate the costs for you,
2. become an expert in estimating costs by doing diligent research, and
3. apply our general rule-of-thumb for cost-per-square-foot improvements for estimating improvement costs on the basis of the complexity level of your rehab.

Familiarizing yourself with all three methods will help you considerably in the evaluation of the true improvement costs for a flip. Use our Top 101 Most Common Tasks in the appendix as a foundational guide for researching your costs to become a better estimator.

Chapter 7

Account for Quiet Costs

After reading this chapter you will know how to
- Understand and calculate the four components of quiet costs:
  - Buying costs
  - Holding costs
  - Cost of money
  - Selling costs

We love watching television shows about flipping houses, but with some of the shows, we find ourselves yelling at the TV when they calculate profit. They start with the selling price and then simply subtract the purchase price and improvement costs *while completely ignoring all the other costs associated with flipping houses*. "Hey, what about real estate commissions, loan interest, and property taxes?"

The myriad costs associated with flipping a house may not make for good TV, but those costs can silently eat up most, if not all, of your profit unless you plan for them. These costs are sneaky: They can surprise you and creep up on you to steal away your profits. That's why we call them quiet costs (it's also why we tend to shout about them). Calculating your quiet costs is the third part of the FLIP Maximum Offer Formula (Figure 7-1).

FLIP Maximum Offer Formula	
	Eventual Selling Price
−	Improvement Costs
−	Quiet Costs
−	Minimum Profit
=	Maximum Offer

Figure 7-1   FLIP Maximum Offer Formula

As we illustrate in the 1202 Fence Post Trail example (Figure 7-2), you could pay the full asking price of $179,000 and still make a nice $31,000 in "TV profit" (if you ignored all the quiet costs).

1202 Fence Post Trail: "TV Profit"	
Eventual Selling Price	$250,000
− Seller's Asking Price	$179,000
− Improvement Costs	$40,000
= "TV Profit"	$31,000

Figure 7-2   1202 Fence Post Trail: "TV Profit"

Figure 7-3 illustrates what it really costs to flip 1202 Fence Post Trail. Note that $33,500 of that TV profit is consumed by quiet costs; if you paid the full asking price, that would leave you with a loss of $2,500—not exactly a made-for-TV moment.

1202 Fence Post Trail: Full Price Purchase	
Eventual Selling Price	$250,000
− Seller's Asking Price	$179,000
− Improvement Costs	$40,000
− Quiet Costs	$33,500
= Profit (or Loss in this case)	−$2,500

Figure 7-3 1202 Fence Post Trail: Full-Price Purchase

In this chapter, we'll give you all the assumptions and formulas that go into determining quiet costs. If you're itching to create elaborate formulas in a spreadsheet or scratch out numbers with a pad and a pocket calculator, power up your computer or sharpen your pencils and get ready to dig in. However, if you'd like us to do the math for you, feel free to skim this chapter and go to our Web site at flipthebook.com to find our online Maximum Offer calculator. Nevertheless, we think it's worth taking the time to understand the concepts even if you use an online calculator to run the actual numbers.

Quiet costs tend to come in at about 12 to 15 percent of the eventual selling price. We group quiet costs into four broad categories: buying costs, holding costs, cost of money, and selling costs. (Figure 7-4).

Quiet Costs Categories	
1. Buying Costs	The costs incurred when you buy the house
2. Holding Costs	The costs accrued while you own the house
3. Cost of Money	The costs related to borrowing the money needed to purchase and improve the house
4. Selling Costs	The costs incurred when you sell the house

Figure 7-4 Quiet Costs Categories

1. BUYING COSTS

Buying costs are incurred when you purchase a house. You need to know the purchase price to get an accurate estimate of those costs. But since the purpose of this exercise is to determine how much you're going to pay for the house, we have a chicken-and-egg problem. The solution is to use a conservative but educated guess as a substitute for the purchase price. You will recall from our discussions with the seller that although he's asking $179,000, we have a hunch that he would accept an offer in the range of $150,000. So, we'll use $150,000 as a substitute for the purchase price, knowing that we may have to fine tune our quiet costs estimate once we have an actual purchase price.

When we say buying costs, we mean the costs to transfer the ownership of the house. This includes fees such as title insurance, inspection, survey, appraisal, and documentation but not the cost of any money borrowed, which we address separately. Many of these costs often are paid by the seller in a real estate transaction, but with your value proposition of quick cash and no hassles, you should plan to pay these costs for the seller. We estimate about 1.5 percent of our educated-guess purchase price for buying costs. In our example, the closing costs are $2,250 ($150,000 multiplied by 1.5 percent) (Figure 7-5).

1202 Fence Post Trail: Buying Costs	
Buying Costs	$2,250
+ Holding Costs	
+ Cost of Money	
+ Selling Costs	
= Quiet Costs	

Figure 7-5   1202 Fence Post Trail: Buying Costs

2. HOLDING COSTS

Holding costs are the various costs that accrue during the time you own the house. These costs consist primarily of property taxes, insurance, utilities, and maintenance costs such as cleaning and yard service. But there may be other costs specific to the house, such as condo or neighborhood association dues.

These costs vary greatly from deal to deal. However, after analyzing hundreds of flips, we have found that taking 1.5 percent of the educated-guess purchase price gives us a simple but surprisingly accurate estimate. At Fence Post Trail, the holding costs come to $2,250 ($150,000 multiplied by 1.5 percent) (Figure 7-6).

1202 Fence Post Trail: Holding Costs	
Buying Costs	$2,250
+ Holding Costs	$2,250
+ Cost of Money	
+ Selling Costs	
= Quiet Costs	

Figure 7-6 1202 Fence Post Trail: Holding Costs

You probably noticed that this is the same formula we used for buying costs. Thus, once you've done this a few times, the obvious shortcut is to calculate buying costs and holding costs in one step by taking 3 percent of the educated-guess purchase price.

3. COST OF MONEY

The next category of quiet costs is the cost associated with borrowing the money you need for the flip. There are three components to calculating the cost of money:

1. Loan amount

2. Loan duration

3. Loan terms

Think of it this way. There are three questions you must answer: how much money am I borrowing, how long will I be borrowing it, and what are the interest and fees I will pay the lender? Let's revisit our example at Fence Post Trail to illustrate how this adds up.

LOAN AMOUNT

The first component is the loan amount. Simply add your purchase price and improvement costs and subtract your down payment to get this number. Using our educated-guess purchase price of $150,000 for Fence Post Trail and the improvement cost estimate of $40,000, we will need $190,000 to purchase the house and pay for the improvements. Recall that we are putting $20,000 down out of pocket. Thus, our loan amount is $170,000.

LOAN DURATION

The second component needed to calculate the cost of money is the loan duration: the time it takes to fix up the house, resell it, and pay off the loan. The biggest variable in determining how long you will hold a house (and therefore pay interest on the loan) is how long it takes to fix it up. Thus, to estimate the cost of money accurately, we first need to estimate the time it will take to complete the improvements.

A few years into doing rehabs at HomeFixers, we had one of those "aha!" moments that changed the way we do business. James Hill, our HomeFixers affiliate in Dallas, Texas, was telling us how quickly he was able to turn out his $40,000 rehabs while we were lamenting how slow a couple of $40,000 rehabs were going for us. The aha! moment came when we realized that the $40,000 rehabs that James was doing were cosmetic updates to 2,500-square-foot suburban houses, whereas our rehabs were for centrally located 1,000-square-foot major remodels. Although the total rehab cost is the same, there's a big difference in the *improvement costs per square foot* ($16 per square foot versus $40 per square foot).

The same number we use to get a quick estimate of improvement costs turns out to be an excellent way to estimate the time it takes to fix up a house. By dividing the cost per square foot by 10, you get the number of *months* you should plan for fixing up the house. Add two and a half months to market and sell the house once the fix is complete and you have an estimate of the number of months you will hold the house (Figure 7-7).

HomeFixers Holding Time Formula	
	Improvement Cost per SQ FT
÷	10
=	Months to Improve House
+	2.5 Months to Market and Sell
=	Total Holding Time

Figure 7-7 HomeFixers Holding Time Formula

Ever since that day, we have used this formula at HomeFixers to estimate the holding time for rehabs.

In the example on 1202 Fence Post Trail, we estimated the improvement costs to be $40,000 on a 2,000-square-foot house, or $20 per square foot. Dividing 20 by 10 gives us two months for the fix-up. With the additional two and a half months of overhead, we estimate that we will hold 1202 Fence Post Trail for a total of four and a half months (Figure 7-8).

1202 Fence Post Trail: Holding Time	
Cost/SQ FT	$20
Months to Fix	2
Overhead Months	2.5
Months Holding the House	4.5

Figure 7-8 1202 Fence Post Trail: Holding Time

With an estimate of how many months you're going to hold the house, you are able to calculate how much money you will pay per month in interest.

LOAN TERMS

The third and final component of the cost of money is the terms of the loan. Our lender for Fence Post Trail is charging an interest rate of 12 percent per year, which is equal to 1 percent per month. One percent of the loan amount of $170,000 is $1,700. This means we'll pay $1,700 in interest every month the loan is out. Multiplying by the four and a half months we expect to hold the house gives us an estimate of $7,650 in interest (Figure 7-9).

1202 Fence Post Trail: Loan Interest	
Interest per Month	$1,700
x Months Holding the House	4.5
= Total Cost of Money	$7,650

Figure 7-9   1202 Fence Post Trail: Loan Interest

In addition to interest, our lender probably will require us to pay points that are due at the time we close on the loan. A point is simply 1 percent of the loan. In our example, the lender charges us 3 points. Three percent of $170,000 comes to $5,100. Adding the interest and points gives us a total cost of money of $12,750 (Figure 7-10).

1202 Fence Post Trail: Total Cost of Money	
Interest	$ 7,650
+ Points	$ 5,100
= Total Cost of Money	$12,750

Figure 7-10   1202 Fence Post Trail: Total Cost of Money

We now have values for the first three categories of the quiet costs (Figure 7-11). Let's move to the final category: selling costs.

1202 Fence Post Trail: Cost of Money	
Buying Costs	$2,250
+ Holding Costs	$2,250
+ Cost of Money	$12,750
+ Selling Costs	
= Quiet Costs	

Figure 7-11 1202 Fence Post Trail: Cost of Money

4. SELLING COSTS

Selling costs include the costs associated with actually putting the house on the market and getting it sold. The two main components of selling costs are real estate agent commissions and closing costs, which generally total about 6.5 percent of the eventual selling price (Figure 7-12).

Selling Costs	
Real Estate Agent Commissions	The fees you pay to a real estate agent to market the house, negotiate, and close the sale
Closing Costs	The amount you pay when you close on the house (title, survey, appraisal, etc.)

Figure 7-12 Selling Costs

It's likely you will pay 3 percent of your eventual selling price (ESP) to a real estate agent representing the buyer. You also should plan to pay 2 to 3 percent more to have a professional handle the sale for you. You may be able to save some money by selling the property yourself, but as a real estate investor, you will find that your time is much better spent looking for the next house. And you may not be familiar with all the procedures and legal issues involved in closing a real estate transaction. It is a lot more complicated than most people realize.

You may recall from the Overview that you need a team to succeed consistently in real estate investing. In our experience, good real estate agents pay for themselves by finding and attracting the right buyers and then handling all the details related to closing. In the example at Fence Post Trail, we chose to work with an agent we had worked with in the past, and she offered to list the property for a 2 percent commission—3 percent for the buyer's agent plus 2 percent for the listing agents means we'll use 5 percent for our total real estate agent commissions.

The same kind of closing costs that you paid at the time you bought the house (title, survey, appraisal, etc.) need to be paid again when you sell it. Some of these costs may be paid by the buyer, but it's likely you will have at least some closing costs. We use 1.5 percent of the ESP to estimate those costs. At 6.5 percent of the ESP, the selling costs for 1202 Fence Post Trail total $16,250 ($250,000 multiplied by 6.5 percent) (Figure 7-13).

1202 Fence Post Trail: Selling Costs	
Buying Costs	$ 2,250
+ Holding Costs	$ 2,250
+ Cost of Money	$12,750
+ Selling Costs	$16,250
= Quiet Costs	$33,500

Figure 7-13   1202 Fence Post Trail: Selling Costs

That's our formula for calculating the quiet costs associated with a flip. Taking the time to count these costs before making an offer will help ensure that you achieve a great profit on your flips, and you may find yourself shouting at the TV right along with us.

The total quiet costs for 1202 Fence Post Trail are $33,500. This is 13.4 percent of the ESP, right in the middle of our rule-of-thumb range of 12 to 15 percent (Figure 7-14).

1202 Fence Post Trail: Quiet Costs	
Eventual Selling Price	$250,000
− Improvement Costs	$40,000
− Quiet Costs	$33,500
− Minimum Profit	
= Maximum Offer	

Figure 7-14 1202 Fence Post Trail: Quiet Costs

There is only one part of the FLIP Maximum Offer Formula remaining. In Chapter 8, we'll set the amount of profit we need to make on 1202 Fence Post Trail on the basis of the risk of the flip.

POINTS TO REMEMBER

The quiet costs associated with flipping houses often are overlooked when one is estimating the potential profit of a flip, hence the "quiet" in quiet costs. Taking the time to calculate the quiet costs carefully *before* you make an offer will help ensure that you will receive a great profit on a flip. Quiet costs are grouped into four broad categories: buying costs, holding costs, cost of money, and selling costs.

Buying costs and holding costs will each be about 1.5 percent of your eventual selling price (ESP) for a total of 3 percent. The cost of money will depend on how much you borrow, for how long, and at what terms. Selling costs will typically be about 6.5 percent of ESP. Together, your total quiet costs will usually be between 12 and 15 percent of your ESP. Don't let quiet costs sneak up on you.

Chapter 8
Set Minimum Profit

After reading this chapter you will know how to

- Calculate your base profit
- Calculate your rehab risk profit
- Determine your maximum offer

Flipping houses for the careless or uninformed can be risky. Our goal with this book is to give you the knowledge and the systems to reduce that risk as much as possible. So far, we've reduced risk by getting firm answers to tough questions such as the following: What will the house sell for once it's fixed up? How much will the improvements cost? and How much will my quiet costs be from the time I buy it to the time I sell it?

Now it's time for the fun part: How much profit should I expect to make from my flip? The final part of the FLIP Maximum Offer Formula is the minimum profit number that bases a reward level on the risks (Figure 8-1).

FLIP Maximum Offer Formula	
	Eventual Selling Price
−	Improvement Costs
−	Quiet Costs
−	Minimum Profit
=	Maximum Offer

Figure 8-1 FLIP Maximum Offer Formula

We often hear investors say that they want to make a specific minimum profit, such as $10,000, on every flip. Other investors completely ignore a profit calculation. They're happy to take whatever money is left after they pay all their expenses. In our opinion, there is too much uncertainty in flipping a house to be so flippant about the profits. We tie the minimum profit to the specific risks associated with a flip.

There are two main factors that increase the risk of a flip: the eventual selling price and the complexity of the rehab. We take both of these risk factors into consideration by dividing minimum profit into two components: a base profit calculated from the eventual selling price and a rehab risk profit that increases with the complexity of the improvements (Figure 8-2).

In our experience, total profits usually fall between 10 and 20 percent of the eventual selling price. As with the quiet costs, you can go online to flipthebook.com to calculate the minimum profit for a flip.

1. Base Profit   A percentage of ESP that you should receive for every flip

2. Rehab Risk Profit   Additional profit that you should receive based on the complexity of the improvements

Figure 8-2   The Two Components of Minimum Profit

1. BASE PROFIT

The first component in determining how much you should make from a flip is a base profit amount, which for us is simply 10 percent of the eventual selling price. We link base profit to the selling price because as you may recall, your risk increases as the selling price increases (the higher the selling price, the higher the base profit). For the 1202 Fence Post Trail example, 10 percent of the selling price of $250,000 gives you a base profit amount of $25,000.

2. REHAB RISK PROFIT

The second component in determining the minimum profit is based on the complexity of the improvements. This is a key part of the FLIP Maximum Offer Formula because it directly associates the most unpredictable part of a flip—fixing the house—with the profit you will receive.

We first looked at the improvement costs per square foot when doing a quick estimate of improvement costs by using rules of thumb. The same number showed up again when we calculated how long it takes to hold a house. We now go back to improvement costs per square foot for the third time to assess the risk of a flip. As the improvement cost per square foot increases, the complexity of the work increases.

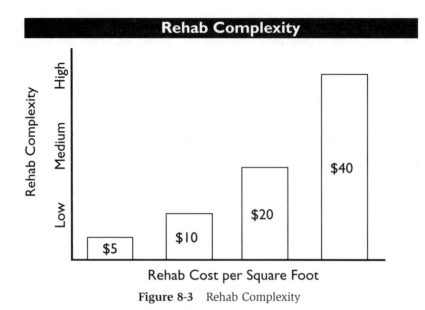

Figure 8-3   Rehab Complexity

Your risk is tied directly to this complexity because with complexity comes unpredictability. Fresh paint and new carpet have very predictable outcomes. But as you increase the complexity to include improvements in areas such as the plumbing and electrical systems, the predictability quickly decreases. By increasing your minimum profit as the rehab gets less predictable, you are building in a profit level that matches your risk.

We recommend that for every $5 per square foot in construction costs you add 1 percent of the eventual selling price (ESP) to your base profit. For 1202 Fence Post Trail, the construction costs are $20 per square foot. Twenty dollars per square foot divided by $5 per square foot is 4, and so we add 4 percent of the ESP to our required profit. In this example, the rehab risk profit equals $10,000 (4 percent of $250,000) (Figure 8-4).

1202 Fence Post Trail: Rehab Risk and Profit		
	Improvement Cost	$20/SQ FT
÷	Rehab Risk Factor	$5/SQ FT
=	Rehab Risk	4% of ESP

Figure 8-4   1202 Fence Post Trail: Rehab Risk and Profit

Combining the base profit of $25,000 and the rehab risk profit of $10,000 results in a total of $35,000 in minimum profit, or 13.5 percent of the ESP. This is on the low end of the 10 to 20 percent range you should expect with most flips. However, because $20 per square foot is not an overly complex rehab, 13 to 14 percent should be an appropriate profit in light of the risk (Figure 8-5).

1202 Fence Post Trail: Minimum Profit	
Eventual Selling Price	$250,000
− Improvement Costs	$40,000
− Quiet Costs	$33,500
− Minimum Profit	$35,000
= Maximum Offer	

Figure 8-5   1202 Fence Post Trail: Minimum Profit

Clearly, your actual profit depends on the final purchase price and costs. You can also make more money if you buy the house below the maximum offer or if you save on improvements. Including a solid profit in your maximum offer calculation sets you up to make a good profit even if there are a few bumps along the way.

FLIPPING POINT

Is it ever okay to make a very small profit margin? Sure it is! The important thing is matching your profit to your risk. We once bought and sold a house where we knew the profit was only going to be 4 percent to 6 percent of the ESP—a deal we'd tell most investors to shy away from. In this case it was a low-risk fix (a $6 per square foot rehab) and Rick had information about the part of town, the neighborhood, the block, the street, and even the house. It was literally the house next door! Rick knew his neighborhood was desirable for investing and that most homes there sold quickly.

YOUR MAXIMUM OFFER REVEALED

We have done the analysis and crunched all the numbers we need to determine our maximum offer for 1202 Fence Post Trail. We have determined that to cover all the costs and make a reasonable profit from rehabbing 1202 Fence Post Trail, our maximum offer is $141,500 (Figure 8-6).

1202 Fence Post Trail: Maximum Offer		
	Eventual Selling Price	$250,000
−	Improvement Costs	$40,000
−	Quiet Costs	$33,500
−	Minimum Profit	$35,000
=	Maximum Offer	$141,500

Figure 8-6   1202 Fence Post Trail: Maximum Offer

One of the things we love about flipping houses is that you can make money in any market, hot or cold. Or as Clay likes to say, flipping is "appreciation-neutral." Your profit is not dependent on the house increasing in value. You don't have to account for appreciation because you don't need it to make a profit. You've taken luck, good fortune, and timing out of the equation. Your formula has taken into account all the key cost and price issues you can accurately estimate. Great flips happen when the estimates are "on the money." As many wise real estate investors would say, "you make your money going in." And when you make the right offer, that's exactly what you do.

Now that you know how to determine your maximum offer, we're on to the Buy stage, where we cover all the steps from presenting the offer to closing on the purchase.

1 – FIND

A House with Investment Potential

2 – ANALYZE

- ✓ Identify Improvements
- ✓ Determine Selling Price
- ✓ Estimate Improvement Costs
- ✓ Account for Quiet Costs
- ✓ Set Minimum Profit

An Offer that Maximizes Profits Given the Risk

3 – BUY

You need to determine your minimum profit. Flipping houses takes substantial time and hard work and, more often than not, some out-of-pocket cash. You need to receive a good profit that accounts for your risk and makes your investment of time and money worthwhile.

Minimum profit consists of two components that take into account the two main factors that increase the risk of a flip:

1. The selling price and
2. The complexity of the rehab.

The first component, which is called the base profit, is a simple percentage calculation tied to the eventual selling price. We recommend 10 percent. The second component is the rehab risk profit, which is based on the construction costs per square foot. To account for it, we recommend adding 1 percent of the ESP to your minimum profit for every $5 per square foot of improvement costs.

Now that you have your minimum profit, you can complete the maximum offer formula. The eventual selling price minus the improvement costs minus the quiet costs minus your minimum profit equals you maximum offer price. If your estimates are as accurate as they should be, you'll have made your money going in.

Samantha

"So when are you going to close?" Ed quipped as he got out of the car.

Samantha felt her face flush. Was it really that obvious?

"I've seen that look before. You haven't even been inside, and you've already made up your mind, right?"

"Of course not," Samantha shot back. "It looks pretty good on paper, but I'm eager to get inside and take a look. Thanks for helping me decide if this is a good deal."

Samantha opened the front door, and they stepped into the entry-way. "Well," she said, her eyes sweeping the room, "here it is. You tell me everything you see that needs to be fixed, and I'll take notes." She pulled a notepad and pen out of her briefcase.

"Not so fast." Ed held up his hands. "Eventually, you're going to want to do this on your own. I'm going to let you drive, but I'll jump in when you need help. Start by making three columns on your pad and label them *Must, Could,* and *Should.*"

"You're one of those teachers who ask questions but never tell the answer, aren't you?" she asked as she labeled the columns.

"Am I?" he asked, walking into the dining room.

She rolled her eyes and followed him. The carpet reeked of cat urine, and cigarette burns dotted the floor. An ugly stain spread across the popcorn ceiling. "Ugh!"

"I've smelled worse," Ed said.

"Not the smell, the popcorn ceiling."

Samantha studied the columns, glancing back and forth from her paper to the room. "The musts are the things that have to be done," she said. "Like that stain on the ceiling needs to be dealt with. I also need to find out if the roof is still leaking. The carpet definitely needs to be replaced." Samantha pressed the pencil to her lips. "Would the popcorn be a must or a should?"

Ed looked at her and shrugged his shoulders. Then he put his hands together. "Ah, young pupil, what do *you* think?" With that he turned and headed into the kitchen.

Samantha's heart sank as she entered the kitchen. The linoleum was cracked and curled up at the edges. The avocado-green laminate counter was laden with stains. One of the cabinet doors was hanging from a single hinge, and several handles and pulls were missing. Two of the drawer faces were gone. "This is a disaster, isn't it?" she asked, hugging the notepad to her chest.

"Actually," Ed replied, "I think this kitchen works in your favor. The last thing the owner wants to do is clean up this mess, especially since he is living in another city."

He squatted and opened the cabinets under the sink.

"What are you doing?" Samantha asked.

"I can't tell you how many times I've seen this," Ed said. "Even small leaks tend to rot out the particleboard under the sink and can leave a real mess."

"I'll put that in the *Must* column," she said, her pencil scratching across the paper.

Ed opened the dishwasher, and they were assailed by the smell of a mildewed dish towel. Rust covered the inside of the appliance. "I'm guessing this hasn't been used in a while and is probably broken."

"Why would anyone leave an old wet dish towel in their dishwasher?" she wondered as she made notes.

"You'd be surprised," he groaned.

"Andy really gave me the impression that it would not be this bad," Samantha said. "Maybe I was just being too optimistic."

"Maybe to Andy, this isn't that bad."

Samantha wandered to the counter. "Should I upgrade this to granite?" As soon as she said "should," a lightbulb went off in her head and she smiled.

"You need to do some research to find out what's normal for the neighborhood. If most of the other houses have granite countertops, go with that," Ed recommended.

"So, the shoulds are the things that bring the house up to par with the neighborhood."

"I also like to think of it as making the house more appealing or beautiful," Ed said.

Samantha tapped her pencil and thought for a moment. "I suppose I need to visit all the houses for sale in the neighborhood to find out what the competition is offering."

Ed nodded in agreement.

"Okay." Samantha looked for something to beautify the kitchen. "All those cheap brass handles and doorknobs should be replaced. And I think I'll change the light fixtures too. What about new cabinets?"

Ed examined the cabinets. "I think that they can be repaired and then painted. If you do all the other things you suggested, you will basically have a brand-new kitchen. You should get a good return on the money you put into it." He paused as if something had just occurred to him. "I would add another thing to your *Must* list. For code you are going to need to install GFI outlets in here and in the bathrooms as well."

Samantha took one more look. "I think I should change the light switches and outlets to a color other than this *lovely* green."

Ed took a step back and surveyed the kitchen from the doorway. "This kitchen is fairly small and dark. How about knocking out this wall and taking advantage of the windows in the family room as well as opening up the layout?"

"It's not a must; it's not a should. I *could* do that," she said, making a note.

Samantha looked at her growing list, and her stomach sank. "Would that be expensive?"

"It doesn't seem to be a load-bearing wall, so it could be done fairly cheaply," Ed concluded.

The master bathroom was in a condition similar to that of the kitchen. The tub was disgusting, with stains and rancid standing water. The tile surround was replete with mildew, and the shower head and bath faucet were turning green. "That's just gross," she said.

Ed reached over and pulled the stopper; the water ran out. "At least the tub drains."

"Shouldn't you be wearing rubber gloves?"

Ed shrugged.

Samantha turned her attention to the sink and the bathroom cabinet. One of the doors was missing, and there was a sizable hole in the side. Samantha took a deep breath. "Let's see. I'll need new tile around the tub, a new shower head, faucet, and handles for the tub. I definitely need a new vanity and sink and of course a new faucet for the sink. How about a matching towel bar and toilet paper holder?"

Ed nodded. "That covers it. And you know, with this long counter, I think there's room for a second sink. People like to have their own space; it's a great value-add."

"I suppose I *could* do that," Samantha said, adding it to the *Could* column.

"You got it." Ed walked over to the toilet and lifted the lid. He tried to flush it, but nothing happened. "That might need to be replaced; at the very least I always change the seat."

"I'm definitely going to bring rubber gloves next time." Samantha flipped the switch next to the light. Overhead they heard a sound like a garbage disposal. Ed pointed toward the ceiling. "Does the pupil think the bathroom needs a new exhaust fan?"

"*Must* the teacher always ask obvious questions?" Samantha said, writing "exhaust fan" in the *Must* column.

On their way back down the hall, Ed paused at each of the doors, scanned the inside and outside, and examined the doorjambs. "Doors can be expensive to replace. Looks like you can save most of them, the ones where the surfaces are intact." He pointed to a hall closet with a hole in one of the panels. "But that one will have to be replaced, and they all have those brass knobs you like so much."

Samantha made a note on her pad and then pulled a piece of peeling burgundy paint off the wall. "I need to paint the whole house."

"Yup," Ed responded nonchalantly. "I always do."

When they got back to the front yard, Ed walked toward the exterior wall and tapped on the lowest piece of siding. It crumbled, and small pieces fell to the ground. "Hmm."

"Is that termites?" Samantha asked. "How bad is it?"

Ed poked at the next higher piece, and it seemed solid. "It's okay. I think it's just a little wood rot. You probably only have to replace the bottom pieces."

Samantha felt a little nervous. There were a lot of things on her list. "So how much do you think the improvement costs will be?"

"How many square feet is it?"

"Almost two thousand," she answered.

"I'd say you're looking at about $30,000 in improvement costs."

"Just like that?" she asked.

"For a house in this condition, the improvement costs usually come in at about $15 a square foot before you pay a general contractor. I haven't seen anything here that would make me want to walk away."

Samantha relaxed. "Me neither," she agreed.

"Of course, you need more than just a rough estimate to make an offer." Ed looked at his watch. "Tell you what, since this is your first flip, why don't I put together a detailed report for you? Let's meet at the Starbucks on Main at six o'clock. In the meantime, check out some of the houses in the neighborhood to see what kind of design choices you should make. I'm not sure granite is the right choice for those countertops. This feels like a standard neighborhood, but let's make sure."

"I'll do that. This has been a huge help," Samantha replied. "Could I at least buy you dinner?"

"That would be a must."

Bill and Nancy

Bill was still charged up from the events of the day. He couldn't wait to tell the others the news. As soon as the waitress took their orders, he kicked things off. "We made an offer on our first house today. We got a call on the way over here, and it was accepted."

There was a brief moment of shocked silence, exactly what Bill wanted. He hoped to be the first one in the group to get a house and now savored the moment of triumph.

"Wow, congratulations!" Amy exclaimed as the others around the table echoed her approval. "How about some details for those of us who are still trying?"

"All right," Bill said, feigning modesty. "It's not that big of a deal. I'm sure you guys remember Tom from the investor meetings." There were some nods around the table. "Well, he and I have been meeting, and he passed along this deal to me because it's too far from his house. Nancy and I bought the house for $66,000, and we plan to sell it for $95,000."

"How many square feet is it?" Mitch asked.

"About a thousand square feet," Bill answered.

"That's $95 a foot," Mitch commented. "That sounds pretty good. Did the comps say that was about average?"

"I'm positive I can get $95,000."

"Oh, I'm just trying to get a general idea," Mitch persisted. "What did your real estate agent say was the cost per square foot for the neighborhood?"

Bill was starting to feel defensive. "I don't need to run comps," he responded. "Tom flipped over fifty houses last year. He was confident I could get $95,000, and I trust him."

A hush fell over the table.

Samantha broke the silence. "Bill, how much do you plan to spend on improvements?"

Bill was glad for the change of subject. "That's the beauty of it; there really isn't much to do. I figured $5,000, tops."

"That's only $5 per square foot," Samantha commented, pictures of her dilapidated flip flashing through her mind. "Is that all?"

"Bill, don't take this the wrong way," Ed said, "but, are you sure you did all your homework on this deal?"

Where did they get off second-guessing him? A quick glance from Nancy and he recognized her "take it easy" look.

"I know it may sound hard to believe," Bill said emphatically, "but this truly is the proverbial paint and carpet deal." He noticed a few skeptical looks, but no one pressed him further.

"How much do you think the holding costs will run?" Samantha asked.

"Well, I'm not a detail guy," Bill said. "But Nancy here has done a great job of crunching the numbers."

Nancy smiled and pulled out a spiral notebook, "I calculated about $11,500 total for our quiet costs. We're lucky to have paid off our house, and we have had a great relationship with our banker for more than thirty years. So Bill was able to work out an interest rate of only 7½ percent to buy the house and finance the construction. I've also accounted for closing costs, insurance, maintenance, and utilities."

"Did you remember to include property taxes in your quiet costs?" Ed asked.

"Oh, yes, I have that here too."

"So how much do you think you're going to make?" Mitch asked.

"We calculated that we should make about $11,000," Bill replied. "Ed, does that sound about right?"

Ed nodded. "That seems to fall in line with a low-risk rehab."

"If I have my math right," Samantha interjected, "your maximum offer would have been about $68,000, and you say you got the house for $66,000. Nice."

"How long is your contingency period?" Ed asked.

"Ten days," Bill replied.

"Great," Ed responded. "That gives you plenty of time to get the inspection and survey done. Also, it really wouldn't hurt to double-check the improvement costs and confirm the selling price. If everything checks out, it sounds like you might have a winner there, Bill."

The others, including Mitch, seemed to agree. Bill turned to Nancy and winked.

Stage Three

BUY

How to Finance, Make an Offer, and Close on an Investment House

BUY Introduction

I will prepare and some day my chance will come.

—Abraham Lincoln

What do Colonial minutemen, expectant mothers, and real estate investors have in common? They're all known for their ability to leap into action at a moment's notice. The minutemen of the American Revolution were always on the alert and could be ready for action in sixty seconds. Women in the later stages of pregnancy have their suitcases packed so that they'll be able to head off to the hospital as soon as the baby is ready. And when real estate investors find a hot lead, they are ready to put an offer on a house and close in just a few days. In each case, the ability to respond appropriately and quickly comes not so much from speed as from preparation.

There are three steps to our process for buying an investment house, and each one requires preparation so that you can respond quickly. The first step is figuring out how you're going to pay for the flip. We'll discuss the various methods for financing deals in the first chapter of the Buy stage. Whether you're borrowing from a private money lender or taking on an equity partner, you should always prearrange your financing so that you can confidently and quickly make an offer when a good deal comes along.

The next step is the offer process. Presenting an offer on an investment house involves more than just filling out a contract. Successful investors take the time to understand the specifics of the situation. They then write an offer that respects the needs of the seller in order to craft a deal that's both fair and profitable.

In the third and final step, we'll take one last careful look at the property before taking ownership of it. Again, it pays to be prepared by establishing relationships with inspectors, appraisers, insurance agents, and all the other professionals involved in the closing process. They'll help you get through closing quickly and smoothly.

Chapter 9
Arrange Financing

After reading this chapter you will know how to

- Understand the importance of paying in full
- Attract financial partners
- Finance through borrowing
- Finance through partnering
- Identify when to borrow and when to partner

Before joining Rick at HomeFixers, Clay lived in the world of high-tech start-ups. Now, as a lender and partner to real estate investors, he draws on his past experiences as both an entrepreneur raising money and as an investor evaluating software business ideas. When Clay and his former business partner, Rob Neville, went out to raise money for their first start-up, Evity Inc., they lacked the experience of running a software business. So they did what most good start-ups do: They captured the fundamentals of their business—a solid strategy in a viable market with a team that could execute—into a business plan that they used to pitch their business to investors. Clay and Rob were able to raise the money to start the business, and their investors received a fantastic return when the business was acquired by a Fortune 500 company.

The same principles apply to buying, fixing, and selling houses. You may have found a great house to flip, but to attract financial investors, you need to *demonstrate* that you have a plan to realize the profit potential of the house and have the skills or team in place to execute that plan.

But before we talk in detail about ways you can attract financial investors, let's first clarify why it's important to be able to pay for a house in full at the closing. With that understanding, we'll show you how to create an investment summary report to pitch your flip to potential sources of financing. Finally, we'll cover the two ways of getting the money for a flip: borrowing and partnering (Figure 9-1).

Financing a Flip

1. Pay in Full

2. Attract Financial Investors

3. Borrow the Cash for a Flip

4. Partner to Get the Cash for a Flip

Figure 9-1 Financing a Flip

Paid in Full

Phrases such as "all cash" and "fast cash" are almost synonymous with flipping. But what exactly does it mean to pay for a house with cash? It doesn't necessarily mean that you show up with a suitcase full of $100 bills, although that certainly qualifies as all cash. It simply means that the seller is *paid in full* at the closing without a long wait and hassle. It's the "no wait" and "no hassle" that distinguish the way investors buy houses from the way most homeowners buy houses. When it comes time to close on the purchase, the investor has the "cash" necessary to pay the seller in full.

Paying for houses with cash fits your value proposition as a flipper. So, in the next section we'll focus on ways to attract financial investors who will provide the cash you need to pay for a house in full at the closing.

Attracting Money: The Investment Summary Report

Attracting financial investors is primarily about demonstrating that the risk they'll take is worthwhile in light of the reward they will receive. Their risk in financing a flip comes from a variety of places, such as the accuracy of the projected selling price and improvement costs, the volatility of the housing market, and the experience of the real estate investor.

To address these risks, we recommend that you create an investment summary that you can distribute to potential financial investors. The purpose of the document is to show that you are capable of flipping the house, have done your homework, and have a clear plan for how you and your financial investors will profit. There are four parts to the investment summary.

1. Your qualifications as an investor
2. The property details, including the address, layout, square footage, and year built
3. The Maximum Offer Formula, including the assumptions that were part of the analysis:
   - A summary of the analysis you performed to determine the eventual selling price
   - A summary of the analysis you performed to estimate the improvement costs (the must-dos, should-dos, and could-dos)
   - The assumptions you used to calculate the quiet costs
4. Most important, how and when the financial investors are going to receive a return on their investment

Figure 9-2 shows a sample investment summary that contains all four elements.

We recommend that you keep the summary to one or two pages so that an investor can evaluate the merits of the deal quickly. However, keep your supporting materials such as comparative market analyses (CMAs) and improvement cost estimates handy so that you can back up your assumptions.

Local investment clubs are excellent places to find financial investors. Plan to get there a little early and stay late to network with other investors. Also, there is often time scheduled at the end of the meetings for people to introduce themselves and pitch a deal or describe their services. That's when you'll be collecting cards and contact information from people who finance deals. Then, when you have a great opportunity and have your investment summary in hand, your chances of finding an interested financial investor will be excellent.

FLIP INVESTMENT SUMMARY

123 ELM STREET

2,000 square feet	Built in 1968
3/2/2 floorplan	2 car garage
2 stories	Slab Foundation

1	Eventual Selling Price............................	$110,000	100%
2	Improvement Costs.................................	- $ 19,000	17%
3	Quiet Costs...	- $ 11,000	10%
4	Minimum Profit..	- $ 20,000	18%
	Maximum Offer...	$ 60,000	55%

Qualifications

I am a new investor; however I have hired a reputable contractor to manage the improvement I am very familiar with the Live Oak Neighborhood as well as have put together a solid team of people to work with:

Cindy Smith	Real Estate Agent	Cindy Smith Team
Judy Russell	Interior Designer	Russel Interiors
Rick Vasquez	General Contractor	Vasquez Construction
Joe Byron	Accountant	Joe Byron, CPA
Fred Kern	Attorney	Kern & Golden

❶ Eventual Selling Price

$55.00 per square foot $110,000

Address	Floorplan	Square Feet	Selling Price	Price Per Square Foot
436 Pecan St.	3/2/2	2,150	$119,000	$55.35
826 Walnut St.	3/2/2	2,300	$127,000	$55.21
927 Hazelnut St.	3/2/2	2,220	$121,500	$54.73
Average		2,223	$122,500	$55.10

❷ Improvement Costs

$9.50 per square foot $19,000

This is a minor rehab, requiring the replacement of the HVAC unit, new appliances, and drywall repairs. I have hired a general contractor to manage the construction process.

Top 5 Improvements

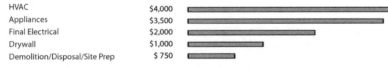

HVAC	$4,000
Appliances	$3,500
Final Electrical	$2,000
Drywall	$1,000
Demolition/Disposal/Site Prep	$ 750

❸ Quiet Costs

$11,000

Buying Costs	Closing Costs, Inspection, Survey, & Appraisal	$ 2,700
Holding Costs	Property Taxes , Insurance, Utilities, & Maintenance	$1,150
Selling Costs	Real Estate Commissions & Closing Costs	$7,150
Total Quiet Costs		**$11,000**

❹ Minimum Profit

$20,000

Excluding the cost of money, the profit on this investment is projected to be $20,000. I am seeking either an equity partner or private money lender to help finance this opportunity. I am putting $10,000 down and need $80,000 to fund the purchase, improvement, and quiet costs. At my estimated selling price of $110,000, $80,000 has a loan-to-value ratio of 73%.

Purchase Price..	$60,000
Improvement Costs...	+ $19,000
Quiet Costs..	+ $11,000
Money Down..	- $10,000
Money Needed..	$80,000

Figure 9-2   FLIP Investment Summary

Two Ways to Get Money

There are two ways to get the cash needed for a flip:

1. *Borrowing:* taking out a loan that will be repaid with interest when the flip is complete
2. *Partnering:* giving an ownership interest in the property to a financial investor in exchange for the necessary cash

In financial lingo, these methods are debt (borrowing) and equity (partnering). Both methods have strengths and weaknesses. First, we'll explain them both and then we'll look at an example to see how the two strategies play out.

For our example, we'll use the following situation. Let's say you found a house that will require $90,000 to buy, fix, and sell: $60,000 to purchase the house and $30,000 in improvement and quiet costs. Your analysis says that the house will sell for $110,000 when it's fixed up (Figure 9-3).

Example Flip	
Eventual Selling Price	$110,000
− Improvement and Quiet Costs	$30,000
− Purchase Price	$60,000
− Expected Profit	$20,000

Figure 9-3 Example Flip

If you financed it all yourself, you would stand to make $20,000 in profit. But in this example we'll assume you're using $10,000 of your own money and need to finance the other $80,000. We'll revisit this example flip throughout our discussion of your two financing options. First, we'll take a look at financing the flip by borrowing the funds.

BORROWING

Borrowing involves getting a loan to pay for any of the costs that you aren't paying out of your own pocket. You have two options when it comes to borrowing the money to finance a flip:

1. *Institutional lenders:* banks and mortgage companies that make loans primarily on the basis of the merits of the borrower
2. *Private lenders:* individuals or groups that make loans primarily on the basis of the merits of the property

Institutional Lenders

If you have good credit, a steady income history, and the ability to put 10 to 20 percent down, you can get a mortgage from a bank or mortgage company to buy an investment property. Institutions base many of their lending decisions on the person who is asking for the loan. If you fit their mold of the type of person who is going to reliably pay back the loan, you have a good chance of qualifying for a mortgage. And because the requirements are so stringent, you'll get a great interest rate compared with private lending.

But even if you meet the requirements, a loan from an institutional lender may not be the best option. That is the case because it's likely to take a month or more to close on the property even if you are preapproved for a loan. For this reason, many investors look to private money to fund their flips.

Private Lenders

Private money lenders, often called hard money lenders, are individuals or groups that lend money for real estate investing projects. The decision to make a loan is not simply based on the borrower's ability to repay the loan but rather on the current or future value of the property. Unlike institutional lenders, private lenders typically are not concerned about your credit history, current income, or tax returns. Some will require credit scores; many do not. They don't because if you cannot pay, they will foreclose, take possession of the property, and then sell it to recover their investment (presumably for a profit.) Their primary concern is whether the property will be worth more than the loan value if they have to foreclose on it.

Because of their focus on the resale value of the property, private money lenders pay close attention to the loan-to-value (LTV) ratio of a deal. Private lenders typically will not lend money above a 75 percent LTV ratio (some are as low as 65 percent). To put it simply, if the value of a property is $100,000, they will not lend more than $75,000. If you need $80,000 for a flip, you would have to use $5,000 of your own money to get the remaining $75,000 from a private money lender.

If you are borrowing the funds for both the purchase and the improvement costs of the property from one lender, that lender often will base the LTV ratio on the eventual selling price of the house (not its current value). For example, if a house will be worth $120,000 when it has been fixed up, you may be able to get a private money loan for the purchase and repairs of up to $90,000 (75 percent of $120,000) even if the current value of the house is only $90,000. Any time a lender lends money for the improvements, you will receive funds only after certain construction milestones are reached. In this way, the lender ensures that the money is being used to improve the value of the house, thus protecting the investment.

Unlike institutional loans, private money loans are not backed by a government-funded entity. Thus, you can expect to pay a much higher interest rate for a private money loan as opposed to a loan from a bank or mortgage company. Typical rates range from 10 to 20 percent interest with 3 to 10 points (a point is 1 percent of the loan amount) due at closing.

The biggest positive for private money loans is the ability to close quickly: in a matter of days rather than weeks. Many private money loans have other perks, such as deferred payments for the first six months. This may cost a little more in interest but can be a nice benefit during the rehab process, when cash is tight. Figure 9-4 summarizes the differences between institutional lending and private money lending.

Institutional Lending versus Private Money Lending		
	Institutional Lending	Private Money Lending
Interest Rate	5–7% since the 1990s	10–20%
Points	0–2%	3–10%
Closing Costs	Similar	Similar
Closing Time	4 weeks or more	A few days
Qualifying	Personal credit and income	The value of the house

Figure 9-4   Institutional Lending versus Private Lending

Let's revisit our example deal and now see how it would look if you financed the flip by borrowing the $80,000 (73 percent LTV) from a private money lender. Assuming an annual interest rate of 12 percent for six months and 4 points down, you would pay $8,000 in loan interest and fees ($4,800 for the six months of interest plus $3,200 for the four points down). Your cost of money in this scenario lowers your expected profit from $20,000 to $12,000 (Figure 9-5).

Borrowing with a 4 Point, 12 Percent Interest Loan	
Eventual Selling Price	$110,000
− Improvement and Quiet Costs	$30,000
− Purchase Price	$60,000
− Cost of Money	$8,000
− Expected Profit	$12,000

Figure 9-5 Borrowing with a Loan at 12 Percent with 4 Points

PARTNERING

When you finance a flip by borrowing, you keep all the profits of the deal but have to pay a lender for the use of his money. In partnering, there is no additional cost of money, but you share the profits with a financial investor by giving her an ownership (equity) interest in the property.

This begs the question, "How much ownership do I give a partner?" The conventional wisdom in flipping houses is to start with a 50-50 split if one partner is doing all the work (finding, analyzing, and managing the fix-up of the houses) and the other partner is supplying all the funds. You then make adjustments on the basis of the specifics of the partnership. For example, if you are supplying 20 percent of the necessary funds and doing all the work and your partner is supplying 80 percent of the funds, you may split the profits, with 60 percent for you and 40 percent for your partner. You and your partner will need to work out a split that you both consider fair.

A less common but nevertheless attractive way for investors to finance a flip is seller financing. This is when you get the home-owner to lend you some or all of the funds necessary to buy the house. You and the seller work out the terms of the loan, including the interest rate and payment schedule. So, in essence, the seller becomes your private lender.

Seller financing often becomes an option when the necessary repairs on a property are so extensive (e.g., major structural or foun-dation work) that conventional lending is not an option. In these instances, seller financing can serve as a "bridge" loan to fund the sale long enough for the investor to make those repairs and then refi-nance with a conventional mortgage lender. Sellers will typically offer more favorable interest terms than hard money lenders. (Remember, the seller is motivated.) These interest savings can be passed along to the seller in the form of a higher offer. For example, if seller financ-ing would save the investor $2,500 in their cost of money, the investor would be able to offer $2,500 more for the property.

There are a number of twists on seller financing, including "sub-ject to" clauses, lease options, lease purchases, assumptions, and wraparound mortgages. These can be good money-saving options, but the legality of some of them (such as lease options) varies from state to state. Do your homework before you purchase a house using any of these methods.

You should create a business entity that defines the business relationship you have with your partner. You have many options for business entities, including limited partnerships, limited liability companies, C corporations, and S corporations. (In addition, you will want to choose whether or not to create one business for all your flips or create a new business entity for each flip.)

For our flips in Texas, we create a unique limited liability company (LLC) for almost every flip. This structure not only defines the ownership interest but also provides liability protection and makes the allocation of income tax responsibilities straightforward. We encourage you to consult an attorney and a tax adviser to choose the business structure that is best for your situation. Even if you are not taking on partners, you should consider creating a business for your flipping activities that provides personal liability protection.

Let's return to our example flip again and now assume that you financed the example flip through an equity partner who provides the $80,000 and takes a 40 percent ownership interest in the house. In this scenario, your expected profit also will be $12,000 (60 percent of $20,000) (Figure 9-6).

Partnering with a 40 Percent Equity Partner	
Eventual Selling Price	$110,000
− Improvement and Quiet Costs	$30,000
− Purchase Price	$60,000
= Total Profit	$20,000
Your 60% Share of the Profit	$12,000

Figure 9-6 Partnership with a 40 Percent Equity Partner

COMPARING BORROWING AND PARTNERING

You may have noticed in Figures 9-5 and 9-6 that if the example flip worked out exactly as planned, financing through both borrowing and partnering would result in a $12,000 net profit for you. The differences between the two methods become apparent when things go better or worse than expected. Figure 9-7 shows what happens when things go very well—when the actual selling price is $130,000 rather than the $110,000 you estimated.

Borrowing versus Partnering with a $130,000 Selling Price

Borrow		Partner	
Selling Price	$130,000	Selling Price	$130,000
− Improvement and Quiet Costs	$30,000	− Improvement and Quiet Costs	$30,000
− Purchase Price	$60,000	− Purchase Price	$60,000
− Cost of Money	$8,000	= Total Profit	$40,000
= Your Profit	$32,000	Your Profit	$24,000

Figure 9-7 Borrowing versus Partnering with a $130,000 Selling Price

If you financed with an equity partner, your 60 percent share of the profits would be $24,000, whereas in the borrowing scenario, your profit would be $32,000. Note that in both of the borrowing scenarios, you pay $8,000 for the cost of money regardless of how much you sell the house for. This is great if you sell for more than you expected, but let's look at what happens if the flip doesn't go as well as you planned. Figure 9-8 shows the results if you sold for $90,000 instead of the $110,000 you estimated.

Borrowing versus Partnering with a $90,000 Selling Price

Borrow		Partner	
Selling Price	$90,000	Selling Price	$90,000
− Improvement and Quiet Costs	$30,000	− Improvement and Quiet Costs	$30,000
− Purchase Price	$60,000	− Purchase Price	$60,000
− Cost of Money	$8,000	= Total Profit	$0
= Your Profit (LOSS!)	−$8,000	Your Profit	$0

Figure 9-8 Borrowing versus Partnering with a $90,000 Selling Price

Selling at $90,000 was breakeven in the partner scenario. You received no profit for the deal. You got back your $10,000, and your partner received the $80,000 he or she put in, but neither of you made a penny of profit off the flip. Putting in all that effort and having nothing to show for it is certainly bad news, but it will be much worse if you financed the deal by borrowing the money. In this case, $88,000 of the entire $90,000 goes to paying off the loan principal, interest, and fees. There's only $2,000 left to pay for the $10,000 you contributed to the flip, and so you're left with an $8,000 loss. This scenario actually could be worse because it's likely you would keep the house on the market for a long time before finally discounting it by $20,000. During that time you would owe even more interest on the loan.

In short, taking on an equity partner reduces the amount you profit from a deal because you are sharing the profits with another party. But when you're sharing the profits, you're also sharing any losses, and so you reduce your risk when you finance with a partner. With borrowing, you keep all the net profits to yourself, but only after you pay back the lender. You have an agreement with the lender stating that you will pay back all the money you borrowed and the interest regardless of how the flip works out. If the flip goes wrong, you may not have enough money to pay off the lender and will end up losing money on the deal. Figure 9-9 summarizes the differences between the two approaches.

Comparing Borrowing and Partnering		
	Borrowing	Partnering
Profit	All Yours	Shared with Partners
Risk	All Yours	Shared with Partners
Repayment	Loan Must be Repaid with Interest	No Obligation to Repay
Cost of Money	Interest, Points, and Fees	None

Figure 9-9   Comparing Borrowing and Partnering

It is quite common to have a mix of both debt and equity partner financing. Taking out a loan and sharing the profits with a partner can allow you to balance the risk of a bad flip with the potential reward of a great one.

It is important to remember the value of being able to pay in full at closing. When you pay in full, you provide your own funds or bring in third-party financial investors so that you can pay "cash" for the house at the closing. Most sellers prefer to be paid in full. In fact, it's a big part of your investor value proposition of providing "fast cash with no hassles."

You can attract financial investors by demonstrating that you have the ability and a plan to flip the house successfully. You will create an investment summary that you can distribute to financial investors so they can easily evaluate the merits of financing your flip.

Borrowing is one of the two main ways to get the cash necessary to pay for a house in full. There are two types of lenders:

1. Institutional lenders such as banks and mortgage companies
2. Private money lenders, who are individuals or groups of individuals

Partnering is the second of the two main ways to get cash for a flip. In partnering, you share the profits by giving the partner ownership in the house in exchange for the cash.

Chapter 10
Present the Offer

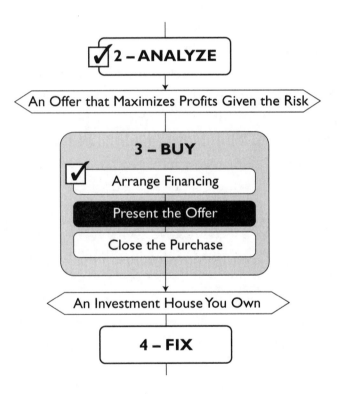

After reading this chapter you will know how to

- Establish trust with the seller
- Make the offer

As in any business, the goal of flipping houses is to create a profit. To that end, we strive to earn a profit on every deal. However, the desire to make a profit does not come at the expense of our personal values. This is the stage in the process at which some people might take advantage of others through deceit or by capitalizing on their ignorance. Our personal experiences and those of many friends and fellow investors have shown that you can make great money flipping houses without compromising your ethics.

One of our good friends and fellow investor goes to great lengths when buying a rehab property to ensure that no one can claim he is taking advantage of people. For each flip, he creates a letter that states that he is a real estate investor and intends to fix up and resell the house for a profit within months of buying it. He puts in the financial details of the flip, including how much profit he expects to make and in what time frame. He then requires the homeowner to read and sign the letter before he buys the house. If the homeowner is elderly, he tracks down any children and gets them to sign the letter as well.

Real estate investing is a business and you have a choice. You can be in the business of taking advantage of people or you can be in the business of helping people get out of difficult situations. You want to profit from this business, but not at someone else's expense. We like to use a simple test for all our business dealings: We must be able to look someone straight in the eye and in all honesty say, "Yes, this is fair."

Presenting an offer to purchase an investment property is a two-step process. The first step is to establish trust with the seller. The second is the actual presentation of the offer contract (Figure 10-1).

STEP ONE: ESTABLISH TRUST

Unlike typical home sales, in which the buyer's agent and the seller's agent act on their respective parties' behalf, buying a house to flip often

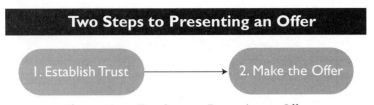

Figure 10-1 Two Steps to Presenting an Offer

requires that you develop a relationship with the seller. Even if you or the buyer are working with a real estate agent, we recommend that everyone sit around the table to discuss the deal. Because your best offer will be substantially lower than the retail value of the house, just sending an offer may insult or offend the seller. Without an explanation of who you are and what you can do for the seller, you may never get a response. The best way to establish trust with a seller is face to face; that allows you to tactfully present the merits of your offer and demonstrate your desire to treat the seller fairly.

If you've ever bought or sold a home, you know that the following maxim almost always holds true: "A homeowner thinks the house is worth more than it is and needs less work than it does." We've seen that even when sellers are in distressed situations, they cling to those notions. This makes it likely that you'll need to directly address the truth about the market value and condition of the property with the seller. In addition, you'll need to communicate your intentions so that the seller understands that you are a business person and need to profit from the buy, fix, and sale of the house.

Although you don't have to go as far as our investor friend and require the seller to sign a document, you should present the seller with a personal cover letter that accompanies your offer. If you're able to meet with the seller in person, you'll probably discuss all the elements in the letter in the course of your conversation. Figure 10-2 lists the seven elements that should be included.

1. An Awareness of the Seller's Situation

2. Your Value Proposition

3. Your Ability to Close

4. The Improvement Costs

5. The Quiet Costs

6. Your Expected Profit

7. The Cost to Sell at Market Value

Figure 10-2   Seven Elements in Establishing Trust

1. AN AWARENESS OF THE SELLER'S SITUATION

Demonstrate that you are aware of the seller's situation. If you have done your homework and qualified the house and seller, you should understand why the seller is interested in selling the house. A quick summary of the seller's situation serves as a reminder of the seller's motivation to sell the house quickly and for below retail market value.

2. YOUR VALUE PROPOSITION

State your value proposition of fast cash and no hassles. Follow up the discussion of the seller's motivation with an explanation of how you can help alleviate the seller's problems by offering a fast and easy closing.

3. YOUR ABILITY TO CLOSE

Provide evidence of your ability to pay in full and pay quickly. Prove to the seller that you are capable of coming up with the necessary cash in a short amount of time. Your proof could be an item such as a preapproval letter from a financial institution, a commitment letter of funds from a private lender, or a letter from your bank verifying that you have the funds.

4. THE IMPROVEMENT COSTS

Show the seller an estimate of what your improvement costs will be. Provide a general summary of what you would do to the house to sell it at retail value and how much it's going to cost to make the repairs and improvements. Keep in mind that your comprehensive improvement plan is valuable intellectual property that you created for this house. Be careful about how much detail you share because it could be used by someone else to do the improvements without you.

5. THE QUIET COSTS

Share the details of the quiet costs you will incur that have a direct effect on your net profit. Many sellers don't consider all the costs required to flip a house. Tell the seller how long you will need to hold the house while improving it and then show the holding costs and interest payments you will incur during that time. This might just open their eyes to the fairness of your offer.

6. YOUR EXPECTED PROFIT

Just like our investor friend, we believe in putting all our cards on the table, even our expected profit. To be clear, you'll be sharing your conservative estimate of your minimum profit, not a "pie in the sky" number that reflects a perfectly executed flip with no room for error. And be sure to have them understand you are taking a financial risk. If things don't go according to plan, you might make a lot less or even incur a loss.

7. The Cost to Sell at Market Value

Finally, make the seller aware that the house will have to be repaired before you can sell it at retail value. Be sure to note continued mortgage payments, other holding costs (insurance, utilities, etc.), and selling costs such as real estate agent commissions and closing costs.

Figure 10-3 shows an example cover letter that you could include when presenting an offer. The letter includes the seven elements described above.

The purpose of this letter is to spell out the facts of the situation in a clear manner that shows the seller that your offer is fair in light of the seller's need to sell the house quickly and easily and your need to fix up the house and resell it for a profit.

Step Two: Make the Offer

If you meet with the seller in person, have a signed offer ready to present after your discussion. When you are unable to meet in person, prepare the offer and send it to the homeowner along with your cover letter. Seek the help of a real estate attorney or agent to draft the offer. There are five main components to an offer that address the purchase price, earnest money, closing costs, the closing date, and the acceptance date (Figure 10-4).

Sample Cover Letter

Dear Mr. Foster,

Thank you for the opportunity to make an offer on the house at 123 Elm Street. I understand that you are facing foreclosure and would like to sell your house as easily and quickly as possible. I am prepared to pay cash for your house and can close five days after the contract is signed. Please see the attached commitment letter from my lender stating that they will provide funds within five business days of my request.

As we discussed on the phone, I operate a business that buys houses, fixes them up, and sells them for profit. If I purchase the property, I estimate I will need to spend $22,500 to fix and update the house. The major repairs include interior and exterior paint, new carpet, a new roof, new kitchen cabinets and countertops, and replacing the vinyl flooring with tile.

During the four to five months that I hold the house, I calculate that I will incur about $17,000 in closing costs, loan interest, real estate agent commissions, property taxes, insurance, utilities, and maintenance. If everything goes as planned I hope to make about $14,500 when I resell the property after making the improvements.

For you to sell the property to a non-investor, you would need to take on all the repairs and some of the updates referenced in the costs above. Keep in mind that to do this, you will also probably need to get a real estate agent to list the house, be prepared to wait the typical time it takes to sell a house, and pay your own selling costs.

Please consider my offer. I am willing to buy the house in its current condition and do all the work required to sell it to a non-investor. I believe it is a fair price for the house given its condition and your desire to sell quickly. I look forward to your reply.

Sincerely,

Jane Buyer

President

Jane Buys Houses

555-1212

Figure 10-3　Sample Cover Letter

The Five Components of Your Offer

1. Purchase Price

2. Earnest Money

3. Closing Costs

4. Closing Date

5. Acceptance Date

Figure 10-4   The Five Components of Your Offer

1. Purchase Price

The purchase price is the price you are offering for the house. The reality of buying and selling houses is that there is almost always a little back-and-forth haggling over the purchase price. As long as you can agree on a purchase price that is at or below your maximum offer, you should be happy. Leave yourself a little wiggle room so that you can raise the price during negotiations and still reach agreement for a price below your maximum offer.

2. Earnest Money

Earnest money is a deposit that demonstrates to the seller that you are a serious buyer. The house effectively is taken off the market when a contract is signed, and so the seller wants some assurance that the buyer will not back out. The amount is as low as you can negotiate with the seller, but 1 percent of the purchase price is common. In a competitive situation, you may want to increase the earnest money to show that you are really interested in buying the house. If the seller accepts your offer, you should deposit the earnest money in an escrow account at a title or escrow company that will handle the closing.

Once your offer has been accepted and the earnest money has been deposited, you will forfeit your earnest money if you change your mind and decide not to buy the house. For this reason, you need to add two clauses to the contract that allow you to get back your earnest money if there are surprises after the contract is signed. These clauses are "subject to inspection" and "subject to marketable title." Real estate contracts often have other clauses, such as "subject to financing." Try to keep these clauses to a minimum since you're trying to make the sale hassle-free for the seller.

Subject to Inspection Clause

The subject to inspection clause allows you to back out of the deal and get your earnest money back if an inspector finds major issues with the condition of the house (e.g., mold, structural problems, or foundation issues) that you were not aware of when you estimated your improvement costs. This means that you probably offered too much for the house and will make less money or you may even incur a loss. If the seller cannot or will not correct them, this clause will protect you. We'll discuss the details of the inspection process in Chapter 11.

Subject to Marketable Title Clause

The subject to marketable title clause ensures that you are able to take ownership of the property. If the title search reveals any judgments or liens against the property, you may not be able to have the deed transferred to your name until those issues are cleared up. As with inspections, we'll cover the details of ensuring a marketable title in Chapter 11.

These clauses don't always come into play in states where the buyer can specify a window of time (called the option period) in which he can cancel the offer unconditionally. The buyer pays the seller a small fee, such as $100, for this opportunity. Once the window expires, the buyer's earnest money is deposited and is at risk if the buyer decides to back out. During this period, the buyer should perform the inspections and title search.

3. CLOSING COSTS

As we discussed in Chapter 7, Account for Quiet Costs, it's common for real estate investors to pay many of the seller's closing costs. If you figured this into your maximum offer, it doesn't really cost you anything because your maximum offer is reduced by the amount of the closing costs; however, it saves the seller some out-of-pocket expenses. This speaks directly to your value proposition of fewer hassles. When you are negotiating price with the seller, offering to pay some or all of their closing costs (by lowering the sales price) can be a great win-win place to start the negotiations.

4. CLOSING DATE

To address the "fast" part of your value proposition, specify a closing date that is as soon as you can get the financing together. There are other tasks you need to do in the days between getting a signed contract and closing on the house, such as inspections and title searches. Arranging financing is usually the most time-consuming task.

5. ACCEPTANCE DATE

The final component of the offer is the date the offer expires. We don't recommend allowing the seller more than a day or two to respond. You've done a lot of work in analyzing the house and crafting your offer, and you don't want the seller shopping your deal around to other investors.

Many investors specialize in "wholesaling" houses, which entails finding houses and handing them to other investors to fix and sell. One method that wholesalers use to hand a house to another investor is to assign the contract for a fee. Adding in a right to assign your contract to someone else gives you the ability to wholesale the house easily if you decide you don't want to do the flip but find it would work for another investor.

It Looks Like We Have a Deal

Keep in mind that when a seller accepts your offer, it probably is a bittersweet moment for him. The seller realizes that he is not getting full price for his home but also realizes that it's a fair deal that solves some of his problems. For you, the investor, reaching this step is a huge milestone. The next step is to close the deal and officially take ownership of the house.

Unlike traditional home sales in which real estate agents do all the negotiating for you, investors want to be personally involved in the offer process. The seller needs to know that your offer is fair considering the amount of work you will put into the house to bring it to market.

In your conversation with and letter to the seller, you will address seven points: the seller's situation, your value proposition, your evidence of cash, a summary of improvement costs and quiet costs, your expected profits, and what it would take for the seller to sell the house on his own.

Before presenting a written offer to a seller, which is most effective if you do it in person, you need to include five components: the purchase price, earnest money with contingencies, the closing costs you will pay, the closing date, and the date when the offer expires.

Chapter 11
Close the Purchase

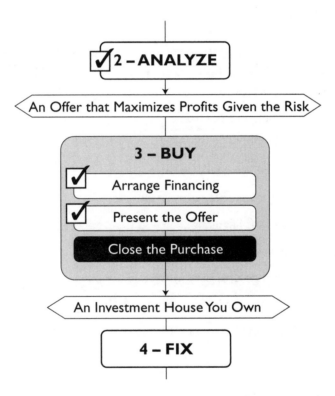

After reading this chapter you will know how to

■ Identify the ten steps to closing on an investment property

The third and final part of the Buy stage includes all the activities that take place after you get an accepted contract through the time when you sign the closing documents and take ownership of the house. Getting to an accepted offer is the tough part. The closing process for an investment house is fairly straightforward and is similar to the closing for any house—it just happens faster. Along the way there are a few things you want to keep in mind as a real estate investor. We've organized this process into ten steps to guide you through closing on the purchase of an investment property (Figure 11-1).

Ten Steps to Closing on a House

1. Set up escrow
2. Arrange inspections
3. Confirm improvement cost estimate
4. Order property survey
5. Request settlement statement
6. Prepare financing
7. Review title search report
8. Arrange property insurance
9. Prepare for improvements
10. Sign closing documents

Figure 11-1   Ten Steps to Closing on a House

The exact closing process varies from state to state, but the concepts are the same. As with drafting a contract, consult with a real estate agent or attorney for at least your first few flips to get comfortable with the process.

1. SET UP ESCROW

When you sign a real estate contract with a seller, you (or your agent or attorney) will submit the contract to an escrow or title company to begin the closing process. An escrow account is set up to hold the deposit or earnest money. An escrow company is a neutral third party that controls the documents and money as well as the way they are distributed to the buyer and the seller. In many states, a title company handles the title issues (discussed later in this chapter) and also acts as the escrow agent. In other states, all of this is done by attorneys or law firms. We'll use the term *closing company* to refer to the actual escrow company, title company, or law firm that performs closings in your area.

FLIPPING POINT

Most closing companies deposit funds in an interest-bearing account. They will earn interest on your earnest money for as long as it is there. Ask the closing company to deposit the funds into an interest-bearing account where you earn the interest during the closing period. This is especially important if you are depositing a large sum of money.

If the deal falls through because of inspection or title issues and you have the appropriate clauses in place, the closing company will return the earnest money to you. Otherwise, the earnest money is forfeited to the seller as compensation for taking the house off the market without the sale going through.

2. ARRANGE INSPECTIONS

The purpose of the property inspection is to assess the safety, function, and general condition of the structural and mechanical systems in the house. Although a detailed walkthrough was the first step in creating the improvement plan, you do not want to skip the home inspection. The purposes of the two walkthroughs are distinct. Although both will uncover many of the same problems, the inspector has an eye for safety issues and code violations that may be overlooked when you are focusing on the potential for improvement.

You should arrange the inspection as soon as the offer is signed and accepted, because you have only a specified period of time (based on the subject to inspection clause) in which to get the property inspected thoroughly. This way, if a major unexpected problem shows up, you can keep your earnest money if you're unable to work out a solution with the seller.

House inspectors come in all shapes and sizes—and qualifications. We recommend going to your network to find a highly recommended inspector, preferably one who is licensed or certified through a professional home inspection association.

Walk through the inspection process with the inspector to learn what to look for when you are evaluating a house. The more you can learn from the inspector, the more informed you'll be during future must-should-could walkthroughs. The inspector will prepare a detailed report listing all of her findings. Ask the inspector to highlight any specific areas of concern. There are three ways to handle any potential showstoppers that turn up during the inspection:

1. Get the seller to make the repairs at his or her expense.
2. Renegotiate the sales price or ask the seller to give you credit for the estimated cost of the repairs.
3. Back out of the deal if the added repairs are too risky relative to the profit you stand to make. If you are within the contingency period, you will get back your earnest money.

In addition to the standard house inspection, you need to order any inspections required by your lender. Finally, you may want to order additional inspections that focus specifically on issues that are particular to the house you want to flip, such as a foundation inspection, a structural engineer inspection, or environmental inspections.

FOUNDATION INSPECTION

Do you feel a little wobbly walking through the house, as if something isn't quite right? If you're sure it's not you, it's probably the foundation. Other signs of foundation problems are lots of cracks in the drywall or doors and windows that don't shut properly. If the house has any of these issues or if you know that houses in that neighborhood often have foundation problems, it's worth your while to get a foundation inspection.

The upside of these inspections is that they are usually free since the foundation company wants you to hire it to fix any problems. We've used the same company for years. Not every inspection results in foundation repairs, but coming out to do our inspections has resulted in plenty of business for that company over the years.

STRUCTURAL ENGINEER INSPECTION

Sagging roofs and bulging walls are the tell-tale signs that there are structural issues with the house. In these situations, it's a good idea to have a structural engineer take a look. Hiring a structural engineer will cost upwards of $400, but is well worth the cost if you have reason to suspect that there are major problems with the roof or framing structure.

CALL IN THE SPECIALISTS

There are many other inspections that are based on the age and condition of the house. We strongly recommend a septic inspection for houses with septic systems. The cost to repair or replace a septic system can equal your entire construction budget for a standard rehab. Other inspection types include the following and, if necessary, will be recommended in the initial inspection report:

- Electrical
- Plumbing
- HVAC
- Chimney
- Well
- Asbestos
- Radon
- Lead paint
- Pool
- Termite or pest infestation

3. Confirm the Improvement Cost Estimate

If you used the rule-of-thumb method to estimate improvement costs, this is the time to get firm numbers for your estimates. You may recall that you can get an estimate from a general contractor or do the estimating yourself. Either way, you want to have a comprehensive and accurate improvement cost estimate before closing on the house.

4. Order a Property Survey

A survey is an examination of the property that results in the creation of a precise diagram that shows the property boundaries, rights-of-way, and easements as well as the location of any improvements. As an investor, you always want to review a recent survey of the property whether it is required by your lender or not. Before ordering a new survey, ask the seller or closing company if a recent copy exists.

Once you have a survey, review it carefully to see if the house or any additions violate the easements, boundaries, or zoning and determine whether your renovation plans will work within the confines of the easements, boundaries, and zoning. If the property is in a floodplain, you should inquire about flood insurance and possibly reevaluate your resell strategy for the house.

5. Request a Settlement Statement

Early in the process, you should ask the closing company for a copy of the settlement statement. The settlement statement details all the numbers associated with the transfer of ownership and ultimately tells you the amount of money you'll pay the seller. Review each column carefully, comparing your numbers with the seller's to make sure there are no accounting errors or miscalculations. The actual values may change a little as you go through the closing process, but you need to get rough numbers that you'll communicate to your financial investor. It's a good idea to get your agent or attorney to review the statement as well.

In addition, get someone from the closing company to go through every line item with you. Closing companies and lenders usually charge fees that they are willing to reduce or even waive. All you have to do is ask. Some of these so-called junk fees include underwriting fees, documentation fees, recording fees, and courier fees. These may represent real costs for the lender or closing company, but they may not materially impact their profit for handling your financing or closing. Ask the closing agent to go through each line of the settlement statement for the details of any line item. If an item seems trivial, ask the agent to remove it.

6. PREPARE THE FINANCING

By the time you get to this stage in the process, you should be pre-approved with a bank or mortgage company, have a commitment of funds from a private money lender, or have an equity partner who is supplying the cash.

This is the time to notify your financial investor that you need funds to close on the house. The rough settlement statement you got from the closing company will have an estimate of the funds that you need to bring to the closing. You also need to fulfill any requirements that the lender has, such as a survey and a professional appraisal. Before closing, check with the closing agent one last time to get the exact amount.

7. REVIEW THE TITLE SEARCH REPORT

Once your contract is set in motion, a title company performs a title search to establish the true owner(s) of the property and whether the title is free to be transferred to a different owner. Some investors prefer to save money by conducting the title search themselves. However, many lenders require that the search be done by a title company.

A title search involves examining public records, generally at the local courthouse, looking for liens, judgments, or other claims against the property. For example, there may be a lien if the owner had the roof replaced but didn't pay the roofing company for the work. As a result, the roofing company placed what is known as a mechanic's lien on the property. The lien has to be settled before the property can be sold. Other examples of claims include unpaid property taxes and legal judgments (divorce, inheritance disputes, etc.).

You have three options if the title search comes back with issues that prevent you from taking ownership of the house:

1. The seller remedies the claim, and the closing moves forward.
2. If the seller is unwilling or unable to remove the claim, you can attempt to pay off the claims yourself. You should renegotiate the purchase price so that your profit remains the same.
3. You can back out of the deal. If you added a subject to marketable title clause, you will be able to get your earnest money back.

TITLE INSURANCE

Title insurance protects you in situations in which there are issues with the title that were not detected until after the purchase closed. Almost all lenders will require you to get a title insurance policy because they want to ensure that there are no claims against the property that take precedence over the loan.

Some investors opt to skip the title insurance when they purchase a house if they don't have a lender who requires it. However, in our opinion, getting a policy is worth it. We have come across several situations in which investors have suffered the consequences when a title problem prevented them from selling the house quickly after it was fixed up. This is a tough situation if you're planning to flip the house. Suddenly that "fix and flip" has become a "fix and rent" that you will now have to manage.

Depending on the state the house is in, you may be able to get two policies for only a little more than the price of one. Some states require title insurance companies to offer an "open commitment" option on their policies, also called a "binder." With an open commitment, you purchase the policy when you buy the house for about 10 percent more than the cost of a standard policy. If the house is sold within one or two years (depending on the state), a second policy is issued with no additional premium. Thus, instead of purchasing a policy when you buy the house and another when you sell it, you get one policy that covers both transactions.

8. ARRANGE PROPERTY INSURANCE

Like title insurance, homeowner's insurance for an investment property is optional. However, it is required by virtually every lender, and we recommend that you have insurance in place before you get started on the improvements. Insurance on your property protects you against two situations:

1. *Liability:* if someone gets hurt or if something gets damaged on your property
2. *Hazard:* if the property is damaged by fire, vandalism, natural disasters, and the like

As we discussed in Chapter 9, Arrange Financing, we recommend that you conduct your flips within a business entity that gives you tax advantages and some personal liability protection. Having a business also gives you the most cost-effective insurance option, which consists of two separate policies:

1. *General liability* provides liability protection for the conduct of your flipping business. You'll get one policy that is renewed each year.

2. *Remodeler's risk* provides hazard protection for a specific property. You need to get a remodeler's risk policy for each house.

If you buy an investment property as an individual, you'll need to take out a homeowner's policy for the house. The policy will provide both liability and hazard protection. Since the house is vacant, you'll pay substantially more than the cost of a standard homeowner's policy. In addition, you may discover that you are unable to get a homeowner's policy for a house that is in very bad shape. You may have to get certain major problems fixed (e.g., repair a bad foundation), before anyone will insure the house.

9. PREPARE FOR IMPROVEMENTS

Clearly, you should not begin improving the house until you own it. But improving the house quickly and getting it back on the market can save you significant money in holding costs, and so you want to get started as soon as possible. You may be surprised to learn how much you can accomplish over the phone within the first thirty minutes of taking ownership of the house if you did a little preparation beforehand (all of the following can be set into motion on the way back from the closing table):

1. Get a locksmith to rekey the locks and install a key lock box.
2. Schedule the utilities to be turned on in your name (or business name).
3. Schedule a pest control company to get rid of termites or other infestations.
4. Have a dumpster delivered to the house.
5. Schedule your cleanout crew to begin trash cleanup and demolition.
6. Have your roofer get started on roof repairs.
7. Begin the installation of or repairs to the HVAC system.

8. Hire a drywall contractor to remove the "popcorn ceiling" texture.

9. Order windows, cabinets, and other materials with a long lead time.

10. Schedule your flooring vendor to measure for new carpet, vinyl, and tile.

11. Schedule your countertop vendors to measure for new kitchen countertops and bathroom vanity cabinet tops.

12 Schedule a meeting at the house with a designer and an architect, if necessary.

10. SIGN THE CLOSING DOCUMENTS

The actual closing can be done at the closing company office with both buyer and seller present, but in most cases the buyer and the seller come in separately. The closing is not complete until both parties sign all the documents needed for the property title to be transferred. Don't be surprised if there's a glitch or two at the last minute. Just be patient and things should fall into place. After all, there are numerous documents and parties involved in a closing, and it entails executing and delivering deeds, signing loan documents, collecting and disbursing funds, and recording the documents.

Buyer's funds have to be provided in the form of a cashier's check, wire transfer, or certified funds (no personal checks). Once the funds clear, the buyer has official ownership of the house. This should take only a few hours, but sometimes funds don't clear for up to twenty-four hours or more if the closing occurs near holidays or weekends.

Closing on your first rehab house is an exciting process. Those who have done it countless times say they still get a thrill at having navigated a good deal to closing.

In the next stage—the Fix—we are going to give you step-by-step guidelines on the best way to plan and complete the improvements, covering everything from how to manage workers to the order in which repairs should be done to save you time, money, and headaches.

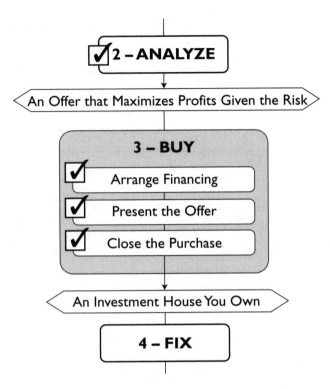

Once you have a signed real estate contract in hand and turn it over to the closing company, the clock starts ticking. There are steps to be taken to ensure that the property is a viable investment before you sit down at the closing table: from setting up escrow to making sure there aren't any surprises during the inspection process that prevent you from gaining clear title. The ten steps to closing on a property are as follows:

1. Set up escrow
2. Arrange inspections
3. Confirm improvement cost estimate
4. Order property survey
5. Request settlement statement
6. Prepare financing
7. Review title search report
8. Arrange property insurance
9. Prepare for improvements
10. Sign closing documents

When all these steps are taken, there should be no surprises when you take possession of the property.

Mitch and Amy

"Sorry about dinner," Amy said. "I got so busy pulling the paperwork together that I forgot to check the time. I can't believe I burned it."

"That's okay; it's not a total loss. We'll just tell Ed it's Cajun chicken," Mitch said, smiling.

"Why would Ed lend us money to fix up a house if I can't even cook a chicken? We barely qualified for this house. I don't see how we could get another loan. Do you really think Ed will lend us the money?" Amy asked just as the doorbell rang.

"We're about to find out," Mitch called as he headed for the door.

As Ed and Mitch made their way to the table, Amy set dinner on the table next to a box overflowing with papers.

"Ah, blackened chicken, just like my mom used to make," Ed said.

"Oh, is your mother Cajun?" Amy asked.

"No, but she worked full-time and raised three boys. Her other specialties were blackened toast and blackened lasagna," Ed replied with a wink.

"Sorry, we forgot about the chicken while putting together our whole lives on paper," Mitch said, motioning to the shoebox. "We've got our bank statements, two months of paychecks, a credit report. . . ." He started sliding things across the table to Ed.

"And don't forget last year's tax returns," Amy said, handing him another stack of papers.

Ed held up his hands as if in surrender. "Whoa, wait a second. What's all this for?"

"Well," Mitch said, glancing at Amy, "don't you need to do some research before you decide to loan us money?"

"I do," Ed said, nodding. He piled all the papers neatly back in the box. "But why are you giving me all this?" he asked, sliding the box back to Mitch and Amy.

"Well, when we applied for our mortgage, they asked for a suitcase of bank statements, pay stubs, and all this stuff," Mitch said. He put his hand on the pile of paperwork.

Ed nodded again. "Okay, I got it. Things work a little differently with private lending. The big things I want to know are how much the house costs, what it will take to fix it up to marketable condition, and what it will sell for once it's fixed up. I really appreciate how seriously you're taking this, but I just need you to tell me about the house."

Mitch sighed and gazed at the pile of now-needless paperwork while Amy fetched a spiral notebook that held all their house notes. "We can do that. Our real estate agent, Monica, did a CMA. It showed five houses that have sold recently and are close to the same size."

"And we drove by and checked them all out," Mitch added, flipping through the notebook. "We're pretty sure we can get $120,000 once it's fixed up."

"Now you're talkin' my language." Ed asked them more questions and plugged the numbers into an offer formula calculator on his Blackberry. "You are aware that private lenders charge a higher interest rate than a bank and you will have to pay some up-front points?"

"Yeah, I remember you talking about that," Mitch said.

"Now tell me, do you want to finance just the mortgage or the repair costs as well?" Ed asked.

"Both," Amy said, blushing. "You'd understand if you looked at all this stuff." She pointed to the pile of paper.

"That's okay," Ed said. "Like I said, what matters most is the house. Investors usually won't lend more than about 70 percent of the property's value. It's called a loan-to-value ratio. That means on a house worth $100,000 you probably won't be able to borrow more than $70,000. If the purchase price and repairs are more than that, you'll either have to come up with the money yourself or maybe pass on the deal."

"Why would a lender only go up to 70 percent?" Amy wondered.

"The same reason the interest rate is higher." Ed leaned forward and rested his elbows on the table. "To mitigate the risk. Private money lenders loan money in situations that mortgage companies won't touch. If the borrower bails on the property, the lender will need to sell the property himself, and he wants to have enough margin built in to clear a profit."

"That makes sense," Mitch said. He motioned toward Ed's Blackberry. "What did you come up with for our offer?"

"It looks like you need to get it for $68,000 or less."

Mitch looked at Amy and smiled a little. She turned to Ed. "They said they were looking for an offer in the low seventies."

"Might be doable." Ed offered.

Amy glanced at the pile of papers on the table and then at Mitch. Who's going to ask? she wondered. He nodded.

"Do you think you can loan us the money?" Mitch asked.

Ed smiled. "It sounds pretty good, but let's talk some more over dessert. If I'm not mistaken, I smell some cobbler in there, and it doesn't smell blackened."

Samantha

Samantha entered the coffee shop and scanned the room. Which one looks like an Andy? she wondered. She'd attended countless important meetings in her business career, presented proposals to rooms full of people, so why was she so nervous?

A tall, thin man stood up and waved. She made her way across the restaurant to his table. "Hi, I'm Andy," he said, holding out his hand.

"Samantha. Thank you for meeting me." They both sat down. "I know you're leaving town in a few hours. It's got to be tough traveling between two cities, not to mention carrying two mortgages."

"It's not so bad," Andy replied evenly, sliding a cup of coffee across the table.

"Thanks for the coffee," she said. "Listen, I know you want to sell your house, and I am interested. I can close in one week. You'll never have to make another trip back to mow the grass or check on the house."

Andy looked up from his coffee cup.

"I've included a letter from my lender with the offer," she continued as she pulled a folder from her bag, "stating that they will loan me the money to purchase the house. I'll provide the cash to fix it up. I'm going to be completely up front with you and show you exactly how I arrived at my offer."

He leaned over his cup of coffee, ready to listen.

Samantha was in her element. It was the same feeling she had in the boardroom. "I plan on spending $30,000 to upgrade the kitchen and bathrooms and to paint and carpet the entire house."

"Look," Andy interrupted. "I don't mean to sound rude, but it really doesn't matter to me what you're going to spend or what you plan to do to the house. You said you could provide a letter from your lender saying you could pay. How much?"

"Before I give you that number, you need to understand that for me to make a profit, I need to fix the house up. Until I can sell it, I'll be taking on those holding costs you've been paying as well. I'm offering $120,000. If all goes well, I'll make about $14,000." Samantha slid the folder across the table.

Andy slumped back in his chair. It was $20,000 less than he'd asked for. His brow furrowed as he looked up. "Hmm," he said. He took a deep breath. "I'm going to have to check with the other person interested in the house."

Did he really have someone else interested in the house, or was he trying to gauge her reaction? "If you have a better offer, you should take it. But I really think this is a fair price, Andy. Remember, I can close in a week."

Andy shifted uncomfortably in his seat. "When can I get back to you?"

"I'd like to have an answer by the end of the day tomorrow. My contact information is on the cover letter," she replied. "Look at the offer and give me a call if you have any other questions."

"Will do," Andy said as he stood up and shook hands with Samantha. "Thanks. I'll get back with you tomorrow."

Andy turned around and walked out. Samantha let out a big sigh. Had she been holding her breath?

Mitch and Amy

Mitch carried a bag of chips as he headed into the fire station. The Braves game was going to be on in an hour, and he was planning to watch it with his buddies at the firehouse. He pulled the door open and touched a helmet mounted on the wall. It was his ritual. The helmet had belonged to a fellow firefighter who had died during a rescue.

He rounded the corner to the kitchen and was surprised to see Amy standing there.

"Guess what?" she said, giving him a big hug. "They accepted our offer."

"Yes!" Mitch did his victory dance. "That's great! When did you find out?"

"Monica called me on my way home from school, so I decided to pop in and give you the news."

Mitch immediately started thinking about closing. "Okay we need to get the inspection done as soon—"

"Done." Amy smiled proudly. "He'll be there tomorrow morning."

"Way to go," Mitch said. He counted off on his fingers, trying to remember all the things Ed had told them. "We still need to order the survey, get an appraisal, run the title search, and set up insurance." Mitch checked the calendar on the kitchen wall. He still had two days to go on his shift. "I can take care of those things in a couple of days, as soon as I get home."

"Uh, Mitch," Amy interrupted. "There's something else I need to tell you. They said we need to close in five days."

"Five days? Wow, Ed said it could be fast. We need to call him right away," Mitch said.

Stage Four

FIX

How to Plan and Manage the Construction Process

FIX Introduction

Truly successful decision making relies on a balance between deliberate and instinctive thinking.

—Malcolm Gladwell

Bucket brigades once were considered the most effective method for fighting fires. Water was transferred in buckets from one person to the next, starting with a water source such as a pond and ending with the last person throwing the water on the fire. With the invention of hand pumps, bucket brigades no longer were used to fight fires, but they linger on as contests at county fairs and on school field days.

In these contests, the goal is to be the team that collects the most water in a specified amount of time. The winning team is often neither the team that passed the buckets the fastest (spilling much of the water) nor the team with the least amount of spills (moving too slowly). It's the team with the right balance of speed and precision.

Think of your potential profit on a flip as the water at the start of a bucket brigade and your actual profit as the amount of water that makes it to the end. Your execution of your improvement plan will determine how much actual profit you end up with at the end of the flip. Every misstep costs you money, but moving too slowly increases your holding costs and reduces your profit. A successful fix requires balancing speedy execution with the demands of staying on budget and ensuring quality. The following chapters will give you a process for achieving that profitable balance.

You may notice that we named the chapters in this stage on the basis of the cliché "Plan the work, then work the plan." In Chapter 12, you will pick up the improvement budget created in the Analyze stage and turn it into a construction plan that will be your guide through the fix-up process.

In Chapter 13, we'll discuss the various ways you can get the work done and a couple of options for overseeing the project. Finally, in Chapter 14, we'll dive in to the details of "working the plan" to have your construction project done well, on time, and on budget.

Chapter 12
Plan the Work

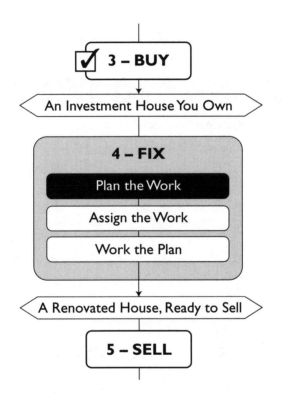

After reading this chapter you will know how to

- Turn an improvement budget into a construction plan
- Rehab a house in fifty steps

Let's get ready to rehab!

Running a successful rehab project is essential to earning a profit. And with careful up-front planning, you'll be in a position to manage a smooth rehab. The improvement budget that you created in the Analyze stage is the basis for the detailed step-by-step construction plan you will put together in this stage.

A good construction plan answers five fundamental questions (Figure 12-1). In this chapter, we'll build on the work we started in the Analyze stage to create a plan that provides practical answers to these questions.

The Five Components of a Construction Plan

1. Scope: What work needs to be done?

2. Specs: What materials are needed?

3. Budget: How much will the work cost?

4. Sequence: When to schedule the work?

5. Trades: Who does the work?

Figure 12-1 The Five Components of a Construction Plan

FROM IMPROVEMENT BUDGET TO CONSTRUCTION PLAN

If those first three questions seem familiar, it is because you answered them in the Analyze stage. When you were still considering whether to buy a promising investment property, it was crucial to come up with the improvement costs to enable you to make a sound offer. You went through each area of the house room by room, inside and out, listing problems that needed to be addressed (the must-dos) along with areas of potential that could be revealed (the should-dos and could-dos).

Next, you took the list and quickly put together an improvement budget based on contractor estimates, your own experience, or rules of thumb. What you ended up with was a list of tasks with accompanying choices of materials and associated costs that probably looked something like the list in Figure 12-2.

Typical Kitchen Tasks: Improvement Budget			
Task	QTY	Material	Total Cost
Install faucet	1	Delta	$135
Install tile backsplash	38 SQ FT	Tile	$475
Install new laminate countertops	25 LF	Wilsonart, Mystique Mount	$450
Install pendant lights	3	Candy apple red	$270
Install gas range	1	GE, stainless	$750
Install cabinet hardware	32	Brushed nickel, knobs	$128
Plumb ice-maker line for ice-maker box	1	plastic, single lever, 1/4 turn valve	$110
Install GFCI Outlets	3 EA	Leviton, ivory	$90
Install new cabinets	24 LF	Stock, oak, 36"	$3,000
Install tile floor	150 SQ FT	Tile	$825
Install sink	1	Sterling	$135

Figure 12-2   Typical Kitchen Tasks: Improvement Budget

Let's take a closer look at the first three questions to see how the work from the Analyze stage carries forward to the Fix stage.

SCOPE: WHAT WORK NEEDS TO BE DONE?

You answered the first question when you listed all the tasks that have to be performed to complete the project. In construction lingo, that list of tasks is called a *scope of work*. Double-check to make sure that the entire breadth of construction activities is listed in detail; don't leave anything out. Making a comprehensive scope of work before you start the project is the first key to staying on budget and on schedule.

SPECS: WHAT MATERIALS ARE NEEDED?

You answered the second question when you made a list of the specific materials needed to perform each task. Builders call this the *material specifications*. The material specifications list all the materials in full detail: brand, style, color, model, size, quantity, and so forth. Most builders say that a well-defined list of material specifications (defined before the job begins) is a major key to ensuring a smoothly running project that stays on budget and delivers the expected outcome.

BUDGET: HOW MUCH WILL THE WORK COST?

Costing out the tasks was an important part of producing an improvement budget when you were considering what to offer for the house. Cost is just as important when it comes to managing the construction process. Verify that your numbers for labor and materials are accurate. If they come in too high, this is the time to get the budget back to what you planned it would be when making your offer. You have two choices: You can either do less (reduce the scope of work) or you can spend less (use less expensive materials).

That leaves two final questions: When to schedule the work? and Who does the work? We answer these two questions by introducing the concept of steps.

STEPS: WHEN THE WORK IS DONE AND WHO WILL DO IT

At HomeFixers, we arrange hundreds of construction tasks into groups of similar tasks called *steps*. A step is just a collection of "like" tasks that are performed at the same time and usually by the same trade. Rolling up many like tasks into fewer steps makes them much easier to manage, so while it takes hundreds of tasks to rehab a house, it takes only about fifty steps. We often refer to these steps as management steps because this is the most effective way to manage all the work done in a rehab project. Instead of trying to assign each individual task, the general contractor or project manager makes assignments at the step level to the appropriate contractors, vendors, and merchants (collectively called *trades*).

Figure 12-3 illustrates how the various tasks that trim carpenters perform (installing baseboards, interior doors, windowsills, closet shelves, etc.) are grouped under a single step, "Interior Doors, Trim and Millwork."

As you can see, now the project manager does not have to think about the individual assignment of windowsills, crown molding, and baseboards; she just has to assign one step (step 32) to one trade (a trim carpenter). Not all steps are limited to one trade, but most are.

Rolling all tasks up under fifty steps also simplifies the job of putting the work in the proper order: You can't execute the paint step until the sheetrock step is completed, and you can't start the sheetrock step until the framing step is completed. All the steps in a job are put in the order in which they are to be performed from the start of the job (demolition) to the end (final cleaning). To do this with the hundreds of individual tasks would be next to impossible.

Step #32: Interior Doors, Trim, and Millwork: Trim Carpenter

Task	Material	Cost
Install Interior Door	30", left-handed, six-panel, hollow core	$90 EA
Install Baseboards	1" x 6", paint grade, medium density fiberboard (MDF)	$1.25 LF
Install Door Casing	1" x 4", paint grade, MDF	$0.85 LF
Install Crown Molding	3 1/2" colonial cove	$1.10 LF
Install Window Sills	1 x window sill stock	$0.72 LF
Install Closet Shelves	Shelf stock	$0.98 LF
Install Shoe Mold	Quarter round	$0.24 LF

Figure 12-3 Step 32: Interior Doors, Trim, and Millwork: Trim Carpenter

Steps answer the last two questions of when the work is done and who does it. Figure 12-4 on pages 250 and 251 shows how HomeFixers has come up with (and ordered) fifty steps that work for almost any kind of rehab project. The steps are grouped into six stages for a broader way to look at a rehab project, which can be very handy when you're communicating with lenders and partners who want a bird's eye view of how the work is progressing. We've also included the trade—who performs the many tasks that roll up into each step (e.g., T: plumber)—as well as any prerequisite steps (e.g., P: 36, 37, 38) that need to be completed before the next step can start.

For example, for step 45, Appliances, we would recommend that you use a turnkey trade: a builder's appliance company. But before you call that company, certain prerequisite steps must be completed. The electrical has to be done (step 41), the plumbing has to be in place (step 40), and the floors have to be finished (steps 37 and 38). Any steps that don't have prerequisites can be started at the same time. In fact, for the average two- to three-month rehab, you'll need to have as many steps going simultaneously as possible to get the project done on schedule. We understand that it can seem overwhelming at first, but bear in mind that most construction projects will not involve all fifty steps. Download a copy of the HomeFixers Fifty Steps to Rehabbing a House at flipthebook.com.

The Fifty Steps to Rehabbing a House

What follows is a detailed description of the fifty steps broken down by the six stages. Beyond telling you in simple terms what a step is, who will complete it, and what the prerequisites are, we wanted to provide you with some insights from our experience to help you avoid common pitfalls and navigate to a profitable flip. Let's take a look at what goes on in each step.

Stage 1: Preconstruction: Steps 1–9

The preconstruction stage gets the house ready for construction, but all these activities can be scheduled before you close on the purchase. You may even complete some steps, such as Step 2 which involves pulling permits and drafting plans. The faster you can get started on the actual rehab after you close, the better your profit at the end will be.

Step 1. House Secured
Trade: Locksmith or Carpenter
Prerequisite: None

You'll want to take precautions against vandalism and theft. Windows and doors should lock or be temporarily fixed shut. We typically send a locksmith to the site to pick the old lock (if we didn't get the keys at the

HomeFixers Fifty Steps to Rehabbing a House

	Step 1	Step 2	Step 3	Step 4	Step 5	Step 6	Step 7	Step 8	Step 9
Stage 1 **Preconstruction**	House Secured T: Locksmith P: None	Plans, Permits & Filings T: Architect, Designer, City/State P: None	House Leveling & Foundation Repair T: House Leveling & Foundation Repair Co. P: 2	Pest Control T: Exterminator P: 1	Temporary Requirements T: Vendors P: 1, 2	Plumbing Pre-Demo T: Plumber P: 5	Electrical Pre-Demo T: Electrician P: 5	Demo, Disposal, Site Prep T: Demo Crew P: 6, 7	Engineering Reports T: Structural Engineer P: 8
	Step 10	Step 11	Step 12	Step 13	Step 14	Step 15	Step 16	Step 17	Step 18
Stage 2 **Rough Structure**	Rough Soil Grading & Drainage T: Landscape Crew P: 2, 3, 9	Rough Plumbing Under House or Foundation T: Plumber P: 1, 2, 3	Framing & Subfloor T: Framing Carpenter P: 9, 11	Roof Decking T: Framing Carpenter P: 12	Exterior Doors T: Framing Carpenter P: 13	Windows & Window Glass T: Window Co., Framing Carpenter, Glass Contractor P: 12	Sheathing, Moisture Protection, Siding T: Siding Framing Carpenter P: 14, 15	Exterior Trim T: Framing Carpenter P: 16	Roof T: Roofer P: 17
	Step 19	Step 20	Step 21	Step 22	Step 23	Step 24	Step 25	Step 26	
Stage 3 **Major Systems**	Fireplace T: Fireplace Vendor P: 18	HVAC T: HVAC Specialist P: 19	Plumbing in Walls, Ceiling, Attic T: Plumber P: 20	Bathtubs & Shower Pans T: Plumber P: 21	Rough Electrical T: Electrician P: 22	Exterior Masonry T: Mason P: 23	Batt Insulation T: Merchant, Handyman, Insulation Co. P: 23	Concrete Work T: Concrete Vendor, Mason P: 24	

Figure 12-4

HomeFixers' Fifty Steps to Rehabbing a House

Stage 4 — Unfinished Surfaces

Step	Name	Trade	Prerequisite
Step 27	Drywall	T: Drywall Crew	P: 25
Step 28	Garage Doors	T: Garage Door Co.	P: 27
Step 29	Gutters	T: Gutter Co.	P: 26
Step 30	Unfinished Wood Floors Installed	T: Hardwood Flooring Co.	P: 27
Step 31	Cabinetry	T: Cabinet Merchant	P: 30
Step 32	Interior Doors, Trim, Millwork	T: Trim Carpenter	P: 31
Step 33	Dust, Sweep, Clean Before Paint	T: Make-Ready Crew	P: 32

Stage 5 — Finished Surfaces

Step	Name	Trade	Prerequisite
Step 34	Paint Interior & Exterior	T: Painter	P: 33
Step 35	Blown Insulation	T: Insulation Contractor	P: 27
Step 36	Countertops	T: Countertop Specialist	P: 34
Step 37	Tile	T: Tile Setter	P: 36
Step 38	Vinyl Floors	T: Flooring Co.	P: 34
Step 39	Final HVAC	T: HVAC Contractor	P: 34
Step 40	Final Plumbing	T: Plumber	P: 36, 37, 38
Step 41	Final Electrical	T: Electrician	P: 36
Step 42	Finish Wood Floors	T: Hardwood Floor Co.	P: 39, 40, 41

Stage 6 — Final Details

Step	Name	Trade	Prerequisite
Step 43	Lockout	T: Trim Carpenter	P: 42
Step 44	Mirrors & Shower Doors	T: Glass Contractor	P: 40, 41
Step 45	Appliances	T: Builder's Appliance Co.	P: 37, 38, 40, 41
Step 46	Carpet	T: Flooring Co.	P: 42, 43, 44, 45
Step 47	Landscaping	T: Landscaping Crew	P: 40, 41
Step 48	Final Cleaning & Make-ready	T: Make-Ready Crew	P: 46
Step 49	Accessories & Decor	T: Decorating Companies & Merchants	P: 48
Step 50	Punch	T: All Trades	P: 48

T = Trade   P = Prerequisite Step

Figure 12-4 HomeFixers' Fifty Steps to Rehabbing a House

It's important to have the utilities (electric, water, gas) turned on as soon as possible so that leaks can be detected and construction can begin without delays. In some cases it can take several weeks to have the utilities turned on. Schedule putting the utilities in your name and having them turned on to coincide with the day you close so that you can start the rehab right away.

closing), rekey the exterior door locks, make three keys, install a combination lock box on the front door (set to a combination of our choice), and put all three keys inside the lock box. One key will stay in the lockbox, so your trades can access the house. One is for you and the last is your backup in case one gets lost.

Step 2. Plans, Permits, and Filings

Trade: Architect, Designer, Project Manager; City or Municipal Authority
Prerequisite: None

Finalize your construction plan: scope of work, material specs, budget, schedule, and trades. You won't need construction drawings (blueprints) on most rehabs, but some projects will require a rough floor plan, site plan, and survey, especially if you are pulling a building permit.

Start making design choices early on. We pay our interior designer, Camille, a flat fee to make many of these decisions for us. Here are the primary design selections that will have to be made: windows, cabinets, exterior door, roof, drywall texture, garage door, trim, paint, countertops, backsplash, floor tile, tub and shower tile, vinyl flooring, sinks, faucets, light fixtures, ceiling fans, hardwood floors, bathroom accessories, cabinet knobs and pulls, doorknobs, appliances, carpet, and landscaping. Camille takes this list and turns it into a comprehensive shopping list of complementary materials (basic, standard, designer, or custom) for a rehab project.

Many rehabs consist of cosmetic-only improvements that don't require permits, but major remodels require permits and inspections—especially when dealing with structural, framing, electrical, plumbing, and HVAC improvements. You or your general contractor should consult your municipal and state authorities to ensure compliance.

Step 3. House Leveling & Foundation Repair

Trade: House Leveling & Foundation Repair Company

Prerequisite: Step 2

There's nothing fun about having to level a house or repair a foundation, so go with a reputable foundation company that's been around for a while and is highly recommended. This is not the time to cut costs at the possible expense of quality work. An established company might cost a little more but they are also likely to have the resources to warranty their work. Select one that offers a comprehensive, lifetime, transferable warranty. A good foundation company will anticipate the plumbing problems that are often associated with foundation work and will formulate a plan to avoid or address them before the work is started.

Step 4. Pest Control

Trade: Exterminator

Prerequisite: Step 1

You can deal with fleas and roaches with foggers and pesticide sprays. Professionals should be called in if there are termites, bees, or rodents. You'll know you have to do this step if there is evidence of pests or if the inspection report dictates it.

Step 5. Temporary Requirements

Trade: Merchants and Vendors

Prerequisite: Steps 1 and 2

If necessary, this is the time to order a portable toilet, put up safety fences or railings, install a silt fence to prevent soil washout, and put down protective coverings on floors and walls.

Step 6. Plumbing Pre-Demo

Trade: Licensed Plumber

Prerequisite: Step 5

Skipping this step can have three potentially disastrous outcomes: (1) a flooded house, (2) a burned-down house, or (3) a house that simply blows up. Thus, it's very important that a licensed plumber always be on the job before the demolition crew gets there to prevent water and gas leaks. Get used to seeing the plumber (and paying him) because he has at least four more opportunities to come back.

At this important stage, the plumber should unhook or detach old plumbing appliances and fixtures that will be replaced or not used again (e.g., gas heaters, gas ranges, gas wall ovens, gas furnaces, gas hot water heaters, gas clothes dryers, as well as sinks, toilets, showers, washing machines, ice-makers, and other plumbing fixtures and appliances). For appliances and fixtures that will be replaced or reused, the plumber should replace the old shutoff valves and fittings with new ones and terminate (or cap) all gas and water lines that will not be used again.

Step 7. Electrical Pre-Demo

Trade: Licensed Electrician

Prerequisite: Step 5

A licensed electrician should terminate wiring that will be in the path of demolition as well as unhook any hardwired appliances and fixtures that will be replaced or not used again (e.g., electric cooktops, ranges, wall ovens, and other electric fixtures, such as lights, fans, and HVAC equipment).

Some houses may not have had electricity (e.g., new construction) or the inside wiring may be unusable because of old age, fire damage, and the like. Temporary power (a "T-pole") may be needed. This requires a city permit and inspection, so it's important to make arrangements before construction begins. If for any reason, it's going to cause delays waiting for utilities to be turned on, rent a generator instead of holding up the project.

Step 8. Demolition/Disposal/Site Prep

Trade: Demo Crew, Handyman, Laborers, Waste and Disposal Vendor
Prerequisite: Steps 6, and 7

Even though you will be using a licensed plumber and a licensed electrician to remove most of the fixtures and some appliances beforehand, it is a good idea to turn off the electricity and water temporarily while the demo is in progress (flip the breakers off and shut off the water at the street). Any suspected load-bearing walls should await evaluation from a structural engineer before demolition.

After a tough day at the office, demolition can be therapeutic. Here are the things we seem to get rid of in most rehabs: bathtub and shower surrounds (tile and plastic inserts), countertops, backsplashes, vinyl floors, exterior storage sheds, patio covers, old appliances, fixtures, faceplates, old carpet, doorknobs, window treatments, cabinet hardware, bathroom accessories, mirrors, picture hangers, nails, screws, and brackets. Everything gets thrown into a 40-yard dumpster. They make smaller dumpsters (20- and 30-yard), but the small savings are a poor trade-off for not getting all your junk's worth out of a 40-yard dumpster.

Once the house is cleared out, we break out the buckets, sponges, and mops and start cleaning and disinfecting. We also use special agents and enzymes to get rid of pet odors. On the outside we get out the chain saws, rakes, lawn mowers, hedge clippers, and weed eaters and start sprucing up the place. There are few more dramatic before-and-after pictures in the life of your project than when the demo and cleanout are complete!

Step 9. Engineering Consultations and Reports

Trade: Structural Engineer, Framing Carpenter, Project Manager
Prerequisite: Step 8

A licensed structural engineer should advise you and your framing carpenters about how to address load-bearing conditions before you attempt to remove or widen walls. The same wisdom applies to building new, or demolishing any structural or roof support systems, elevated patios, decks, and porches. An engineer can also advise you of any drainage issues and how to address them.

STAGE 2: ROUGH STRUCTURE: STEPS 10–18

The rough work starts in Stage 2 and continues through Stage 3. If a house were a human body, Stage 2 would be the skeletal and muscular system. This is the framework that gives shape, form, support and protection to a house. As a general rule, this rough work has a high ratio of labor cost to material cost. The two-by-four studs may not be particularly expensive but the labor to frame the house will likely be paid by the hour. In other words, you'll be managing people during the rough work. It's important to be at the job site as often as possible during these stages, as this is where most projects can get off track.

Step 10. Rough Soil Grading and Drainage

Trade: Structural Engineer, Plumber, Laborers, Framing Carpenter, Dirt Vendor, Landscapers, Bobcat Operator, Drainage and Waterproofing Contractors

Prerequisite: Steps 2, 3, and 9

Follow the advice of a licensed engineer for addressing drainage issues. The engineer can give you specifications on where and how to install area drains, French drains, grade soil, and add gutters with extended downspouts as well as other measures to address drainage and excessive moisture (wet or damp basements, etc.). Surprisingly, drainage issues are the most frequently found problem that comes up on inspection reports.

Step 11. Rough Plumbing Under House or Foundation

Trade: Licensed Plumber

Prerequisite: Steps 1, 2, and 3

This is the visit from the plumber that you dread the most, because it can be expensive. Thankfully, it isn't always necessary. Rough plumbing comes into play when you're doing major layout changes or when the inspection has revealed a major problem. Repairs can also be the result of house leveling and foundation repairs. The work in this step is repairing or installing new water supply lines and sewer lines. These are the main lines underneath the house or foundation. They must be worked on by a licensed plumber and they almost always require permits and inspections.

Problems with a septic system or water well should have been detected by a professional (licensed) inspector before you closed on the house. Begin repairs as soon as possible. With septic sytems, pumping the septic tank is sometimes all that's required. Wells should be repaired by a licensed water well contractor.

Be at the job site as often as you can during the rough plumbing and be a friend to your plumber. Have the site cleared of any debris and do your part to help make the work go as smoothly as possible.

Step 12. Framing and Subfloor

Trade: Framing Carpenter, Structural Engineer
Prerequisite: Steps 9 and 11

In a typical rehab project, you'll mostly be removing and replacing rotten or termite-eaten two-by-fours and mushy subfloor, especially around water sources such as kitchens, baths, and utility rooms. You also may have to frame a curb for a walk-in shower or frame out a bathtub support or a deck for a Jacuzzi-type tub. Occasionally, you'll frame a new stud wall or possibly an entire addition. Follow the advice of a licensed structural engineer before removing any existing framing. The engineer also will design the appropriate framing for windows, widened openings, long spans, and entries.

The roof system, trusses, joists, ridge board, rafters, collar beams, and other support members should be done by professional framers under the guidance of a structural engineer. Any structural or roof framing will have to be permitted and inspected.

Step 13. Roof Decking

Trade: Roofer or Framing Carpenter
Prerequisite: Step 12

On typical rehabs, the roofer will replace any rotted or damaged plywood or board decking to which the new felt and shingles will be applied. Make sure decking is included in the roof bid and ensure that problem areas actually were addressed. You don't want to cover up a hole in the roof with new felt and shingles—it eventually will leak. If the roof system is being replaced completely or built from scratch, the framing crew will take care of the decking.

Step 14. Exterior Doors

Trade: Framing Carpenter or Handyman

Prerequisite: Step 13

Cost, design, safety, and how much light you want to let in are some of the deciding factors in the choice of an exterior door. Most municipal building codes now require a solid-core (exterior) door from the house into the garage. If you're just repairing the current door, look out for bad jambs and rotted thresholds.

Step 15. Windows

Trade: Framing Contractor, Window Contractor

Prerequisite: Step 12

Replace and or repair all broken single-pane window glass and fogged double-pane windows where the seal has broken. Order any new windows right away—they usually have long lead times. A few new windows in key places (front of the house, a dark room, etc.) can maximize your overall return. Windows come as single-pane, double-pane insulated, aluminum, vinyl, and wood. Keep in mind that there probably will be some siding (step 16) and sheetrock (step 27) repairs along with casing and exterior trim when you are installing new windows.

Step 16. Sheathing, House Wrap, and Siding

Trade: Framing Carpenter, Siding Contractor

Prerequisite: Steps 14 and 15

Siding replacement was ranked as delivering among the highest returns on investment in the 2005 Cost vs. Value report in *Remodeling* magazine. Siding comes in all sorts of varieties, styles, brands, and materials: wood, fiber-cement, vinyl, and aluminum. Your handyman or framing carpenter can handle the small patches, while your framing carpenter or specialty siding company will handle residing an entire house. Siding an entire house can be very expensive in both removing and disposing of the old siding and applying the new material. You'll also need to include new exterior trim in the budget as well.

House wrap is a protective layer that goes under the siding and over the wood/foam sheathing. It's both water-resistant and wind-resistant and goes on only if you are redoing the siding or an addition.

Step 17. Exterior Trim

Trade: Framing Carpenter, Siding Contractor
Prerequisite: Step 16

It's in this step that the wood will be replaced for any rotten window trim, windowsills, corner trim, eaves, door trim, fascia, or soffit. Replacing rotted fascia boards and soffits can be tricky—it often involves, splicing, scabbing, or surgically removing and replacing the old boards. This can be time consuming and therefore the expense can get out of hand.

Depending on the design level, a large variety of types of decorative wood can dress up the exterior of a house and add some wow factor for curb appeal: columns, corbels, brackets, gingerbread, louver gable vents, and shutters.

Step 18. Roof

Trade: Roofer
Prerequisite: Step 17

Roofers measure the amount of shingles to remove and replace by the square: one square equals one hundred square feet. They'll usually charge extra for removing more than one layer of old shingles but disposal and minor decking replacement is usually included. Besides replacing the roof shingles, the roofer can install the appropriate air vents (ridge, turbine, etc.). The common repairs include replacing small areas of bad shingles, replacing flashings, replacing vents, caulking exposed nails, painting pipe protrusions, gently pressure washing a stained roof, and installing a new chimney cap.

STAGE 3: MAJOR SYSTEMS: STEPS 19–26

This is an extension of the rough work that started in Stage 2 but with a focus on the systems of the house rather than the structure. If a house were a human body, Stage 3 would include the respiratory, circulatory, digestive and nervous systems (HVAC, plumbing, and electrical). Like Stage 2, a lot of this work won't be seen in a finished house (materials go above the ceiling, below the floor, or inside the walls, out of sight). As with the other rough work, your focus here will be on people management since labor costs can get out of control if they're not managed tightly. Again, we recommend that you or your general contractor follow the work in these steps closely.

Step 19. Fireplace
Trade: Fireplace Vendor, Chimney Sweep
Prerequisite: Step 18

Installing a fireplace probably won't be necessary in most rehabs, but this is the stage in which it is done in new-construction projects. Sometimes an old fireplace and chimney will have so many years of buildup on it that it may be a fire hazard (it could be flagged by a home inspector when you sell the house). You may need to hire a chimney sweep to clean the buildup. But, as Mary Poppins says, "When you're with a sweep, you're in glad company."

Step 20. Rough HVAC

Trade: Licensed HVAC Specialist

Prerequisite: Step 19

HVAC stands for "heating, ventilation, and air-conditioning." The V for "ventilation" means that if "moving air" is involved, your HVAC specialist will be in charge of getting it done. Examples are exhaust fans and ducts for bathrooms and utility rooms and venting systems for cooking (up- or downdraft). This is the appropriate time to do these things, and your HVAC person is the go-to guy for these tasks as well as for repairing and installing a new heating and air-conditioning system.

Step 21. Plumbing in Walls, Ceiling/Attic

Trade: Licensed Plumber

Prerequisite: Step 20

This is the third plumber visit. This task usually is referred to as the plumbing top out because they build on top of the plumbing they began underneath the house. It's the repair, replacement, or new installation of any water lines, drain lines, vent lines, and gas lines in the walls and ceilings of the house. Besides repairs, this is when the plumber will install new lines to plumb for fixtures and appliances that will be moved to a new location: sinks, toilets, tubs, walk-in shower, washer connections, ice-maker box, hot water heater, and hose bibs. If you're installing or moving a gas HVAC system, stove, dryer, hot water heater, or logs in a fireplace, the plumber will have to run gas lines to them at this stage. A lot of this work requires permits and inspections.

Step 22. Bathtubs and Shower Pans

Trade: Licensed Plumber
Prerequisite: Step 21

This is the fourth plumber visit. By now, you know his favorite soft drink and country music station. After the proper water lines, drain lines, and vent lines are installed, the bathtubs and walk-in showers (adjustable drain and shower pan) should be put in (a garden or Jacuzzi-type tub will go in after step 37, Tile). There will be a top out inspection to ensure that the tubs and shower pans are holding water.

Step 23. Rough Electrical

Trade: Licensed Electrician
Prerequisite: Step 22

The licensed electrician will install junction boxes and pull wire for outlets, switches, appliances, systems, lights, and fans. The location of some of these items will be dictated by a city code. The electrician will upgrade the service panel if necessary (e.g., when putting in central air and heat for the first time).

Step 24. Exterior Masonry

Trade: Mason
Prerequisite: Step 23

The mason will repair or replace brick, stone, or stucco exteriors. This is especially important if there has been any foundation work or settling. For brick and stone, you will want to match your materials as closely as possible for repairs. For stucco, you need to consider whether to use an integral color stucco (color mixed in the stucco) or the type you have to paint after applying it. Other considerations are the application system, the expansion joints, and the texture. Your mason can advise you on the pros and cons for each of these choices.

Step 25. Batt Insulation

Trade: Handyman, Insulation Vendor
Prerequisite: Step 23

After the plumbing and electrical are in and any inspections have been passed, you can go on to insulating exterior walls with rolls called batts. We use a turnkey insulation company, but a handyman also can get the job done. Blown-in insulation in the attic is installed in step 35.

Step 26. Concrete Work

Trade: Concrete Vendor
Prerequisite: Step 24

Most of the crawl-space work has now been completed (for plumbing and electrical), and so this is usually the best time to repair or replace the concrete underpinning that skirts around a house with a pier and beam foundation. We also fill cracks and make repairs in driveways, walkways, patios, and porches.

STAGE 4: UNFINISHED SURFACES: STEPS 27–33

The ratio of labor costs to material costs begins to balance out in this stage, and you will start to manage materials and quality assurance more closely. Ensure that each trade sticks to the schedule and to your material specifications. Always prep for the next trade that will come in by making sure the area is clean and any needed materials are on site.

Step 27. Drywall

Trade: Drywall Crew
Prerequisite: Step 25

Putting up drywall is like closing the hood on your car after overhauling the engine. Now you can concentrate on the stuff that people see: the design finishes. The sheetrockers will hang, tape, float, and texture the walls and ceilings. They'll repair cracks, patch holes, retape seams and corners, remove any acoustical texture (popcorn), and retexture the house to give it a newer appearance. Our drywall crew also handles removing any old wallpaper or simply floating and texturing over it. Wallpaper and texture removal can start as early as the Demo step (step 8) if the house is not crowded with people wielding sledgehammers, wheelbarrows, and reciprocating saws.

Step 28. Garage Doors

Trade: Garage Door Company
Prerequisite: Step 27

There are companies that install garage doors for builders that should be able to give you a good price. There are a number of design choices: from several gauges of aluminum doors to decorative wood doors (with or without windows). A new garage door can add great curb appeal.

Step 29. Gutters

Trade: Gutter Vendor
Prerequisite: Step 26

We install gutters and downspouts only to address drainage problems. Most home inspectors want extended downspouts to keep water 4 feet away from the foundation.

Step 30. Unfinished Wood Floors Installed

Trade: Hardwood Floor Vendor
Prerequisite: Step 27

If we're rehabbing a custom or even a designer house, it's at this step that we install new hardwood floors (the kind that need to be sanded and finished after they are installed). Some design considerations in wood flooring are wood species, stain color, engineered (glue down), and all wood (nail down over plywood). Unfinished wood floors run half-inch to three-quarter-inch thick, and you will need to consider floor height transitions to other rooms, door height, trim height, and so on.

Step 31. Cabinetry

Trade: Cabinet Vendor, Cabinet Maker, Cabinet Installer
Prerequisite: Step 30

Cabinets will be stock (premade) for most rehabs and usually will be constructed of oak, maple, or cherry. Using a turnkey cabinetry company was a huge leap forward for us. Our cabinet rep comes out and measures, orders the cabinets, and installs them within three weeks (lead times can run long, so order cabinets early). For basic or standard bathroom vanity cabinets, we still use a lot of preassembled 24-inch and 30-inch vanity cabinets, the ones that come with simulated marble sink tops. They are available at big home improvement centers.

Step 32. Interior Doors, Trim, Millwork

Trade: Trim Carpenters
Prerequisite: Step 31

There are a couple things you need to know about interior doors. The prehung ones are easier to install (they come attached to the jambs, with hinges and with the doorknob hole already drilled), but you have to remove the old trim and doorjamb during demolition. You'll also need to trim the new door with new door casing once it's installed. If you don't want to have this expense, you can buy an unassembled door (often called a blank); the trim carpenter will need to mortise and install hinges and drill a hole for the doorknob. Other interior door considerations are door swing (left-hand or right-hand), hollow core versus solid core, panel versus flat, and pocket doors that slide inside a wall, especially for custom homes. For wide shallow closets, bypasses (sliders) and bifold doors often are used.

The interior trim items you'll be dealing with the most are baseboards, door casing, windowsills and aprons, pantry shelves, laundry shelves, and closet shelves and rods. For designer and custom homes, you'll probably ask the trim carpenter to leave room so that tile or finished wood flooring can be installed underneath the baseboards. For basic and standard houses, have the trim carpenter install baseboards flush with the existing floor; he will come back and install shoe molding over any finished flooring in step 43, Lockout.

Step 33. Dust, Sweep, Clean Before Paint

Trade: Make-Ready Crew

Prerequisite: Step 32

This step consists of the interim removal of construction debris, dirt, and dust before painting: a rough cleaning. You don't need to be able to eat off the floors, but the majority of the drywall dust and sawdust should be gone.

STAGE 5: FINISHED SURFACES: STEPS 34–42

Now that all the rough work is done, this is the time to focus on the design finishes.

At this stage, your job will consist mostly of managing materials and assuring a high-quality finish from the trades. This is where the house will start to look less like a construction project and more like a home.

Step 34. Paint (Interior and Exterior)

Trade: Painter

Prerequisite: Step 33

There are three things you need to understand about paint: type, sheen, and color. There are two main types of paint: latex and enamel. On drywall, you'll use latex. On hard surfaces, you have a choice between oil-based and latex-based enamel.

As for sheen, or gloss level, the shinier the paint is the more washable the finish will be. You'll choose between flat, eggshell, satin and semigloss.

1. *Flat:* nonreflective. Flat is best for hiding imperfections in drywall and siding. We use it on ceilings, walls, and the entire exterior.
2. *Eggshell:* just slightly more reflective than flat and more washable. Eggshell is good for walls.
3. *Satin:* a step above eggshell in shininess and washability. We often use satin paint for the trim, especially in custom homes where we don't want anything too shiny.
4. *Semigloss:* shiny and very washable. Semi-gloss is best for cabinets, trim, doors, and millwork.

Finally, when we paint the interior of a designer house, we usually paint the ceilings one color (white) and the walls a richer color. For a standard or basic house, we paint the ceilings and walls the same color, typically linen or off-white. Sometimes we bring an accent color into the master bedroom, living room, or kitchen. The trim, doors, shelves, and millwork are another color, usually a shade of white.

Step 35. Blown Insulation

Trade: Insulation Vendor

Prerequisite: Step 27

On rehabs you typically won't put extra insulation in an attic unless an inspection report (when you bought the house) reveals that there was inadequate or no insulation in the attic. If so, this is the time to get it done.

Step 36. Countertops

Trade: Countertop Vendor

Prerequisite: Step 34

Here are some of the countertops you may have chosen: granite, engineered stone (e.g., Zodiaq, Cambria, and Silestone), solid surface (e.g., Avonite, Corian, Swanstone), stainless steel, concrete, butcher block, ceramic tile, and the ever-popular plastic laminate (e.g., Formica, Nevamar, and Wilsonart). Some of the more expensive choices have a couple of weeks' lead time and will require that you purchase a sink and a cooktop before the countertop installation. You also have to consider how the edge of the countertop will be finished.

Countertops line up with our four design levels as follows:

- Basic: laminate
- Standard: laminate
- Designer: high-end (designer) laminates, tile, solid surface, low-end granite
- Custom: high-end granite (bull nose edge and/or honed), engineered stone, stainless steel, concrete, and wood

Step 37. Tile

Trade: Tile Setter, Tile and Flooring Vendors
Prerequisite: Step 36

All tile is installed at this point for floors, kitchen backsplash, tub sur-rounds, shower surrounds, and fireplaces. Tile comes in ceramic and porcelain (most common), quarry tile, natural stone (marble, granite, limestone, travertine, quartz, slate), glass, terra-cotta, and terrazzo, among others.

We don't use tile for basic houses. For standard houses, we use a low-end tile on the floors (usually found on sale at the end of the aisle at one of the big home improvement centers). For designer houses, we use a natural stone, such as travertine (especially if we can get it on sale). For custom homes, we use high-end travertine, slate, glass, etc.

Step 38. Vinyl Floors

Trade: Flooring Vendor
Prerequisite: Step 34

Use sheet vinyl (linoleum) in the kitchens, bathrooms, utility rooms, and entryways of basic houses and some standard houses where tile is not cost-effective. In smaller, older houses with existing hardwood floors, it sometimes looks better to use higher-end vinyl composition tile (VCT) squares instead of sheet vinyl or less expensive tile.

Step 39. Final HVAC

Trade: HVAC Specialist
Prerequisite: Step 34

This is the last time you'll see the HVAC crew. Even if we're not installing a new system, we have our HVAC specialist install brand-new air vents and a programmable thermostat in every house we do. It's at this stage that the condenser is put on a concrete pad outside, if you're installing a brand-new system. Make sure that the condensate line is properly installed; this is often an inspection item.

Step 40. Final Plumbing

Trade: Licensed Plumber

Prerequisite: Steps 36, 37, and 38

This is the plumber's last visit. Honest. He'll install the sinks, faucets, toilets, toilet seats, washing machine connections box trim, ice-maker box trim, and vacuum breakers for the hose bibs. He'll install the hot water heater at this point if he didn't install it at top-out. If you don't use a turnkey appliance company, the plumber also will install the gas range, gas cooktop, gas ovens, dishwasher, and disposal.

Step 41. Final Electrical

Trade: Licensed Electrician

Prerequisite: Step 36

It's during the final electrical that all the outlets, switches, jacks, and plates go in. The electrician also installs the lights, fans, smoke detectors, and the door chime. If you're not using a turnkey appliance company, the electrician can install the vent hood, microwave vent hood, electric range, electric cooktop, and electric wall ovens.

Step 42. Finish Wood Floors

Trade: Hardwood Floor Vendor

Prerequisite: Steps 39, 40, and 41

We go back and forth about when to sand and finish wood floors (before painting or afterward). We usually seem to end up here, after the painting is complete and a lot of the major traffic has cleared out. This is also the time when we install prefinished wood or laminate (simulated wood) floors.

Stage 6: Final Details: Steps 43–50

Details is the keyword here. By the time you get to this stage, the house is coming together. But to realize your full profit potential, you need to complete all the small items at the end of the job or you will diminish the overall value. You can do a major rehab on a kitchen complete with granite countertops and stainless appliances, but the buyer's eyes will be drawn away if there are blemishes in the paint or gaps between the switch faceplate and the wall. It's time to finish strong. Your reward is waiting for you.

Step 43. Lockout
Trade: Trim Carpenter, Handyman
Prerequisite: Step 42

This is where the trim carpenters come back to install doorknobs (lock sets) and deadbolts in addition to doorstops, window locks, towel bars, towel rings, paper holders, cabinet knobs and pulls, shoe molding, framed mirrors, and other miscellaneous hardware. On the exterior, house numbers, mailboxes, brass kick plates, and door knockers are installed.

Step 44. Mirrors and Shower Doors
Trade: Glass Contractor
Prerequisite: Steps 40 and 41

The same glass contractor who replaced the broken window glass can install custom-cut vanity mirrors, shower glass wall (enclosures), and shower doors. We use a more specialized bathroom glass company for our higher-end glass shower surrounds.

Step 45. Appliances

Trade: Appliance Vendors
Prerequisite: Steps 37, 38, 40, and 41

For years we let plumbers and electricians install our appliances. Now we use a turnkey appliance company that specializes in working with builders and remodelers. The cost is a little higher, but the predictability and warranty are worth every penny. The big home improvement centers usually offer similar services.

Step 46. Carpet

Trade: Flooring Vendor
Prerequisite: Steps 42, 43, 44, and 45

When it's time to put in the carpet, wait. And then wait some more! It's likely that three more contractors will be tramping across the floors before you're done. Once the carpet is in, cover it with plastic construction film until buyers are at the door. In general, lighter-colored carpets are more attractive.

Remember, this is a massive surface area in the house, and people will notice if you make a bad color decision. For the four different design levels, use plush for basic, Berber for standard, frieze for designer, and wool for custom.

Step 47. Landscaping

Trade: Landscaper, Landscape Company, Nurseries
Prerequisite: Steps 40 and 41

Few things have more curb appeal than nice landscaping. Trimming the trees and bushes alone can make a big difference. Of course plants, flowers, and mulch add the wow factor. We put fully sodded lawns and stone pathways (usually crushed granite) in a lot of our designer homes. This is also the time when we construct patios, decks, porches, and fences. Although you trimmed and removed in the demo step, wait until the end to add any new landscaping as you don't want it to get trampled or destroyed by all the trades coming into the house. You also don't want to begin yard maintenance until the last possible moment.

Step 48. Final Cleaning
Trade: Make-Ready Crew
Prerequisite: Step 46

A good make-ready crew is the difference between getting your car washed and getting it detailed. A thorough final cleaning that includes perfect, spotless windows can make a house look practically new. Lita and Robert are the dynamic duo who have been with HomeFixers since our first house. Their passion for cleaning and attention to detail are unrivaled in the Austin area. A good make-ready crew will catch things that you can add to your punch list. Besides windows and floors, they'll detail appliances, countertops, baseboards, cabinet shelves: everything. We did a walkthrough recently and found Lita staining the wooden blades of a ceiling fan because she couldn't remove the overspray caused by the painters. That's a passion for perfection!

Step 49. Accessories and Decor
Trade: Decorating Vendors
Prerequisite: Step 48

Blinds, shades, and other window coverings; doormats; shelf paper; and shower curtains are little touches that can dress up parts of the house that you didn't improve during construction.

Step 50. Punch

Trade: All Trades, but Mostly Sheetrockers and Painters

Prerequisite: Step 48

Your punch list is the to-do list you create of all the things that are incomplete or unsatisfactory and have to be fixed before the final walkthrough. Punch can go on forever, but don't let it do that. We did a house for an investor where the improvement cost was $300,000 (not recommended for one's first house). Knowing that the punch list items could get away from us, our project manager and contractors swarmed the house to get the job done in days instead of weeks. These last little details go a long way and often are rewarded by a quick sale and a nice selling price.

Getting Your House in Order

After the quick overview of the fifty steps, we're ready to take the improvement budget and turn it into a construction plan by putting the tasks in order. We do this on the basis of the steps they fall into and assign a trade to each task to show who does the work.

Your job is to look at each task and note what step it falls into. Figure 12-5 shows how the improvement budget from Figure 12-2 has been modified into a construction plan by adding step and trade columns. If you are doing it yourself, set aside a few hours to reorganize your improvement plan according to our fifty steps. You'll find that the process gets faster each time you do a new flip, since you'll be able to use your last improvement plan as your jumping off point.

Even if you hire a general contractor to handle the construction, knowing which tasks need to be done, who is doing them, and in what order they are being done will help you stay on schedule and on budget.

Typical Kitchen Tasks: Construction Plan					
Step	Task	QTY	Material	Cost	Trade
21. Plumbing in Walls, Ceiling, Attic	Plumb ice-maker line for ice-maker box	1	Plastic, single lever, 1/4 turn valve	$110	Plumber
23. Rough Electrical	Install GFCI Outlets	3 EA	Leviton, ivory	$90	Electrician
31. Cabinetry	Install new cabinets	24 LF	Stock, oak, 36"	$3,000	Cabinet Co.
36. Countertops	Install new laminate countertops	25 LF	Wilsonart, Mystique Mount	$450	Countertop Co.
37. Tile	Install tile backsplash	38 SQ FT	Tile	$475	Tile Setter
37. Tile	Install tile floor	150 SQ FT	Tile	$825	Tile Setter
40. Final Plumbing	Install sink	1	Sterling	$135	Plumber
40. Final Plumbing	Install faucet	1	Delta	$135	Plumber
41. Final Electrical	Install pendant lights	3	Candy apple red	$270	Electrician
43. Lockout	Install cabinet hardware	32	Brushed nickel, knobs	$128	Trim Carpenter
45. Appliances	Install gas range	1	GE, stainless	$750	Appliance Co.

Figure 12-5 Typical Kitchen Tasks: Construction Plan

Congratulations on completing your construction plan. Over time, you'll find yourself looking at a task and knowing exactly where it falls in the process. Next up is assigning the work.

Planning is crucial. It will help you stay in control of the time, the cost, and the desired outcome as you rehab a house. A good construction plan is the fundamental way to organize all your planning efforts.

1. It defines the work to be done (all the construction tasks that are the scope of work)
2. It defines the materials that will be used (the specifications)
3. It defines the cost (the project budget)
4. It defines the major contracting categories (the sequential steps and trades under which each set of like tasks is ordered)

Ordering all the tasks in a job by referring to our fifty steps allows you to manage hundreds of construction activities by arranging them into smaller, more manageable groups according to when they have to be managed and who will perform them.

Stages and steps give you or your general contractor a big-picture way of determining which group of construction tasks has been accomplished and which group of tasks needs to be performed or scheduled next.

Having and using this well-organized and detailed construction plan will put you, as the rehabber, way ahead of those who wing it or try to manage things on the fly.

Chapter 13

Assign the Work

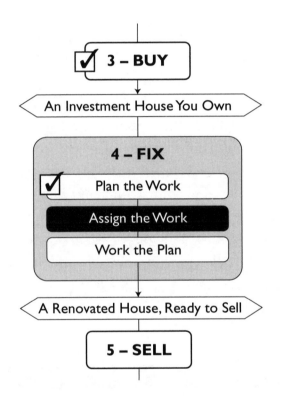

After reading this chapter you will know how to

- Decide who to hire and manage for your rehab:
  - A general contractor
  - Specialized trades
  - Individual workers
- Find and qualify the people who will do the work
- Use contracts to set expectations and protect your interests

Predictability is everything in the world of house flipping. You've staked your profit on accurately estimating all the variables: the eventual selling price, the improvement costs, and the overhead costs. When it comes to fixing up a house, completing your improvements in a predictable manner (without serious setbacks or do-overs) is a must. It is a measure of how well you can stay on schedule, stay on budget, ensure quality, and navigate unexpected surprises or deal with them head on.

In assigning the work, you'll be balancing the need for predictability with the desire to minimize costs. There are three main ways to get the work done in a construction project: hiring a general contractor, hiring specialized trades, and hiring individual workers. Each has its own level of predictability, cost, and personal involvement. A general contractor is an experienced construction manager who takes responsibility for the entire project. Specialized trades are typically businesses (e.g., a plumbing, countertop, or roofing company) that are highly skilled at performing a specific task from start to finish. Individual workers simply show up to do the work, but you'll have to provide the management and materials. The challenge with individual workers is that they usually do not guarantee their work. No matter who you choose, you always will have oversight responsibility (Figure 13-1). The question is, How much?

Three Ways to Get the Work Done			
Who You Manage	Predictability	Cost	Personal Involvement
1. A General Contractor	High	High	Low
2. Specialized Trades	High	Medium	Medium
3. Individual Workers	Low	Low	High

Figure 13-1   Three Ways to Get the Work Done

To illustrate the differences, imagine that you drop by your investment house to check out the newly installed tile floor in the master bathroom. You're disappointed to discover the tile has been laid straight instead of set on a 45-degree angle as specified by the designer to make the bathroom look bigger. The plumber is on his way to the house to install the toilet which must be done after the tile is installed. Depending on who you are managing, there are three ways this plays out:

1. If you hired a general contractor, you call him to come fix it, which he'll do at his own expense. He'll also manage rescheduling the plumber and everything else that is affected by this mistake.

2. If you used a specialized trade, in this case a tile company, the trade has to redo the work free of charge. You have to reschedule the plumber and deal with any delays.

3. If you used an individual worker, you have a decision to make. To get the full benefits of the improvement, you could incur the additional cost and delay ripping out the incorrectly installed tile, buy more, and have it reinstalled. You'll also have to reschedule the plumber and hope he can fit you into his schedule. Or you can live with it and try to convince yourself that it won't affect the selling price.

As you can see, a general contractor brings a high degree of accountability to the construction process. It's also clear that this is the most expensive option. Let's take a look at why a general contractor is an expense you should consider seriously. We'll also consider the pros and cons of using specialized trades and individual workers.

1. HIRE A GENERAL CONTRACTOR

One of the wisest moves you can make is to hire an experienced general contractor to manage the construction of your first rehab project. A general contractor is an expert at improving houses and will handle all the challenging tasks associated with a construction project, from managing the materials, people, and money to solving problems on the fly.

The general contractor orchestrates the entire rehab project. He'll take your vision and objectives for the house and, if necessary, work with architects and designers to come up with a scope of work, budget, and timetable (Figure 13-2).

What a Good General Contractor Should Do

1. Manage the entire rehab project
2. Consult with you on your improvement plan
3. Collaborate with architects and designers
4. Draw up a comprehensive scope of work and material specifications
5. Create a budget and timetable
6. Pull permits and schedule inspections
7. Schedule, order, and make payments for all materials
8. Hire, schedule, and make payments for all trades
9. Ensure adherence to budget, schedule, and quality
10. Manage risk and solve problems that arise

Figure 13-2 What a Good General Contractor Should Do

When you hire a general contractor, your responsibility is to communicate the improvement plan, objectives, vision, and expectations for the rehab clearly. Once you've approved the budget, scope of work, and specifications, the construction can begin. You will have milestone meetings to make sure the job is on track. You may or may not want to be involved in making design decisions. Finally, you'll write checks or direct funds from your lender. That's it. Everything else is the general contractor's responsibility.

There are many practical reasons why hiring a general contractor makes sense on an investor's first flip. It could be that she's too busy, or maybe needs more experience or time to fill out her roster with the trades and material resources that will help execute a smooth rehab. This could be a golden opportunity to learn from a pro, someone who knows how to manage all the resources as well as the building permits and inspections. Plan to spend 25 percent or more for a general contractor's markup. However, you will benefit from his volume buying power with trades and materials plus the influence he can wield to keep a project moving swiftly and efficiently. All this can mean cost savings for you, which can offset a portion of his fee.

FLIPPING POINT

As Greg and Eursula Clarkson, our HomeFixers affiliates in Orlando, will attest, Florida is one of many states that requires a licensed general contractor to pull permits. Greg's road to becoming a licensed general contractor included a combination of a college degree and years of practical and managerial construction experience, culminating in a two-day examination testing his administrative, financial, and technical understanding. We recommend that you search the Internet to find out if you live in one of the states that requires a licensed general contractor to pull permits.

Finally, the biggest reason we recommend using a general contractor is predictability. Construction is a general contractor's full-time job; most are insured, and many are licensed and bonded. Like any other professional, a general contractor will use all of his experience to deliver the expected outcome, and he'll do it while sticking to the schedule and the budget and creatively dealing with the pitfalls and surprises along the way.

2. MANAGE THE WORK YOURSELF THROUGH SPECIALIZED TRADES

If you plan to manage the project yourself, you are going to be responsible for the improvement plan, the detailed scope of work, the budget, and the materials list. To help you, consult the HomeFixers Fifty Steps to Rehabbing a House. This step-by-step process will help you understand when to schedule the work and what trades are needed. To get the work done, we recommend that you hire specialized trades.

Specialized trades handle all aspects of completing their tasks with expertise, and so minimal management is required. They typically supply both the labor and the materials and give you a hard bid for completing the work before they start.

Managing the rehab yourself by using specialized trades can be the next best thing to using a general contractor for a low-hassle solution. This is especially true if you're sticking to projects at the rehab intensity level as defined in Chapter 6 (see "Use Rules of Thumb" on page 153). In that case, you might be able to use the trades to complete most of the job. You're not getting the overall expert management experience that you would with a general contractor, but you're not paying for it either. You are, however, getting experts at the individual tasks they perform who bring a high-level of predictability with very little management from you. In many cases, it takes just a phone call. The majority of the specialized trades we employ are turnkey solutions, meaning that one call is all it takes to get the job done. That's why, at HomeFixers, we call them the "one-call wonders" (Figure 13-3).

Ensuring predictability fits right in with using these professionals. There are a lot of specialized trades on our job sites, and we often are asked about them: "Why do you use a countertop specialist for your kitchen laminate instead of getting your carpenter to pick it up at the home improvement center? Isn't that more expensive?" At first

Specialized Trades			
(In Order of Appearance)			
1. Locksmith ♀	8. Glass and Mirror ♀ Contractor	15. Sheetrock Crew	22. Paint Contractor ♀
2. Designer	9. Window ♀ Contractor	16. Garage Door ♀ Company	23. Laminate Countertop ♀ Company
3. Exterminator ♀	10. Roofer ♀	17. Gutter Company ♀	24. Granite Countertop ♀ Company
4. Plumber	11. HVAC Specialist ♀	18. Hardwood Floor ♀ Company	25. Tile Company ♀
5. Electrician	12. Mason	19. Cabinet Company ♀	26. Flooring Company ♀
6. Demo and Cleanout Crew	13. Insulation ♀ Company	20. Trim, Door and Millwork Carpentry Company	27. Appliance Company ♀
7. Framing Carpenter	14. Concrete Company	21. Cleaning Company	28. Landscape Company ♀

♀ = Turnkey Trades

Figure 13-3 Specialized Trades

glance, it is. The same kitchen countertop that Ken, our laminate guy, charges $315 for might cost $225 or less if our carpenter picked it up at an improvement center and installed it himself. When we pay for turnkey trades, we're paying for predictability: the certainty that the task can be done for a set amount, at a specific time, and with very little management.

That's why we leave the countertops to Ken. He's installed over 100 kitchen countertops for us in Austin, and he's scratched only a couple of them. The best part is that he calls and tells us about the mistake and has it corrected within a day (no charge, of course). Our role in managing Ken is simply to ask Camille, our designer (also a specialized trade), to pick out a laminate design from her sample of hundreds and call Ken with a style number and the address of the house. That's it. Ken orders the material, shows up as scheduled, and installs perfect countertops.

Using an army of specialists is a great way to build a predictable, consistent house-fixing team. With hundreds of successful rehabs under our belt, we can say with confidence that hiring specialized or, even better, turnkey trades is a great way to go.

3. Do the Work Yourself with the Help of Individual Workers

On our first rehab, we used individual workers (the "handyman model") and five guys did all the work: demo, carpentry, roof, plumbing, electrical, drywall, cabinets, trim, doors, painting, countertops, tile, vinyl, carpet—everything. With no management markup, we saved a bundle.

It was kind of nice: five guys working with brushes, trowels, chisels, wrenches, and hammers. We'd meet for coffee each morning, talk about our objectives for the day, go to the improvement center to pick up supplies, and head to the job site. There are a lot of people who can think of no better way to spend a day than being out in the fresh air, tools in hand, fixing up a house; it can be a beautiful thing.

On our second rehab things started off smoothly, but a couple of weeks into the job our carpenter began to get flaky. We finally had to fire him. Unfortunately, he was also the sheetrocker, painter, and tile setter. That was a bad day, but we recovered and settled into a groove. Overall, our jobs were turning out great and the houses were selling quickly, but the rehabs were taking too long. If we had used the system we have in place today (made up predominantly of turnkey and specialized trades), those projects would have taken three to four weeks instead of ten to twelve.

If you choose the handyman model, you're responsible for creating the schedule and budget as well as picking up and paying for all the materials, supplies, and equipment rental. As crew chief, you also may be picking up and dropping off the workers each day. The quality of work doesn't necessarily suffer; the painter you pick up today may be the same guy painting a million-dollar home the next week.

If you enjoy doing the work yourself (and a lot of people do), it boils down to a business decision: Can you do enough jobs to make a living? Remember that you have to find, analyze, buy, and sell the houses as well

The first $20 per square foot of improvement costs in most rehab projects is made up of the most predictable and easy-to-manage tasks. In fact, the first $20 per square foot is full of potential one-call-wonder tasks. Knowing this, we quantify how difficult a job is to manage simply by looking at the construction cost per square foot. Any rehab project that costs less than $20 per square foot in improvement costs is going to be relatively easy to manage, and rehabs that cost over $20 per square foot will be much tougher. This is a great way to determine who should manage the project (Figure 13-4).

Using Rehab Intensity to Determine Who Should Manage the Work

Rehab Cost/SQ FT	Who You Manage
More than $20/SQ FT	General Contractor
$5–$20/SQ FT	Specialized Trades
Less than $5/SQ FT	Individual Workers

Figure 13-4 Using Rehab Intensity to Determine Who Should Manage the Work

If your project costs less than $5 per square foot in improvement costs, you should consider doing it yourself with individual workers. If it costs $5 to $20 per square foot, you can manage the work using predominantly specialized trades. If the project costs more than $20 per square foot in improvement costs, you should consider hiring a general contractor.

as fix them up. Once you find a house, it takes an average of four to five months between the time you buy it and the time you sell it (longer if you're doing the work yourself). However, if you're flipping houses as a hobby, doing it yourself might be the perfect therapeutic way to make some extra money each year.

FINDING AND QUALIFYING CONTRACTORS

Now that you have a better idea about who will help you do the work, it's time to start looking for the general contractor, specialized trades, or individual workers who will help you take the rehab to its completion: a fully renovated house that is ready to sell. Contractors are precious assets in the rehab business, and so when you find a great one, you don't want to lose him or her. Conversely, when you hire a bad one, you could lose your profit. In this section, we'll help you identify some of the ways we find contractors and make sure they're qualified to do the job (Figure 13-5).

Figure 13-5   Two Steps to Hiring Contractors

FINDING CONTRACTORS

Here's the truth: Finding contractors isn't hard. They're in business, they advertise their business, and they want to be found. It can be as easy as browsing online or in the Yellow Pages or jotting down a number from a construction site sign or the side of a truck. There are a lot of similarities in the ways you go about finding a general contractor, specialized trades, and individual workers. Thus, we will refer to all three groups together as contractors for the purposes of this discussion.

Networking is without a doubt the most powerful way to find contractors. That's how we have gotten the best contractor referrals for our business. Getting a contractor through your network often comes with a built-in reference and can jump-start the qualifying process. Figure 13-6 shows sources that may help you find contractors.

Good Sources When Networking for Contractors

1. Real estate investors

   – Real estate investor clubs (meetings and email distribution lists)

   – Your circle of real estate investors

   – Private money lenders

2. Construction professionals

   – General contractors and specialized trades

   – Merchants, vendors, and supply-store workers

   – Architects and interior designers

3. Real estate–related professionals

   – Real estate agents

   – Lenders specializing in construction loans

   – Home inspectors

4. Friends, neighbors, relatives, and coworkers

Figure 13-6   Good Sources When Networking for Contractors

QUALIFYING CONTRACTORS

We said above that finding contractors is relatively easy because they want to be found. Qualifying is another story: Contractors don't always want to be *found out*. In this section, we'll outline seven factors to consider to "find out" if a contractor is going to be a good fit for you (Figure 13-7).

Seven Factors to Consider When Qualifying Contractors

1.	Longevity	How long has the contractor been in business?
2.	Licensed and Registered	Does the contractor have the appropriate license and registration?
3.	Real Estate Investment Experience	Has the contractor worked on real estate investment projects?
4.	Insurance	Is the contractor properly insured to protect you?
5.	Business References	Does the contractor have good business relationships?
6.	Customer References	Does the contractor have satisfied customers?
7.	Competitively Priced	Did the contractor provide a comprehensive and accurate bid?

Figure 13-7 Seven Factors to Consider When Qualifying Contractors

1. Longevity

How many years has the contractor been in business? Many small businesses go out of business within the first five years, and contractors are no different. Thus, when you find a general contractor with five years of experience, chances are that you'll be working with a competent businessperson. For specialized trades and individual workers, look for two years in the business. There are always exceptions. Marvin is the best full-time trim carpenter we ever had, and he came to us straight from his management job at Motorola, where he was not a carpenter. Throughout his high-tech career he did woodworking as a hobby before coming to work with us.

2. Licensed and Registered

Does the contractor have the appropriate license and registration? General contractors must be licensed or adhere to the state's registration or regulatory requirements (for example, in Texas, general contractors do not need to be licensed, but they do need to be members in good standing with the Texas Residential Construction Commission). Other trades also need to be licensed, especially electrical, plumbing, and HVAC.

3. Real Estate Investment Experience

Has the contractor worked on real estate investment projects? For general contractors, you're looking for someone experienced at doing rehabs where the entire house is being remodeled (from light fixtures to landscaping), not just a kitchen or a bathroom. Find out how many rehab projects the contractor has done and when. For specialized trades and individual workers, real estate investment experience is a plus but is not required.

4. Insurance

Is the contractor properly insured to protect you? As the owner of the property, you can be held liable for anything that happens on it. A general contractor or a specialized trade should be insured with a general liability policy. A million dollars is standard for most policies. Obtain proof of the policy to ensure that it's current. Once a contractor is hired, ask the contractor to list you as an additional insured on his or her policy.

5. Business References

Does the contractor have good business relationships? Get three or four current business references: suppliers and other trades that the contractor does business with on a regular basis. Make sure there has been activity within the last three months. Some specialized trades and most individual workers do not work directly with other businesses. With them, you'll have to rely on customer references.

6. Customer References

Does the contractor have satisfied customers? Get the names and phone numbers of his three most recent jobs. It is important to follow up on these references. If contractors have satisfied customers and have done quality work, they will be eager to let their most recent customers vouch for them. You should expect to hear that the contractor has good business habits: professional, punctual, responsive, and organized.

7. Competitively Priced

Did the contractor provide a comprehensive and accurate bid? Even if you're just interviewing a contractor for future work, you should set the expectation that you want a competitive bid and that it's customary for you to get other bids for the work. We recommend a minimum of three bids. Don't automatically go for the lowest bid. Often the old adage "you get what you pay for" is true.

FLIPPING POINT

If a contractor is going to work at a home where a family is living, we recommend that you conduct a criminal background check. This also should be done when you are building a team of contractors that you may be working with again and again. There are many places on the Web to conduct background checks.

Using Contracts to Set Expectations and Protect Your Interests

Once you have a short list of qualified contractors, you will make the business engagement official by signing a contract before work starts. In some cases, you'll have to provide the contract; in others, you'll be working with their contracts. A general contractor most likely will present you with a contract. It is important to remember that his contract probably is designed to protect the contractor's business, not yours.

Figure 13-8 is a fifteen-point checklist to make sure the contract also represents your interests. If your contract does not contain some of these key provisions, they can be added in amendments or clauses. There are acceptable standard boilerplate contracts available from the American Institute of Architects, the American Homeowners Foundation, and the Associated General Contractors. Seek the help of an attorney if you have any questions.

For most specialized trades and individual workers, you will usually be working from a signed work order, proposal, or bid. Make sure to include basic information, scope of work, material specifications, and total costs. If you're dealing with a business, also make sure it shows proof of insurance.

When you're considering the level of detail that can go into drawing up a contract, it is important to remember why you are going to all this trouble. As Gary Keller said in *The Millionaire Real Estate Investor*, "For me, contracts are agreements for disagreement. When everyone is in agreement, no one looks at the contract. It's only when there is a disagreement that it gets pulled out and gone over with a fine-tooth comb. As a rule, write agreements to resolve any possible disagreements as agreeably as possible." A good contract provides protection for you and the contractor.

Fifteen Key Provisions of a Construction Contract

1. Basic Information

   - Contract date, start date, and substantial completion date
   - Your name, address, and phone numbers
   - Contractor's name, address, and phone numbers
   - Address of the job site
   - Contractor's license number or registration number
   - Contractor's tax ID or Social Security number

2. Scope of Work—Describes the project in detail (usually listed in an appendix to the contract).

3. Material Specifications—Details a complete list of materials that will be used (usually listed in an appendix).

4. Total Cost—Specifies the amount due, including material, labor, and management costs.

5. Proof of Insurance—Requires that the contractor maintain coverage and specifies policy numbers.

6. Not to Exceed—States that the contractor is not to exceed the cost for any of the listed tasks. Overruns must be paid for by the contractor.

7. Payment Schedule—Lists the total number of draws and dollar amounts of each that will be paid along the way (when and at which milestone).

8. Architectural Drawings and Plans—Provides copies of the originals (usually listed in an appendix).

9. Change Orders—States that you or your contractor has a right to make changes after the contract has been signed through separate, individual change-order contracts signed by both parties.

10. Compliance (zoning, permits, inspections)—States that the contractor is responsible for pulling permits and complying with state and local ordinances and codes.

11. Cleanup—Designates that the contractor will clean up each day and keep a neat job site.

12. Mechanics' Liens—Requires a general contractor to provide you with documented evidence that subcontractors have been paid for completed work. Alternatively, the contractor can provide a "release of lien" for the work performed by subcontractors.

13. Warranties—States what is covered and the length of time coverage applies.

14. Dispute Resolution—Specifies how unresolved disputes between you and the contractor will be resolved (e.g., arbitration, mediation, etc.).

15. Termination—Gives you the right to terminate the agreement for breach of contract (e.g., due to poor workmanship, failure to meet the contract requirements) or for bankruptcy or insolvency.

Figure 13-8 Fifteen Key Provisions of a Construction Contract

Next, we'll discover the best ways to stay on schedule, stay on budget, and ensure top quality for all your rehab projects.

POINTS TO REMEMBER

Just as you want to use the right tool for the right job, you want to be careful to choose the right people to get the job done.

1. General contractors provide intense management with almost no involvement on your part.

2. Specialized trades can perform a substantial part of the work on most standard rehabs expertly, but you will be required to schedule and monitor progress.

3. Tackling the job head on with the help of some individual workers can yield a high sense of accomplishment for people who enjoy doing it themselves. The rehab might take twice the time, but it could be the perfect hobby that earns you some extra money on the side.

Always perform due diligence on the contractors who will help you take your job through completion and use written, signed contracts to keep things straight.

Chapter 14
Work the Plan

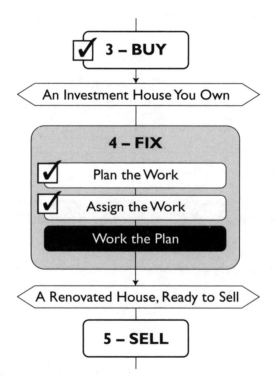

After reading this chapter you will know how to

- Stay on schedule
- Stay on budget
- Ensure quality

A series of experiments was conducted in the 1920s and 1930s at the Hawthorne Works factory of the Western Electric Company in Chicago to measure employee productivity. Researchers noted that productivity increased as a direct result of the participants' knowledge that they were part of an experiment. In other words, people performed better when someone was watching them and interested in what they were doing. This phenomenon has become known as the Hawthorne effect. Although researchers go to great lengths to keep it from corrupting their studies, we recommend that you harness its power to improve the quality of your rehabs.

If you are taking on the responsibility of managing the construction of an investment property, we recommend that you become a familiar figure at the construction site. Taking the time to get to know the trades and what they are doing can go a long way toward keeping a project on track. Coffee and breakfast tacos don't hurt either. In this chapter, we'll cover methods to help you and your contractors stay on schedule, stay on budget, and ensure quality (see Figure 14-1).

The Three Main Project Management Goals

1. Stay on Schedule
2. Stay on Budget
3. Ensure Quality

Figure 14-1 The Three Main Project Management Goals

Let's start with the keys to effective project scheduling.

STAY ON SCHEDULE

Managing a construction project is a lot like a police officer directing traffic through a busy intersection. There's no exact amount of time that the officer should allow traffic to move in any direction. The officer continually assesses the situation and manages the flow so that the highest number of cars can make it through the intersection with the least amount of waiting. If the officer does a poor job of managing the intersection, collisions can happen. Worse, a collision can cause a pileup that really delays traffic.

It's the same thing with construction project management. Scheduling trades in the wrong order or before the project is ready for them disrupts the entire schedule and can result in major delays. The goal in scheduling is to *do everything you can, as soon as you can*, but that's easier said than done. Figure 14-2 shows the three keys to making that possible.

The Three Keys to Effective Scheduling	
1. Sequence	The order in which work gets done
2. Lead Time	The time it takes to start work
3. Duration	The time it takes to complete work

Figure 14-2   The Three Keys to Effective Scheduling

SEQUENCE: DO THE WORK IN ORDER

In Chapter 12 we introduced the concept of grouping hundreds of tasks into fifty manageable steps. Those sequential steps make it easy to mark the progress in any rehab project. The beginning and end of each step are milestones that mark the advancement of the project. Using the HomeFixers Fifty Steps to Rehabbing a House (see page 250) is an effective way to organize the workflow.

For example, instead of trying to remember when to install all final plumbing tasks, including toilets, the kitchen sink, a disposal, shower heads, the bathroom sinks, and all the faucets, all you have to do is alert your plumber to start step 40, Final Plumbing, when the prerequisite steps are completed, as illustrated in Figure 14-3.

When to Start Step 40				
☑ Step 36 Countertops	☑ Step 37 Tile	☑ Step 38 Vinyl Floors	Step 39 Final HVAC	Step 40 Final Plumbing
T: Countertop Specialist	T: Tile Setter	T: Flooring Co.	T: HVAC Contractor	T: Plumber
P: 34	P: 36	P: 34	P: 34	P: 36, 37, 38

Figure 14-3   When to Start Step 40

Since many construction activities can't start until others are completed, it's important to know the order in which things are done and make sure to do them in that order. In our example, final plumbing is dependent on vinyl floors, tile, and countertops, and so as soon as those tasks are done, the plumber can get to work.

Remember, the goal in scheduling is to do everything you can, as soon as you can. You want to have your radar up, constantly scanning the project plan, noting when steps are completed, and looking for opportunities to get other steps started. Let's zero in on stage 5, Finished Surfaces, to get an idea of what steps can be done at the same time. As you can see in Figure 14-4, countertops, vinyl floors, and final HVAC can start as soon as you're finished painting the interior, step 34.

However, it's important to understand that rehab projects are very fluid. If you're too rigid in your planning, you probably will find yourself with periods of time when no progress is made on the house, and that will cost you profit. For example, there's no reason why step 41, Final Electrical, cannot start as soon as the walls are painted. However, because the plumber and the tile setter have to wait for the countertops, we recommend that the electrician stay out of the kitchen also until the countertops are installed. In this way, the countertop installer can do the job

Stage 5: Timeline for Finished Surfaces

Steps	Week 4							Week 5							Week 6						
	Su	M	T	W	Th	F	Sa	Su	M	T	W	Th	F	Sa	Su	M	T	W	Th	F	Sa
Step 34—Paint Interior & Exterior			▓	▓	▓																
Step 35—Blown Insulation	▓	▓																			
Step 36—Countertops						▓															
Step 37—Tile										▓	▓	▓									
Step 38—Vinyl Floors						▓															
Step 39—Final HVAC						▓	▓														
Step 40—Final Plumbing												▓	▓								
Step 41—Final Electrical									▓	▓											
Step 42—Finish Wood Floors															▓	▓	▓	▓	▓	▓	

Figure 14-4   Stage 5: Timeline for Finished Surfaces

quickly, and then the tile setter, plumber, and electrician can get started. It also means that the electrician can (and probably should) be working on other parts of the house so that when the countertops are done, only the kitchen electrical work remains.

This is what we call working the plan. A good general contractor will use his knowledge of construction to keep the project moving. With experience and knowledge of the construction sequence and dependencies, you can do that too.

LEAD TIME: PLAN IT IN ADVANCE

To keep a project moving and maximize your investment profits, you need to have everything in place for the next step to start as soon as the previous steps are complete. Lead times, the amount of time it takes before a task can start, can have a big impact on your schedule. Figure 14-5 shows the three factors that affect lead time.

The Three Factors That Affect Lead Time	
1. Material Availability	Some materials must be ordered in advance.
2. Labor Availability	Some crews are often backlogged and need advance notice.
3. Paperwork and Processing Time	Some tasks require paperwork, such as permits, to be in place.

Figure 14-5 The Three Factors That Affect Lead Time

1. Material Lead Time

Materials can have a long lead time for a variety of reasons. Some materials are hard to find, such as certain tile selections. Other materials have to be constructed before they are ready to be installed, such as cabinets. The following materials can have long lead times:

- Roof trusses: step 12
- Windows: step 15
- Cabinets: step 31
- Granite countertops: step 36
- Cultured marble countertops: step 36
- Special-order tile: step 37
- Special-order lighting: step 41
- Hardwood flooring: step 42
- Special appliances: step 45

Long before these steps begin, place your orders. It's better to have materials waiting in a storage area than for you to be waiting on materials to get the job done.

2. Labor Lead Time

Most trades only need a few days' notice before they show up. Others need several weeks. The lead time is related to the difficulty and duration of the installation. For instance, hardwood flooring crews often have a long lead time because the process takes up to five days. You need to get on their schedule early because it takes only a few projects ahead of yours to have a delay of two weeks or more. In our experience, there is often a wait for the following labor crews:

- House leveling and foundation repair crews: step 3
- Concrete contractor (for driveways, sidewalks, patios): step 26
- Granite countertop installers: step 36
- Hardwood floor finishing: step 42
- Glass contractors (for glass shower enclosures and doors): step 44
- Landscapers: step 47

You may find that in your city, plumbers are particularly hard to come by. You also may notice that at certain times of the year (e.g., the busy summer building season) contractors' schedules tend to tighten up. The point here is to know that some contractors may require a longer lead time than others, so book them in advance.

3. Paperwork and Processing Time

Some tasks require that paperwork be in place before the work can begin. Examples of required paperwork include the following:

- Architectural plans: step 2
- Permits: step 2
- Engineering reports: step 9
- Inspections: all stages

A lot of the paperwork is front-loaded in our process. The notable exception is inspections, which happen frequently throughout the construction process. You need to account for these disruptions to keep the project moving ahead.

DURATION: HOW LONG IT WILL TAKE

Now that we have covered sequence and lead time, let's turn our attention to duration, the final key to successful scheduling. New home construction is predictable. It's common to have a timeline for the entire project that shows each task and how long it is expected to take to complete the work. A plan with a specific duration for each task is possible because the work in each step is fairly consistent from house to house. If you're always building from the ground up, you should know what to expect along the way.

However, in most rehab and remodeling projects, the actual work required in each step varies significantly from one project to another. For example, in one very simple project, the extent of step 32, Interior Doors, Trim, and Millwork, might be to install only one bifold closet door in a bedroom. However, in a major rehab, step 32 might include the installation of twelve doors, 300 linear feet of baseboards, 420 linear feet of door casing, and ten windowsills. In this example, the duration of step 32 jumps from as little as an hour to as long as a week.

Additionally, it's not just the scope of work in each step that changes from one rehab project to the next; it's also the way the task is performed. For example, in a house that has a slab foundation, installing 135 square feet of kitchen floor tile may take two days: one day to set the tile and the next day to grout it. In an older house built on a pier and beam foundation, the kitchen may have old hardwood floors that are decayed, warped, and uneven. This easily can add an extra day because of the extensive floor prep (including installing tile backer board) that must be done before installing the tile.

Finally, every rehab project has surprises. Even after a thorough walkthrough, we almost always come across something we didn't expect, especially if it involves removing sheetrock. It's not uncommon to discover termite-eaten studs, unsafe wiring, and, in one memorable flip, a major infestation of rats.

Therefore, we believe that rehab projects are too unpredictable for it to be worth the effort to schedule a specific start and finish date for each step at the beginning of the project. One minor mishap could throw off the entire schedule. Instead, like a police officer directing traffic, keep a close eye on the changing nature of the project. As steps get closer to being ready, you'll have a more accurate picture of exactly what is involved in the upcoming work and how long it will take to get it done. Monitoring the progress of the work and staying in close communication with your contractors are the keys to successfully accomplishing this.

STAY ON BUDGET

In our experience, staying on budget is 80 percent planning and 20 percent execution. This is good news if you've created a solid construction plan that is both comprehensive and accurate: Most of the work needed to stay on budget is done before you write the first check. Let's look at how effective planning and execution keeps a project on budget (Figure 14-6).

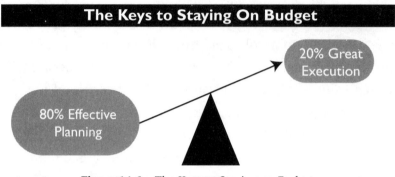

Figure 14-6 The Keys to Staying on Budget

PLAN TO STAY ON BUDGET

By the time you get to this stage, you have an improvement plan that you created to determine your offer. The foundation for this plan was laid during your must-should-could walkthrough. Next, you developed a detailed scope of work and material specifications that precisely delineated *what work you were going to do* and *what materials you were going to buy*. Finally, you came up with an accurate cost assessment by getting bids and estimates from contractors, vendors, and merchants. The result was a full-blown improvement budget (Figure 14-7).

Why do so many construction projects go over budget? One of the main reasons is that not enough attention is focused on ensuring accuracy and thoroughness during the planning phase. You'll notice that in Figure 14-7, all your planning builds up to contractor bids and estimates. If these bids and estimates are not solid and reliable, your planning is for naught. That is why we recommend that you obtain fixed bids

The Process of Developing an Improvement Budget

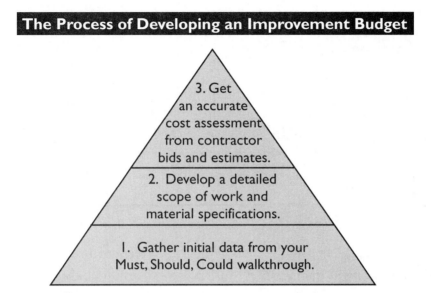

Figure 14-7   The Process of Developing an Improvement Budget

for as much of the work as possible. A fixed bid is a legally binding contract to perform a defined amount of work at a fixed price. To get the best bid, you need to present a detailed scope of work and material specifications (Figure 14-8).

Why a Detailed Scope and Specs Get You the Best Bids

1. Shows the trades that you completely understand the work to be done.
2. Eliminates ambiguity.
3. Eliminates trades taking liberties with what should be done.
4. Provides for apples-to-apples comparisons among several bids.

Figure 14-8   Why a Detailed Scope and Specs Get You the Best Bids

You won't always be able to get a fixed bid. An example of this would be the rough work (e.g., demo, framing, and sheetrock repairs). For these tasks, you will be working off estimates and probably pay the trades by the hour. With rough work, there's only so much you can do up front to

Talk about money before the work starts. Clear up-front communication about your budget and how you will pay trades (per hour, per job, per piece, etc.) can prevent misunderstandings down the road. Don't pay for labor until you have verified that the work has been completed to your satisfaction. It's also a good idea to implement a payment schedule that carries a penalty if the work extends beyond the agreed-on completion date.

stay on budget. Controlling costs with these types of tasks will require your attention and management during the execution phase.

EXECUTE TO STAY ON BUDGET

The difference between what you expect the project to cost and what it will end up costing will be a direct result of how well you manage the rough work, labor, scope, and spending. Even a perfectly planned project can get off track during execution. Your ability to wield a clipboard, a cell phone, and sometimes even a hammer can make the difference between a slightly profitable venture and a highly profitable one (Figure 14-9).

Execute to Stay on Budget

1. Manage Rough Work

2. Manage Labor

3. Manage Scope

4. Monitor Spending

Figure 14-9   Execute to Stay on Budget

1. Manage Rough Work

If there is a time when your project costs can get away from you, it is during the rough work (most of the work from steps 6 through 27 on the HomeFixers Fifty Steps to Rehabbing a House). Rough work typically has a low materials cost but a high labor cost, which translates to more people management. And *speed* isn't a word typically associated with rough work. There are sometimes multiple inspections to pass and many successive tasks to complete. Finally, the outcome is tougher to measure: What does a perfectly soldered elbow joint look like, anyway?

FLIPPING POINT

This is the case of the not-so-simple stud wall. It is an example of the many successive tasks and inspections that can result when one is putting up an exterior kitchen wall with a door and plumbing:

1. You decide where to put the wall with the help of an architect or designer.
2. The framer puts up the wall.
3. You request a framing inspection.
4. An electrician wires outlets and switches in the wall.
5. You request an electrical inspection.
6. A plumber runs a water line through the wall.
7. You request a plumbing inspection.
8. An insulation company insulates the wall.
9. You request an insulation inspection.
10. Sheetrockers hang the drywall.
11. You request a wallboard inspection.
12. A trim carpenter hangs the door and installs trim.
13. A painter caulks and paints the wall, trim, and door.
14. A trim carpenter returns to install a doorknob and doorstop.

Make frequent visits. It is during these rough stages that you should be driving out to the house as often as possible to check on the progress and to keep things moving.

2. Manage Labor

Managing labor boils down to two things: the trades being ready for you and you being ready for the trades. Remember, time is money, so you want to keep work moving as quickly as possible.

How do you know the trades are ready for you? Schedule all your contractors in advance, paying special attention to those steps which have long lead times. We've learned that the best way to make sure our contractors are ready to go is to remind them the week before and again the day before they are to start work. If that's not enough, we also let them know that we will meet them on the job site the day the work begins to review any specific instructions. Monitor your contractors frequently to make sure they stay on the job and follow up to make sure they finish on time.

How do you know you're ready for the trades? For starters, make sure everything they need to do the work is in place before they start. Confirm that the utilities are on, the permits have been pulled, and any engineering reports or construction drawings are posted. If necessary, cover walls and floors with protective coverings; there are few things worse than scratching and denting original hardwood during the demo process. If the plumbing is not up and ready, make sure temporary facilities are on site. Ensure that all the materials that the trades need to complete their work are on site. Make sure that any visual cues or instructions are clearly marked. This is particularly useful during the demo stage to make sure there is no ambiguity about what does and does not get the sledgehammer. Last but not least, always consult the HomeFixers Fifty Steps to Rehabbing a House to make sure that all the prerequisite steps are completed before you call in the new trades for the next step.

Trades should work, not shop. There's nothing more nerve racking than watching a much-needed contractor head off to the hardware store, announcing that he will be "right back." As hard as it can be to get workers on the site to begin with, you never want to see one leave, get sidetracked, and not come back.

It's the project manager's job to have the materials waiting for the contractor to begin work. Double-check the shopping list before the work is started to make sure nothing has been left out. If you don't have a truck, most home improvement centers will make even the smallest deliveries for a nominal fee.

3. Manage Scope

Stick to the original scope of work and resist the desire to make changes once the project begins. These changes can cause "scope creep." This occurs when the original scope of work expands during a construction project because of poor planning or lack of commitment to the improvement plan. It is imperative to stay true to the original plan throughout the construction process. Changes during construction can throw off your schedule, increase your costs, and reduce your profit.

4. Monitor Spending

Frequent monitoring of your spending is one of the big keys to staying on budget. Our point is that you won't know you're off track unless you're keeping track. We recommend accounting all your expenses at the end of each week and checking the actual spending against what you budgeted.

It's helpful to use a business accounting software application such as QuickBooks, but a spreadsheet or ledger system also will work. The benefit of professional software is that it allows you to know where the money's going, down to the specific step and contractor. You can visit flipthebook.com to download the QuickBooks chart of accounts that's based on the Fifty Steps to Rehabbing a House. The point is not choosing a particular system to use but using a system and using it often.

Another benefit of carefully monitoring spending is that any pricing updates you make on your current project will feed directly into the planning of the next project budget. For example, if you blew the budget for sheetrock by a few hundred dollars, by updating the price of sheetrock you can avoid that mistake on the next flip. Your present execution is always great preparation for future planning.

ENSURE QUALITY: THE WIN-WIN FOR YOU AND YOUR TRADES

Communicating your high expectations about quality before the work begins is one of the best things you can do to ensure a positive outcome for your project. Don't just tell your trades that you want them to do a good job; communicate exactly what makes a job good. You've already set your trades up for success by giving clear instructions and prepping the job site before they arrive; now ensure their success by communicating clear expectations.

Figure 14-10 illustrates the expectations we share with our tile setters when they are tiling the backsplash in a kitchen. Notice that the actual installation of the tile is only one small part of the expectations.

Holding your trades to preset expectations will make them better trades. In essence, you become their training program for achieving excellence. Clear expectations will reduce management time, callbacks, and warranty work while increasing quality; your trades may even thank you. You can develop these quality assurance checklists for many of the tasks in your rehab project by doing a little research on the Web or reading one

Quality Assurance Checklist: Tiling a Kitchen Backsplash

✔ Countertops must be masked prior to tile work to prevent scratching the countertops.

✔ Outlets and switches must be unscrewed and pulled away from the wall so that they are not "tiled or grouted in."

✔ Tile must be cut outside the house to prevent covering the interior with tile dust.

✔ Tile should be laid according to design specs, such as straight, at a 45-degree angle or in a specified pattern.

✔ Tile must be laid perfectly straight and spacers should be used to ensure grout lines are perfectly even.

✔ The grout must be checked to ensure there are no missing or unfilled areas.

✔ Faceplates should be held up to all outlets and switches to ensure that there are no gaps in the tile or grout around them.

✔ Grout must be thoroughly wiped off the tile before it dries.

✔ All scraps should be removed from the premises (inside and out) once the job is completed.

✔ Excess mortar and grout should never be left on the premises and there should be no mortar or grout residue left on grass, plants, hoses, etc.

✔ There should be no evidence anywhere on the job site (inside or outside) that a tile job was ever done except for the tile work that was performed.

Figure 14-10   Quality Assurance Checklist: Tiling a Kitchen Backsplash

of our favorite books, *The Reader's Digest Complete Do-It-Yourself Manual,* and then gradually filling in with personal experience. Figure 14-11 gives some general pointers that apply to the entire rehab process and will help you achieve a high-quality outcome.

It's important never to lose sight of the fact that you are improving a property for profit. Everything that we have covered in the Fix stage, from planning the work to working the plan, is designed to protect the poten-

Six Tips to Ensure Quality

1. Link payment with performance. Communicate that quality is checked before payment is authorized. Consider putting a bonus structure in place for consistent, exceptional work over multiple projects.

2. Monitor and measure progress often. As the saying goes, "inspect what you expect" to ensure that your expectations are being met along the way.

3. Address problems immediately. Quickly raise the red flag if you notice errors, especially if they cannot be fixed later in the process or would be cost or time prohibitive if not addressed right away.

4. Prepare for the work. Just like staying on schedule and on budget, a quality outcome is ensured by a house that is properly prepped and ready for the trades to start work:
   - ✔ Work is clearly defined
   - ✔ Job site is clean
   - ✔ Prerequisite steps are completed
   - ✔ All of the needed materials are on site (trades should work not shop)

5. Manage the rough spots. Intensify your focus on the rough work or work that serves as the foundation for future work.

6. Pay for predictability. Cheaper isn't always better. When applicable, don't hesitate to use turnkey trades who will guarantee a good job. Use materials that have a tried and true track record of looking good and being installed easily.

Figure 14-11   Six Tips to Ensure Quality

tial profit you worked so hard to get when finding and buying the house. When you've reached this stage, your vision for the house has become a reality. What's left is to turn your hard work into hard cash in the Sell stage.

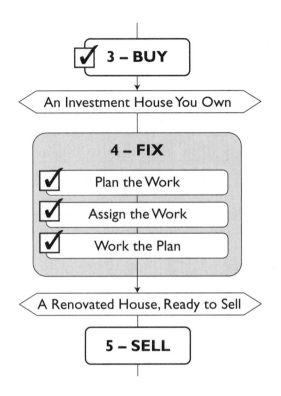

POINTS TO REMEMBER

A construction project, with all its complexities, needs to have someone in charge to monitor its progress and keep things on track.

- Use the HomeFixers Fifty Steps to Rehabbing a House to create your construction plan, establish your schedule, and to assign the work.

- Trades need to have clear instructions about what is expected of them, how they will be paid, and who will be monitoring their work.

- Their materials should be ready when they are ready: You don't want to pay your trades to shop.

- Streamlining the materials choices as well as the material-ordering process can save you time and money.

- Rough work, such as framing, plumbing, and electrical, is the area that needs most of your attention because if these things aren't done correctly, fixing the mistakes later will affect your bottom line negatively.

- You and/or your general contractor are the captain of your construction ship. If you aren't careful and if everyone is not on task at the right time with the right materials and instructions, you risk running aground.

Samantha

The massage therapist worked out a knot next to Samantha's shoulder blade. I could get used to this, she thought. Samantha couldn't decide which was better: getting a massage or having her afternoon free. She had six weeks of vacation saved up and had decided to use most of it during the couple of months it was going to take to fix up her investment house. She wanted to manage the job and even do some of the work herself. So far, the rehab was going well. It was time to treat herself.

"How did this happen?" the therapist asked as she continued to work on Samantha's knotted muscle.

"Sledge-hammering," Samantha said, relishing the memory of swinging the heavy hammer. She had taken the first blow at the kitchen wall Ed had recommended removing. It had been kind of a reverse ground-breaking ceremony. The crew had helped out after that first hit, and it had felt good to do some physical work, much better than sitting in meetings all day.

"I see," said the therapist. "Renovating your house?"

"No, actually I'm working on an investment property," Samantha answered.

"Oh, I've got a couple of other clients who are investors," the therapist replied as she moved to Samantha's feet. "You get sore feet, I hear, from chasing after all those contractors."

Samantha's thoughts drifted back to her project plan. She wasn't chasing after anyone. If the roofers could finish today, she would be two days ahead of schedule.

"Feeling better?" the therapist asked.

"I'm doing great," Samantha replied.

Bill and Nancy

Bill shook Mitch and Amy's hands as he opened the door to his newly renovated investment house. "Come on in," he boomed. The smell of cinnamon wafted from the kitchen.

"Cooking something?" Amy asked, incredulous. She tried to forget the state of the kitchen in their own flip. No flooring, no cabinets, no oven, or even electricity to turn one on.

"Just a candle. Isn't it nice?" Nancy asked as she came into the room.

"Smells great! Thanks for inviting us," Mitch replied. "It gives me a chance to get away from working on our house for a while. We can't believe you two got the house ready so fast. Maybe you can give us some tips on how to speed things up."

Amy took a deep breath. "I smell more than a candle," she said. "Something even better. Fresh paint. New carpet. Ahhhh."

"Just finished up yesterday," Bill said. "We actually had someone look at the house this morning."

"Wow!" Mitch said, trying not to be jealous. "The paint looks great. Did you do it yourself?"

"No." Bill rubbed his hand across his short buzz haircut. "I have to confess that I haven't done any of the work. The paint was done in two days; would have taken me at least a month." He laughed. "There wasn't that much that I wanted to do myself, so I concentrated on using my charm to encourage my contractors to get everything done quickly."

"He used his big marine body to do some encouraging too," Nancy whispered to Amy. "When those contractors saw him on the job site every day, they knew he meant business." She cleared her throat to catch Bill's attention.

"Oh, yes, and they were all quite fond of Nancy's fudge," he said. "She promised a fresh batch each afternoon as long as they showed up and stuck around."

"How many crews did it take to get this ready?" Mitch asked, kneeling down to examine the baseboards. They looked a little scuffed; they hadn't been replaced.

"I've only had three crews come in here," Bill boasted. "Painters, the carpet guys, and a handyman. I always say, make a plan and stick to it. That's just what I did."

Nancy took Amy's hand. "Would you like to see the kitchen?" she asked.

"Sure," Amy said, allowing herself to be led away from the living room, where the two men were getting into a discussion on the merits of new baseboards. As she entered, she took a look around.

"We painted the walls and put some new knobs on the cabinets," Nancy said, watching Amy's face carefully. "That was Bill's original plan, and like he said, he stuck with it. He wanted to keep the budget down and get it ready to sell quickly. Personally, I wonder if we should have done a little more. What do you think?" Her eyes peered anxiously into Amy's.

"Well," Amy said, trying hard to be positive. Nancy looked so concerned. "Everyone has a different strategy." She rested a hand on the worn and yellowed countertop, noticing the stained grout in the tile backsplash. "Our house is taking a lot longer because of the extra work, and sometimes we have had to wait for the designer materials we ordered to show up. You've already had a potential buyer walk through. This may work out great for you."

"Oh, do you really think so?" Nancy said, giving Amy a hug.

Samantha

It was a little after 11 a.m. as Samantha pulled up to the house. The plumber's truck was not there. Maybe he's taking an early lunch, she thought.

Samantha went inside. The bathroom was untouched. It was evident that the plumber had not been there at all. This wasn't supposed to happen. Samantha had confirmed with him the previous afternoon. He was going to be there at eight this morning and had assured her he would be done by the end of the day.

She had it all planned out. She had more contractors coming the next day and Friday, and they couldn't do their work until the plumber was done. She flipped open her cell phone and dialed his number. She waited as it rang and finally went to voice mail. "Joe, this is Samantha. I am at the house, and it is eleven o'clock. I was expecting you this morning at eight. Call me as soon as you get this message."

No phone call. No messages. How could he just not show up? This sort of thing would *not* happen at the office.

She redialed the number and listened to it ring and ring.

Okay, Samantha thought, regrouping. You take care of problems for a living.

Samantha walked back to her car and pulled out her laptop. She got on the Internet and went to the investment group Web site. Within minutes she found the names of five plumbers. Three phone calls later she found one who would be out within the hour.

She rolled up her sleeves and grabbed her tools from the trunk. She was looking forward to doing some sheetrock on the half-wall between the kitchen and the living room.

Samantha's cell phone rang. She checked the caller ID. It was Ed.

"This is Samantha," she said, eyeing the frame where the half-wall would go.

"Hi, Samantha. You finish that house yet?"

"Ha, ha. Not yet, but I'm getting pretty close. I'm going to hang a little sheetrock today."

"First time?"

"First time. I can't wait to get my hands dirty."

"You've got a strange idea of fun," Ed said.

"Speaking of fun," Samantha replied, "I've got to go. My mom is flying in from California in a few weeks, and I need to get this sheetrock done by tomorrow to finish the house before she shows up."

"Well, don't stress out trying to hit an exact deadline." Ed offered. "Flipping can be messy, especially your first one."

Just then Samantha noticed a small blue pickup pull up to the curb. "Paul's Plumbing" was printed on the side. "You don't say?" Samantha said, smiling. "I think I can handle a little deviation from the original plan. My new plumber just showed up; see you later, Ed."

• • •

Her mother would arrive at any minute. Samantha had offered to pick her up at the airport, but of course, Eleanor insisted on taking a cab. She didn't want to inconvenience anyone.

Eleanor wasn't crazy about Samantha quitting her high-paying job to flip houses, and she had told her so in no uncertain terms. Samantha had tried to explain that she wasn't quitting her job, not yet, anyway. But her mother was worried and had questioned her during each of their weekly phone calls. Finally, she had put her foot down. "I'm going to come check up on my girl," she had insisted the last time they'd talked. "I'll be there next Thursday."

Samantha walked from room to room, keeping an eye on the front windows. The carpet had gone in the previous day. She was down to the final touches. The landscapers were planting a few bushes in front, and a cleaning crew was finishing up in the kitchen. Her mother wouldn't recognize this as the house that was pictured in the e-mail Samantha had sent her when she bought the place.

A flash of yellow pulled into the driveway: a taxi. Samantha tucked her hair behind her ears; her mother always hated it when hair hung in her face. She stood up straight, threw her shoulders back, and walked out the door.

"Samantha!" her mother called.

She gave her neatly dressed, perfectly manicured mother a hug. Then she turned to the house, "So, Mom, what do you think?"

Mitch and Amy

Mitch pulled into the empty driveway and parked the car but left the headlights on to illuminate the front door until he could get it open.

Frankie claimed to have finished about half of the kitchen tile, and so if Mitch was lucky, he'd be finished, back home, and in bed by 2 a.m. Mitch fumbled with the lock, stepped inside the door, threw the switch, and gasped. "Oh, no!"

Mitch noticed the mistake immediately. That was why Frankie wouldn't return Mitch's calls. The nitwit had used the bathroom tiles on the kitchen floor. Then he had left the job without fixing his mistake.

Perfect.

Mitch called Amy as he drove to the hardware store to get more bathroom tile. He hoped it wasn't closed.

"Hey, do we have money in the account?"

"Why, what's wrong?" Amy asked, worry creeping into her voice.

"Frankie did the tile wrong. I've got to get more and don't want to write a hot check." He had another long night ahead of him. He had to tear up the bathroom tile in the kitchen, lay the proper one, and then tile the bathroom as well.

"Oh, Mitch. Yes, the account is fine. But I'm so sorry. You must be exhausted."

"Yeah, well, it won't be forever. I guess I'll see you later, babe." He hung up the phone and swerved into the hardware store's parking lot. It was almost empty, but the lights were still on. "Hey, Mitch," the manager called from the back of the store. They were on a first-name basis.

As he drove back to the house, he stopped for a quick hamburger. How long was it going to take to retile the kitchen and tile the bathroom? *Frankie!* He lingered over the French fries, dreading the work ahead.

When he got back to the house, the lights were out. "Funny, I know I left them on," he mumbled. He grabbed a crowbar and walked to the front door. He could feel his heart beginning to race. Who had turned off the lights and why? Couldn't be thieves; there was nothing to steal. Maybe vandals?

He opened the door, not sure what he would find. He reached behind him for the light switch and heard something move. He raised the crowbar, and the lights came on.

"Surprise!"

It was Amy and three of his firefighter buddies.

"What are you guys doing here?" Mitch asked, lowering the crowbar.

"Amy called us and said you could use a little help," Chuck offered.

Amy smiled at Mitch. "I couldn't just sit home alone while you stayed up half the night."

"Besides," Al said, smiling, "we figured if we helped you finish this up, we wouldn't have to listen to any more of your whining."

"Don't talk to me about whining until you've crawled on the kitchen floor for an hour removing that tile," Mitch said, handing Al a hammer and chisel. "Thanks, guys. I owe you big time."

"We'll settle for some of Amy's cookies," Ken said.

"A few of them are blackened on the bottom," Amy said. "My specialty."

Stage Five

SELL

How to Prepare and Market an
Investment House for Sale

- ✓ **I – FIND**
  - A House with Investment Potential
- ✓ **2 – ANALYZE**
  - An Offer that Maximizes Profits Given the Risk
- ✓ **3 – BUY**
  - An Investment House You Own
- ✓ **4 – FIX**
  - A Renovated House, Ready to Sell
- **5 – SELL**
  - Profit in the Bank

SELL Introduction

Between two products equal in price, function and quality, the better looking will outsell the other.

—Raymond Loewy, twentieth-century industrial designer

In a classic *Seinfeld* episode, Jerry and company yield to a friend's constant prompting—"You've got to see the baby!"—and head out to the Hamptons to see the baby and spend a weekend at the beach. The baby's mother introduces her child with the question, "Isn't he gorgeous?" Although we never see the baby, it's clear from Jerry and Elaine's reaction that the baby is anything but gorgeous.

After spending months analyzing and fixing up an investment house, it's likely that it will feel like your baby. And like the mother in the Seinfeld episode, you may lose your objectivity. This can be a problem when it comes time to set the price, decide who is going to handle the sale, or respond to an offer, all of which demand an investor's clear-eyed objectivity.

We divide the Sell stage into two steps. In the first step, you will prepare your house to go on the market. In the second step, we'll prepare you to field offers, reach agreement, and then close on the sale.

Chapter 15

Prepare to Sell

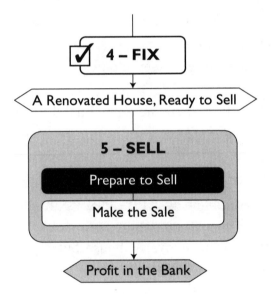

After reading this chapter you will know how to

■ Decide who will handle the sale

■ Set the selling price

■ Analyze the four staging levels

When the fix-up is complete, it's time to sell the house and reap your reward. Let's revisit the good decisions you need to make along the way that will make selling the house a quick and profitable process. The road to success starts in the Find stage when selecting a target neighborhood where people want to live. The neighborhood must have good sales activity, be in a nice location, and in general, have homes that are well cared for. In the Analyze stage, you must identify improvements that make for a desirable house in your target area. In addition to spotting everything that needed to be fixed, you need to select design choices and lifestyle upgrades that buyers would expect.

In the Buy stage, you must purchase the house for a price that allows you to receive a reasonable profit on a quick sale. Even if you have a few bumps along the way during the Fix stage (one always does), your good decisions up to that point will keep a quick sale and a nice profit within reach.

Now, in the Sell stage, there are a few final decisions to make before putting the house on the market. First, you have to decide how you want to sell the property: by yourself or through your real estate agent. Second, you need to revisit your eventual selling price to see if it's still on target. Third, you should stage the house according to its design level of basic, standard, designer, or custom so that buyers can visualize the house not as just a clean renovated house but a place they could call home (Figure 15-1).

Preparing to Sell

1. Decide Who Will Handle the Sale—You or Your Agent
2. Set the Selling Price
3. Stage the House Based on its Design Level

Figure 15-1 Preparing to Sell

MANAGING THE SALE

In the Fix stage, we covered the one-call wonders: the specialists who with one phone call handle all the details of a specific rehab task. When we call our roofer, he measures the roof, picks up the materials, removes the old roof, and installs a new one. One call and we're done.

When it comes to selling the property, your real estate agent can also be a one-call wonder. They can save you time and hassle as well as make you more money by getting a higher selling price than you would likely get on your own. Unless we quickly sell the house before we've finished fixing it up, we always use a real estate agent when selling our investment properties because it allows us to focus on aspects of flipping houses in which we can add the most value. But there is a cost associated with hiring a real estate agent, and we know investors who prefer to save this money by selling their houses themselves. We'll cover the basics of each approach to help you decide which method is best for you (Figure 15-2).

Two Ways to Sell an Investment House

1. Hire a Real Estate Agent

2. Sell the House Yourself (For Sale By Owner)

Figure 15-2   Two Ways to Sell an Investment House

HIRING A REAL ESTATE AGENT

A good real estate agent is like a general contractor who manages the entire process of selling a house. She supervises all the different people involved in the real estate transaction, making sure that all the paperwork is done properly and on time and that all the pieces are in place when it's time to close on the property. She spends time and money marketing the house by listing it in the Multiple Listing Service (MLS) and on other Web sites, advertising it appropriately and effectively, and working with buyers' agents to preview and show the house.

Ideally, what you are looking for in a real estate agent is someone who is familiar with your target neighborhood and regularly works with people who want to live in that neighborhood. In essence, you want to hire a real estate agent who has a history of delivering qualified buyers to houses in your target area.

You and the real estate agent will sign a listing agreement that authorizes her to market and sell the house and outlines the responsibilities, terms, and conditions of the agreement. There are three points that you want to pay close attention to in the listing agreement (Figure 15-3).

Key Points of the Listing Agreement

1. Commissions

2. Term

3. Agent Bonuses

Figure 15-3 Key Points of the Listing Agreement

1. *Commissions.* Commissions are, by law, always negotiable. However, given the costs of doing business, there will not be a wide range. Usually, half the commission you pay your agent will actually go to the agent who brings the buyer. We suggest that in most circumstances you stick with the local commission structure; you don't want to demotivate either your agent or a buyer's agent by paying a lower commission than the one on the house down the street. If you accounted for these fees in the Analyze stage, a real estate commission won't keep you from realizing your expected profit. In fact, it could increase your chances of getting a higher selling price.

2. *Term.* A listing agreement usually specifies that your agent will receive a commission if the house sells within a specified number

of days. Most agents will agree to 90 to 120 days (depending on the market), which fits your plan to close on the house within two months.

3. *Agent bonuses.* Personally, we like to add a couple of commission bonuses. The first one is for our real estate agent if she closes within two months. We also add a bonus for buyers' agents to encourage them to show the house to more prospective buyers. These bonuses can be a percentage of the sales price (e.g., 1 percent) or a fixed dollar amount (e.g., $1,500). It's up to you to decide when to offer them and how much.

FLIPPING POINT

Most real estate agents carry errors and omissions insurance to protect them (and you) from any mishaps during the listing and closing process. For this reason alone, hiring an agent can be a good idea, because you get some benefits from their coverage.

SELLING THE PROPERTY YOURSELF

Just like making the decision about whether you have the time and skills needed to manage the rehab of a property yourself, you have to decide if you have the resources to handle the sale on your own [For Sale by Owner (FSBO)]. If you decide to go FSBO, you will have to market the property yourself by putting up signs, making flyers, possibly mailing postcards throughout the neighborhood, and placing advertisements in the newspaper and on searchable Internet Web sites that list FSBO properties. You also will be the one to show the property, hold open houses, and field calls from prospective buyers.

It will also fall to you to access the reliability, trustworthiness, and creditworthiness of the buyer. When you accept an offer and sign the contract you have taken the house off the market. If it falls through, you get the house back and begin the sales process again. If you are not using a licensed real estate agent, we highly recommend hiring a real estate attorney for your first few flips.

SETTING THE SELLING PRICE

When it is time to sell the house, it may have been months since you estimated the selling price. Were your assumptions about market trends and the seasonal selling cycle accurate? If you're lucky, the real estate market (and your house) may have appreciated a bit. Either way, you need to go back to the comps to determine the price at which you're going to list the house.

If you follow our formula for holding time, you will budget for about two months of interest, taxes, utilities, and other holding costs once the house is listed. To find a buyer and close on the sale, you want to get the house under contract within the first few weeks that it is on the market. This requires a selling price that is realistic for a quick sale in the neighborhood. Again, it may be difficult to stay objective. Be sure to let the current market information tell you how much you can get for the house.

FLIPPING POINT

Do not base the price on how much it cost you to buy, improve, and hold the house. Making mistakes along the way is painful, and you'll be tempted to try to erase those mistakes by selling the house for a higher price than it is worth. In reality, you're adding to your mistakes by increasing your holding time and incurring more costs. Price the house according to the market.

Staging: A House Becomes a Home

The final bit of work to prepare your house for the market involves turning the renovated house into a home where buyers want to live. In recent years, staging houses has become a popular way to give prospective buyers a glimpse of what life would be like in the house. Professional staging companies fill vacant houses with furniture by the truckload and create visual impressions throughout the house, from a cookbook and cookware in the kitchen to a hardback novel and reading glasses on a nightstand in a fully furnished master bedroom.

Although professional staging may be a good idea for certain houses in certain neighborhoods, we don't recommend spending the money to stage every house fully. In the Analyze Stage, when identifying improvements, you assigned a design level to the house that was based on other houses in the neighborhood. We recommend that you choose the extent of your staging efforts on the basis of that design level.

Staging a Basic House

You may recall that basic design includes no frills. Staging for a basic house is similar. The house should be kept spotless, and the grass should be mowed and watered regularly. You want your house to give a good visual impression from the street. A few small, low-maintenance plants in the beds and a welcome mat are all you might need to stage a basic house. But grass and plants require maintenance. In some cases, you may skip landscaping altogether to keep the costs as low as possible.

Staging a Standard House

When you are staging a standard house, you begin to incorporate some inexpensive touches that give the house a homey feel. Don't skip basic lawn maintenance in a standard house. In addition, put some potted plants by the entry or front porch. Again, low maintenance is a must. You don't need to hassle with furniture, but make use of the surfaces of the house to create a nice visual impression:

- Place a bowl of fresh fruit or a vase of flowers on the kitchen counter. (Keep them fresh!)
- In a hallway or powder bath, add soap, a soap dish, and a hand towel (in addition to toilet paper, which is available but not displayed).

STAGING A DESIGNER HOUSE

For a designer-level house, your staging options increase. If you bring in rented furniture, your ability to create a visual impression expands greatly. Focus on areas of the house where you can highlight the effective use of space:

- Furnish patios and porches to create appealing outdoor living areas that increase the square footage of the house.
- Add chairs and a lamp to an oversized master bedroom and stage it with books and blankets to give it a cozy feel.
- Add a single bed and a small dresser to a smaller bedroom to dismiss any concerns that a room can't be furnished adequately.
- Place furniture so that it directs buyers to notice a nice view or desirable features of the house such as a fireplace.
- Add bar stools and a couple of breakfast place settings to a kitchen bar.

STAGING A CUSTOM HOUSE

For a custom-level house, consider hiring a professional staging company that will handle the process of setting up and taking down an elaborate home furnishings and decorations. Although this is expensive, the effect on the selling price of your house may be well worth it. Custom staging often involves completely furnishing and decorating the major rooms in the house such as the master bedroom, the kitchen, and the dining and living areas. This marketing approach can be similar to that of the "Parade of Homes" events put on by custom builders in some metro areas.

With the house staged, you're ready to put the house on the market and make a quick and profitable sale.

POINTS TO REMEMBER

Just like figuring out who will manage the Fix, deciding who will manage the sale of a house will require you to determine the best use of your time and energy.

- If you decide to sell the house by yourself, not only will you have to market the property (via signs, direct mail, and advertising as well as showing the property and holding open houses), you will have to manage all the appropriate contracts, legal procedures and paperwork to get to the close (discussed in Chapter 16).

- Hiring a good real estate agent to sell the house for you is akin to hiring a general contractor: You oversee the sale of the house, but can spend the bulk of your time on other things, such as your primary career or generating leads for another house.

- When you put the house on the market, you also need to make sure that you create the best impression possible as time is of the essence for a quick sale. This means staging the property according its design level: basic, standard, designer, or custom.

Chapter 16
Make the Sale

After reading this chapter you will know how to
- Put the house on the market
- Consider offers
- Close the sale

At this late stage in the flipping process, you already may have bought the champagne, but before you pop the cork, remember the sage advice of Yogi Berra: "It ain't over till it's over." You need to put the house on the market, and of course you need to get an acceptable offer and close the sale. Last but not least, you have to perform the final analysis to pay the tax man and then see how much profit you truly made on the flip. That's when you uncork the bubbly.

Put It on the Market

Once you've decided whether you're going to market the house yourself or with the help of your real estate agent, the next decision to make is *when* to market the house. That can be before you've completed the improvements or after the house is totally fixed up, spotless, and staged.

Seller's Disclosure Statement

Before putting the house on the market, you probably will have to fill out a document that details almost everything you know about the current and past condition of the house. It's called the seller's disclosure statement, and it's required by law in most states. It would be a major mistake and a serious legal risk not to do this or to do it inaccurately.

When selling a house, you should expect prospective buyers to review carefully the seller's disclosure statement that you produce. It is one of those formalities that should be completed as soon as you are ready to market the house. Not only will you check off what systems are in place and what kind of condition they are in, you also should disclose any major problems (e.g., water damage, pest infestation, structural issues) that existed when you bought the house and what you have done to fix them. You also must disclose any work that was done without the required permits.

This is a good opportunity to list all the improvements you have made to the house since you bought it (new carpet, new HVAC system, new roof, etc.). In our view, you should disclose everything you can think of so that there is never any question about what you did or didn't do to the house.

WHEN TO MARKET

There are two schools of thought among investors about when to make investment properties available to prospective buyers. Some go for a quick strike, and others go for maximum impact.

Certain investors like to offer their houses to the public before they are completely fixed up and ready to be marketed seriously. They do this by some combination of the following:

1. Putting up a "For Sale" sign in the yard
2. Advertising the property in the newspaper or on local real estate Web sites
3. Sending out postcards to mailing lists and other houses in the neighborhood

Their hope is to make a quick sale without having to do all the work of finishing the improvements, staging the house, and hiring an agent. This method is most successful when the local housing market is heating up and there are more buyers than available houses.

The other school of thought involves holding the public back until the investment house is completely ready for viewing. These investors believe that you maximize the selling price when you not only fix up the house but also create a place that a buyer could call home. By adding the finishing touches, including a thorough final cleaning, some tasteful landscaping, and the staging of the house, they are presenting the house in a way that appeals to homeowners looking to move in immediately. This approach makes sense when there are a lot of homes on the market and you need yours to stand out from the crowd.

> **FLIPPING POINT**
>
> During the rehab process, we put a for sale sign in the yard to get the word out to the neighborhood that we're fixing up the house for immediate resale. This is a great way to find the neighbor down the street who wants to move to a larger or nicer house in the same neighborhood. Once the fix-up is complete, if the house has not sold, our real estate agent lists the house on the Multiple Listing Service (MLS) and begins marketing and showing the property. Then we move on to focus on other opportunities.

Whether you are marketing the house before or after it is completely fixed up, the goal is to get an offer as soon as possible. But what if you get a quick offer, possibly even before it's officially on the market? And what if the sales price is a little lower than you think you can get? Let's discuss what to do with offers that don't meet your expectations.

CONSIDERING OFFERS

A friend and fellow investor was finishing up an investment property that she planned to list for $250,000 once it was ready. Before she officially put the house on the market (and before she finished sealing the wood floors), she got an offer for $235,000. She decided to reject the offer and finish the house first to see if she could sell it for the full price.

The next week, the wood floors in the house were sanded and sealed. After completing the job, her flooring contractor told her that the doors were locked and that no one should be allowed to enter for twenty-four hours while the floors dried. He posted signs in English and Spanish that said "Do not walk on the floors!" and even took the keys to the house just to be safe. The same day, however, our friend let a couple of contractors in to work on the tile in another part of the house. She gave them explicit instructions to stay off the wood floors, but you can guess what happened next: When our friend returned the next day, she discovered footprints and scratches so deep in the sealant that the wood floors had to be resanded and resealed.

The moral to this story? First money is best money. A bird in the hand is worth two in the bush. Pick your favorite cliché as long as you *accept the first legitimate offer*. By legitimate offer, we mean a serious one from a buyer with the ability to close. What you don't want to do is take the house off the market immediately for a buyer who may not be qualified or even very interested.

The Six Considerations of an Offer

1. Letter from Lender
2. Quick Inspection Period
3. Not Contingent on the Sale of Another House
4. Short Closing Period
5. Reasonable Down Payment
6. Reasonable Earnest Money

Figure 16-1   The Six Considerations of an Offer

You need to do a quick assessment of every offer to verify that the prospective buyer is considering the house seriously and is financially capable of buying it. Whether you are thinking about rejecting an offer in hopes of getting a better one or weighing offers in a multiple-offer scenario—may you be so blessed—you will want to pay close attention to several parts of the offer in addition to the sales price listed on the contract (Figure 16-1).

1. *Letter from lender.* If a buyer if going to finance a portion of the purchase, he should demonstrate that he has the means to purchase the house with a prequalification (or, better yet, a preapproval) letter from his lender. Be wary of the buyer who does not provide one.

2. *Quick inspection period.* The inspection period should be a few days instead of a few weeks so that you can get your house back on the market quickly if the buyer backs out or you are unwilling to do any requested repairs.

3. *Not contingent on the sale of another house.* In most cases, you should avoid the situation where the buyer needs to sell her house first to come up with the money to pay for your house. That is too uncertain and time-consuming for an investor planning for a quick sale.

4. *Short closing period.* You've already been paying for quiet costs throughout the construction process. If a buyer has stated that she needs two to three months before she will be ready to close, are you prepared to keep incurring holding costs while the house is off the market?

5. *Reasonable down payment.* If a buyer can come up with only 5 percent or less of the sales price for a down payment, there's an increased chance he will have difficulty securing a loan. However, in lower-end neighborhoods, many offers have relatively small down payments, so don't be too quick to reject an offer in that situation.

6. *Reasonable earnest money.* If a buyer is serious about the house, you can expect her to offer around 1 percent earnest money.

Anything less than a month's worth of holding costs will not protect you if the sale doesn't go through. If the earnest money is non-refundable, you have a greater assurance that the buyer will not back out.

Let's be clear: We're not suggesting that you reject every offer that doesn't meet every element in the list. But they are all factors that can help you decide whether you want to accept an offer or take your chances on waiting for another one.

If our investor friend had accepted that first offer, she would have made a nice quick profit on the flip. But instead, she spent more money on the floors, incurred additional holding costs, and still had to find another buyer. The old adage "good things come to those who wait" isn't necessarily true in flipping houses. Sure, good things can happen, but in our experience the potential negatives outweigh the positives when it comes to rejecting a legitimate but early offer. The market can turn, the house could be vandalized or robbed, holding costs could increase, the roof could be damaged in a storm, and so forth. An alternative to rejecting an offer that you think may not pan out is accepting the offer but also accepting backups, with a short time period for any contingencies.

BACKUP OFFERS

Backup offers are great insurance policies in case the first offer falls through. When an initial offer is accepted, you can still accept additional offers and even include the proviso "accepting backup offers" on the MLS listing. The beauty of a backup offer is that it not only gives you another opportunity to sell the house but also gives you more leverage in negotiating with the buyer who submitted the first offer. Once the first buyer is aware that there are one or more backup offers, he suddenly realizes that his ability to negotiate has been lessened considerably.

But again, even if the local market is hot, it is our advice to go with the first reasonable offer. Backup offers can fall apart just as easily as a primary offer can. You may find yourself rejecting an offer to accept the backup only to have it fall through as well.

In any case, make sure you seek the advice of a real estate agent or attorney before accepting multiple offers, even back-up offers. When you sign a contract you must fulfill all the obligations of that contract. A helping hand from a real estate professional can help you avoid accidentally agreeing to sell your house to two different parties (when you intended to sell it to one and have the other as a backup). This happens more often than you might think and sellers often have to pay damages to get out.

CLOSING THE SALE

Once the contract and earnest money are submitted to the closing company, it's time to put the champagne on ice but not yet time to break out the glasses. Just like buying a house, it's not over until everyone signs all the papers. Figure 16-2 shows the five-step process for getting to the closing table.

Five Steps to Closing on the Sale of a House

1. Show a permit paper trail
2. Respond to repair requests
3. Provide a survey
4. Purchase title insurance
5. Request a settlement statement

Figure 16-2   Five Steps to Closing on the Sale of a House

1. Show a Permit Paper Trail

We recommend that you always obtain any necessary permits and get the required inspections for construction projects. When it comes time to sell, you'll need to have copies of all the permits and inspections available to prospective buyers to show that, when necessary, the work was done by licensed professionals and inspected by the local authorities.

2. Respond to Repair Requests

The buyer should order the house inspection and any other inspections required by the buyer's lender as soon as the offer is signed. This way the results will be available before the inspection period expires. You have three options if the buyer requests that you make a repair:

1. Make the repair yourself at your expense
2. Get your contractor to fix the problem free of charge for a repair that was part of the scope of work
3. Decline to make the repair, allowing the buyer to back out of the deal or renegotiate

Again, if you have backup offers, you can take a tougher stance on making any repairs, but the next prospective buyer may make the same requests. It's often better to keep the deal going by making small repairs or offering the buyer a fixed amount of money at closing.

3. Provide a Survey

The survey you acquired when you bought the house should be acceptable to the buyer's lender provided that you made no additions or improvements on the property beyond what existed before. If your work affected the property lines, easements, or boundaries, the buyer will order and typically pay for a new survey.

4. PURCHASE TITLE INSURANCE

In most real estate transactions, it's customary for the seller to purchase the title insurance policy. However, in a real estate *investment* transaction, the investor often buys the title policy when she buys the house. Thus, you probably will be buying two title insurance policies for a flip: one when you buy the house and another when you sell it. If you happen to live in a state that requires title insurance providers to offer the "open commitment" option we covered in Chapter 11 on page 228, this is when you'll take advantage of the option instead of buying a second title insurance policy.

5. REQUEST A SETTLEMENT STATEMENT

The last step before signing the paperwork is to take a look at the settlement statement to review all the costs and charges as well as your proceeds from the sale. As in the Buy stage, it is important to go over this document early in the closing process to make sure there aren't any errors or overcharges. Contact the closing company if you have any questions, and a representative will be able to go over every line item. Ask your closing agent to waive any "junk" fees that show up on the statement.

Next up is closing day. This is the time to close the books on the flip and calculate your profit.

CLOSING THE BOOKS

Closing the books on your first—or fiftieth—flip can be an exciting and educational event. Take the time to analyze what went right and what went wrong so that you can learn from the experience and do an even better job on the next flip. Most important, before you reinvest your profits in the next house, you have to set aside money for taxes and any other expenses that have not been paid.

A TAXING SITUATION

We sometimes hear people say that they didn't make any money because all their profit was eaten up by taxes. In reality, this can't happen. Your taxes are a portion of your profit, and the tax rate is never 100 percent. Be sure to account for and deduct every expense you incurred buying, holding, and selling the house before calculating how much tax to pay.

The biggest tax hit comes if you flipped the house in less than a year. In this situation you will pay the "short-term" capital gains rate, which is the same rate as that for ordinary income such as wages and salary. Once you have held the house for a year and a day, you pay the "long-term" capital gains rate on your profit, and in most cases that results in a sizeable tax savings. So, in the unlikely event that your flip is getting close to that first year mark from when you bought it, consider delaying closing until after a year and enjoy a tax break.

If you choose to live in your house while you flip it, a whole new world of tax savings opens up, but only if you live in the house for two years. If you are single, you can deduct up to $250,000 in profit from the sale of the house. Married couples can deduct $500,000. Thus, a married couple pays taxes only on profits that exceed $500,000, in which case paying taxes isn't nearly as painful. You can do this multiple times as long as you have lived in the house for two of the last five years and you do not sell more than once every twelve months. In investment circles, the strategy of living in a house while you fix and flip it is often called "homesteading."

Tax Scenarios for a $50,000 Profit		
Scenario	Tax on $50,000 Profit	Explanation
Flipped in Less than 1 Year	$10,000–$15,000	Varies based on other income and deductions
Flipped in More than 1 Year, but didn't live in it	$7,500	15% of profit
Lived in the House for 2 Years	$0	Exempt from taxes since profit less than $250,000 ($500,000 if married)

Figure 16-3   Tax Scenarios for a $50,000 Profit

Figure 16-3 shows a comparison of the taxes for three flips that had a $50,000 profit. Tax laws change frequently, so be sure to check with your accountant for the latest details on calculating the taxes on a flip.

There is a way to defer taxes by executing a 1031 Exchange (Section 1031 of the Internal Revenue Code). A 1031 Exchange allows investors to roll the profit from the sale of one investment property into another property without having to pay any capital gains taxes. To qualify, both the old property (the one you flipped) and the new property (the one you'll be flipping next) have to fit the IRS definition of property held for investment or used in a trade or business and you must identify the new property within forty-five days. Also, you must exchange "like" properties: a house for a house. If you find the next house quickly, we encourage you to explore the 1031 Exchange program with your accountant. You will also need a qualified 1031 company to act as your escrow agent between the sale of your first property and the acquisition of your next one.

BREAK OUT THE BUBBLY

Once the house is sold, it's time to celebrate. Let's hope you'll make a nice profit on every flip, but even a small profit means you got a paid education.

Most investors learn their flipping lessons while still employed at their day jobs. That way, they have something to fall back on if they decide that flipping isn't for them or if the profits from their first few flips don't pay the bills. We don't recommend quitting your day job to flip full-time until you've done several flips that have generated a good profit. We'll dive into this topic and others in Chapter 17.

Congratulations, you now understand the anatomy of a flip—the steps, the checklists, the systems, and the key decisions.

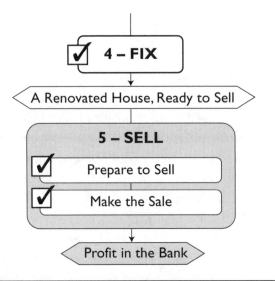

POINTS TO REMEMBER

All your hard work is about to pay off when you begin to entertain offers on your property. You can choose to premarket the property before it is completely finished, although some investors prefer to wait until all the finishing touches have been completed before showing the house to buyers. Either way, the longer a property sits on the market, the more risk there is of your profit being eaten up. Any offer on the property should be considered and evaluated seriously.

Before an offer is accepted, you must provide a detailed seller's disclosure as well as any permits obtained for the project and give them to the buyer's agent for review. After an offer is accepted, there probably will be the usual inspection, title insurance, and survey before you can close on the house.

Finally, it is important to take the time to go back to the books to reevaluate how well you did in your calculations. Whether you got paid well for your flip or simply got a paid education, you want to learn from any mistakes and flip your next house with more knowledge and confidence.

Bill and Nancy

Bill pushed the door open and pumped his fist in the air as he walked out of his real estate agent's office. *Yes! We did it!* He had just signed a contract to sell their investment house for $95,000. It was $5,000 under their asking price but was the exact amount Bill and Nancy had estimated for the eventual selling price. They had stuck to the plan and would receive a nice profit.

He quickly dialed Nancy on his cell phone as he strode down the sidewalk toward his car. "You're not going to believe this," he crowed.

"What?" Nancy replied. He could hear the grandchildren in the background, probably jumping on the couch. "Johnny, get down, honey, you'll hurt yourself," Nancy said. "Now, what were you saying, Bill?"

"We sold the house!"

"No way. We just put it on the market yesterday. Johnny, get down!"

"I know! Doug called about two hours ago and said that an offer had come in and the buyer wanted to get it signed right away. I headed straight to Doug's office so I could call you after the deal was done."

"Bill," Nancy pleaded. "If this is some kind of practical joke. . . ."

Bill laughed. It was happening so fast. "No, no joke. He offered $92,000. I countered at $95,000, and he took it. I just left Doug's office with a signed contract in hand."

"That's fantastic," Nancy exclaimed. "So that's it? Selling our house is easier than a weekend with the grandkids!"

"Oh, just a few formalities: survey, appraisal, inspection." Bill opened the door of his car. "They have a two-week contingency period to get it all done, and then we close."

The first one in the group to buy a house and the first one to sell. Yes!

• • •

Nancy called. "Bill, pick up the phone. I think it's the real estate agent."

"Hi, Bill. It's Doug."

It had been twelve days since they had signed the contract, and the closing was scheduled for the next day. "So Doug, what time do we close?"

Nancy walked in, holding her calendar.

There was a pause. "We don't," he said finally.

"What? What happened?" Bill thundered.

Nancy grimaced. "Oh, dear."

"The buyer was another investor," Doug explained. "He was trying to wholesale the house. He didn't find another buyer and backed out of the deal."

Bill shook his head. Two weeks wasted while the house was off the market. "What do we do now, Doug?"

"Well, not much else we can do now except put it back on the market."

"We've got another house we want to make an offer on," Bill confided. "I can't pull the trigger on it until this house sells."

Doug's tone became more upbeat. "Hey, we got the first offer pretty quickly. I bet it won't be too long before we get another."

"Okay, thanks, Doug. Let us know if you hear something." They hung up.

Bill reached for Nancy's hand and gave it a squeeze. "He's right. After all, how hard can it be?"

"As easy as a weekend with the grandkids?" Nancy asked with a weak smile.

Samantha

Samantha laid the flowers aside and pulled the card from the envelope.

> Sam,
>
> Congratulations on the sale of your house! You did a great job, and as always, I am so proud of you. When do you start the next one?
>
> Love and kisses,
>
> Mom

Samantha smiled and glanced at the calendar. The inspection for her next flip was scheduled for Tuesday.

Mitch and Amy

Mitch moved a chair into place while Amy put down the welcome mat. They had moved almost half of their own furniture and had borrowed some from their friends to stage their open house.

"It looks fantastic," Mitch said, surveying the room. "You've done an incredible job decorating this place, Amy."

"Thanks. You've done an incredible job fixing up the house for me to decorate. Remember the tile disaster?"

Mitch could almost laugh in hindsight, but not quite. Not until after it sold. "We stayed on budget, even if we did finish a month later than we planned."

"And not a moment too soon; it's two o'clock," Amy announced.

They walked to the front door, and Mitch opened it just in time to see a couple walking up the sidewalk.

Bill and Nancy

"It's been five weeks since we put it back on the market, and the only offer we have is for $82,500." Bill's fist pounded the table.

Doug cleared his throat. "Sometimes these things just take time," he said, eyeing Bill's clenched fingers.

"I'm sorry, Doug. I know it's not your fault. Shoot straight with me. Why isn't it selling?" he asked, staring directly into Doug's eyes.

Doug took a deep breath. "I don't think the improvements on the house compare favorably to the other houses in the area."

"What? The baseboards?" The fist unclenched, and he held his hands palms up.

Doug sat back, letting his breath out in a whoosh. "It's not just the baseboards. Most of the homes for sale in that area have remodeled designer kitchens and updated bathrooms." Doug's cell phone went off, and he checked the caller ID. "Hold on. This is the other agent," he said.

Bill got up to pace the small office.

Doug picked up and listened intently. "Okay, I'll need to talk to my client; I'll get back to you." He hung up. "They countered," he said. Bill stopped pacing. "It's $85,000."

That wouldn't leave any profit, but he and Nancy needed to sell because they were really excited about the house they had found recently. He knew Nancy would approve; holding on to this house made her nervous. Bill heaved a deep sigh. "Take it."

Mitch and Amy

"Ed, it's Mitch. I have Amy with me on the speaker phone."

"How did the open house go?" Ed asked.

"It went okay. . . ." Mitch left the explanation dangling.

"Oh, I'm sorry. Maybe next time."

Amy interrupted, "What he's trying to say is that we got *two* offers!"

The Millionaire Real Estate Investor Club

"All right, this is our first meeting since everyone sold their flip. We have a rough idea of how everyone did, but this is bottom-line time," Ed said. "Let's hear your final profit after you closed the books."

Bill leaned forward. As usual, he was the one to start.

"Well, let's see," Bill said. "We bought our house for $66,000, spent about $5,000 on improvements, and then sold it for $85,000." He paused for dramatic effect, and said "We made $14,000."

The group remained quiet and exchanged puzzled looks. They knew Bill and Nancy's deal was tight.

Nancy grinned and shook here head. "Bill conveniently left out the quiet costs, which totaled almost $14,500," she added, referring to her notepad.

Bill held up his hands in mock surrender. "Guilty as charged. We actually lost a little less than $500, but I see it as a fair price for a good education." He looked at the table. "We learned a big lesson here. We didn't follow the process and it cost us. Thankfully, it didn't cost us much."

"I know it's not what you were hoping for, but I'm really proud of you guys," Amy said.

"Here, here," Ed announced. He held up his glass and tapped a spoon against the side. "To Bill and Nancy, lessons learned and on to your next deal." The others joined in for a chorus of clanging glasses.

Nancy put her arm around Bill and smiled at everyone gathered at the table. "It was our first try. Next time we'll do better. We've already found our next flip."

"You're not the only one who learned some lessons," Mitch said. "The good news is we made about $12,500."

They all clanged their glasses for Mitch and Amy. "Congratulations!"

"We could have made an extra $500," Amy added when the spoon celebration died down. "If we hadn't spent it on gas, driving back and forth to the house."

"Do not, under any circumstances, buy a house outside your target neighborhoods," Mitch added.

Everyone chuckled, well aware of Mitch's driving dilemma from past meetings.

"To stay on budget after a couple of mishaps, I ended up spending way too much time doing the work myself," Mitch confessed. "We don't have any leads on another house yet because we completely stopped lead generating to finish this one."

"Not to worry," Ed said, smiling. "There are plenty of houses to rehab out there, and I'd be willing to work with you two again anytime." He turned to Samantha. "I think Samantha has some good news to report."

Samantha tried not to sound too pleased. "I made over $26,000," she admitted.

Another round of clanging spoons drew disapproving glances from the people at other tables in the restaurant.

"So," Ed said, looking around the table, "it sounds like you are all interested in doing another flip."

Everyone in the group nodded their heads, and Samantha added, "Definitely. We've all got some work ahead of us if we're going to reach that seven-figure mark, but at least we all took a step in the right direction."

"A toast," said Bill.

They raised their glasses together and said, "To the Millionaire Real Estate Investors Club."

Chapter 17
Putting It All Together

After reading this chapter you will know how to
- Flip in any market
- Flip part-time and full-time

We hope you have enjoyed your journey through *FLIP*. We also hope you gained some insight from following Samantha, Bill, Nancy, Mitch, and Amy find, fix, and flip their first rehab investments. We wish them the best of luck on their next ones.

Before wrapping up the book, we'd like to share a few thoughts on flipping that extend beyond the model. At the start of the book we touched on the fact that flipping works in any market. Now we'll take a closer look at how market conditions can affect your strategy. We'll also give you some pointers on how to most effectively use your time and resources whether you're flipping part-time or full-time.

STILL FLIPPING OVER THE FLIP

One of the things we love about flipping houses is the ability to invest in rehab properties regardless of current market conditions. However, that doesn't mean you should always approach flipping a house the same way. You'll want to know which way the market winds are blowing and act accordingly.

When it comes to making market related decisions on a flip, all that really matters is what's happening in and around your target neighborhoods. National trends eventually may affect the local scene, but that impact is far from immediate or even certain. We recommend that you pay close attention to factual articles in the local papers and business journals and, more importantly, pay attention to the number of houses that are selling in your target neighborhoods, how quickly they are selling, and for how much.

Those local indicators will give you a sense of whether supply and demand are favoring buyers or sellers. That understanding will direct your focus and determine your immediate strategy.

FLIPPING IN A SELLER'S MARKET

In general terms, a *seller's market* is when there is an abundance of buyers looking for houses and fewer houses for sale. To put it in economic terms, demand is greater than the supply. In a seller's market, homeowners expect to sell quickly, at or above market value.

In buying an investment property, a common frustration in a seller's market is getting outbid on a house by people who are going to fix up the house and live in it. As an investor, more often than not, you can't match their offer and still be able to pay for the improvements, account for quiet costs, and resell the house for a profit. So, in a seller's market, concentrate on lead generation strategies that connect you with properties *before* they go public on the Multiple Listing Service (MLS). This is clearly a time for prospecting for vacant houses and advertising to all the residents in a neighborhood with your message of fast cash and no hassles. The good news is that once you've found and purchased an investment house in a seller's market, you're well positioned to receive a better than average profit. Not only should there be plenty of buyers for your house, you may benefit from the house appreciating in value while you are fixing it up.

FLIPPING IN A BUYER'S MARKET

A *buyer's market* is when there is an abundance of houses for sale and fewer buyers interested in them. In this case, supply is greater than the demand. For homeowners, this usually means a lower selling price and a longer time to sell.

When looking for houses in a buyer's market, you're not as likely to compete with people who are willing to move into a house in bad condition, because there is a ready supply of houses that don't need major repairs. Thus, mining the MLS becomes an easier strategy for finding investment properties. In addition, the foreclosure market tends to heat up when the housing market is cold because individuals facing foreclosure have difficulty selling their homes. However, although buying opportunities increase, selling becomes more challenging. You'll need to buy a house on the basis of a very conservative and realistic eventual selling price, possibly accounting for further softening in the market. When you're ready to sell, you need to price it right and fix it up so that it stands out from the crowd. To sell quickly in a buyer's market, the house must be completely ready to become a home.

Figure 17-1 shows the five stages of the FLIP model and explains that your focus in each stage may change on the basis of the market conditions.

PART-TIME OR FULL-TIME FLIPPING

An old joke asks, "What's the difference between bacon and eggs for breakfast?" The answer: "The chicken was involved, but the pig was committed." In flipping houses, it's not a matter of whether it's better to do it part-time or full-time; we know plenty of successful part-time and full-time investors. It's a matter of your commitment. Is it extra cash or a new career you're looking for?

PART-TIME FLIPPING

Flipping houses part-time while working full-time is a great way to earn extra money, but even if you're flipping part-time, you must treat it like a

Strategies for Flipping in Different Market Conditions

	Buyer's Market	Seller's Market
Find	Easier than seller's market. MLS and foreclosure markets can be good strategies.	Often difficult. Find houses before they are publicly for sale. Scouting for vacant properties and mailers to neighborhoods can be effective.
Analyze	Consider extra holding time and further softening of the market when estimating the selling price.	The house may appreciate, but never count on it when estimating the eventual selling price.
Buy	Often room for price negotiations.	Resist the urge to exceed your maximum offer.
Fix	Make the house stand out in the crowd.	Stay in the neighborhood norm.
Sell	Challenging. Good price, staging, and marketing are musts.	Easier than buyer's market. Consider listing before it's even finished.

Figure 17-1   Strategies for Flipping in Different Market Conditions

business. The advantages of having a team become evident when you are trying to flip houses profitably on a part-time basis. Finding houses is challenging even for a full-time investor. As a part-time flipper, you'll want to devote time to keeping your lead generation activities going. Whether it's driving through neighborhoods or sending out regular mailers, consistency is the key. Hiring a scout can be an inexpensive way to keep your prospecting going while you're at work.

When you get to the Fix stage, hiring a general contractor to manage the job while you're at work is well worth the extra expense. We think that good general contractors almost always pay for themselves, especially if you can't be at the job site consistently during the day. Finally, when you are selling the house, let a real estate agent manage the sale to save you the time and hassle of marketing and showing the house, as well as in closing the transaction.

The income from your regular job also takes a lot of the stress out of flipping houses and allows you to make better decisions. Imagine being three months into a full-time flipping job and still not finding a house. You would start to feel pressure to buy a house. That pressure can cloud your judgment at a time when you need to be completely objective.

We know many investors who make good money flipping one to four houses a year on a part-time basis. The money can pay for college, weddings, vacations, charities, and so on, or you can put it away in preparation for going into flipping full-time.

FULL-TIME FLIPPING

When you're ready to take the plunge and go into full-time flipping, we recommend that you have a nest egg that allows you to get through any surprises that may delay your profits. You need to be financially secure even if you can't find a house for months or if a contract falls through at the last minute.

Flipping full-time gives you the ability to ramp up your lead generation efforts. You'll also be able to take on more than one flip at a time. Once you've got your lead generation humming and have the team and infrastructure in place to handle multiple projects, you'll be well on your way to becoming a millionaire real estate flipper.

Money aside, we love being in real estate investing full-time. We both have spent time at big companies, working in tiny cubicles where we couldn't even crack a window to let in a bit of fresh air. The lifestyle and freedom that come with being a real estate investor are very rewarding, and our goal for this book is to help many people take that step. There's something satisfying about walking up to an investment house on a bright sunny morning and surveying the tangible fruits of your labor.

We also get personal satisfaction from seeing something old and neglected become new again. We've had the opportunity to turn a crack house into a home that was donated to a family in need. We're blessed to be in a business that can help people, and we would love to hear stories about people who are inspired to be a blessing to others. So will you flip or won't you? We hope this book has helped you learn about flipping and maybe learn a bit more about yourself. We wish you great success.

POINTS TO REMEMBER

Flipping houses works in any market at any time, but you should base your efforts on the conditions of your local housing market.

- In a seller's market, it's harder to buy houses at a good price. Focus on the Find stage and aim your lead generation efforts on houses that aren't publicly for sale.
- In a buyer's market, it's harder to sell houses. Be sure to price the house well and make improvements so that a homeowner can move in immediately.

Both part-time and full-time flipping are fine choices depending on the time and resources you're willing to commit to investing.

- When you are flipping part-time, focus on putting a team together that can manage finding, fixing, and selling when you can't be there.
- When you are flipping full-time, strive to compound your profits by flipping multiple houses at the same time. Look for efficiencies and economies of scale.

Never underestimate the potential rewards of real estate investing—both the personal and the financial rewards.

Appendix

The 101 Most Common Tasks

With the help of James Hill, our HomeFixers affiliate in Dallas, we have assembled the 101 most common tasks that we perform on construction jobs for our investor customers. The tasks are organized into the HomeFixers Fifty Steps to Rehabbing a House. Some of the steps have no tasks because those steps aren't involved in our typical rehabs. In fact, only the most complex rehabs require all fifty steps. Similarly, not every task associated with each step will be performed. For example, in the HVAC step you could replace either the entire system or a portion of it; you wouldn't do both. With this list in hand, you can get a head start on costing out labor and materials. This will help you make confident and quick decisions when estimating improvement costs to make your offer.

Step 1: House Secured

- Install lockbox and keys

Step 2: Plans, Permits, and Filings

- Obtain necessary permits

Step 3: House Leveling and Foundation Repair

Step 4: Pest Control

Step 5: Temporary Requirements

Step 6: Plumbing Pre-Demo

- Pull and terminate water and gas fixtures, appliances, and lines before demolition

Step 7: Electrical Pre-Demo

- Pull and terminate electrical fixtures, appliances, and wiring before demolition

Step 8: Demolition/Disposal/Site Prep

- Order dumpster
- Perform demolition (not walls, just finishes such as tile, cabinetry, doors, and trim)
- Remove debris (interior)
- Trim and remove trees
- Clean yard (remove junk, rake, cut, trim)
- Haul away junk and debris

Step 9: Engineering Reports

Step 10: Rough Soil Grading and Drainage

Step 11: Rough Plumbing under House or Foundation

Step 12: Framing and Subfloor

- Repair subfloor
- Minor replacement of damaged two-by-fours

Step 13: Roof Decking

- Install new roof decking

Step 14: Exterior Doors

- Repair exterior door, jamb, and threshold
- Install new front door
- Install new exterior doors (not including the front door)

Step 15: Windows and Window Glass

- Replace glass window panes
- Install window locks

Step 16: Sheathing, House Wrap, and Siding

- Repair siding

Step 17: Exterior Trim

- Repair fascia
- Repair garage door jamb (two-by-eight jamb and trim)
- Repair exterior trim (one-by-four window, door, and corner)

Step 18: Roof

- Repair roof
- Replace bad patches of roof decking
- Install new roof

Step 19: Fireplace

Step 20: Rough HVAC

- Service HVAC system
- Replace HVAC indoor unit (furnace and evaporator coil)
- Replace HVAC outside condenser unit
- Install entire new HVAC system

Step 21: Plumbing in Walls and Ceiling/Attic

Step 22: Bathtubs and Shower Pans

- Replace bathtubs
- Build shower pan for walk-in shower

Step 23: Rough Electrical

- Install new junction boxes (for outlets, switches, fixtures, fans, etc.)
- Upgrade electrical service

Step 24: Exterior Masonry

Step 25: Batt Insulation
- Install batt insulation in walls

Step 26: Concrete Work

Step 27: Drywall
- Repair sheetrock
- Texture sheetrock
- Remove wallpaper (remove, float, texture for paint)

Step 28: Garage Doors
- Install new garage doors

Step 29: Gutters

Step 30: Unfinished Wood Floors Installed

Step 31: Cabinetry
- Install new bathroom vanity cabinets
- Replace sink base cabinet bottom
- Repair cabinets
- Install new kitchen cabinets

Step 32: Interior Doors, Trim, and Millwork
- Repair interior doors and jambs
- Install interior doors
- Replace baseboards
- Replace interior door trim
- Install closet shelving
- Repair interior window trim (sill, apron, casing)
- Install attic access hatch

Step 33: Dust, Sweep, and Clean Before Painting
- Clean construction debris and dust before painting

Step 34: Paint Interior and Exterior

- Paint interior ceilings, walls, doors, trim, shelves, and cabinetry
- Paint exterior siding, doors, and trim

Step 35: Blown Insulation

- Add blown insulation in attic

Step 36: Countertops

- Install laminate countertops
- Install laminate backsplash
- Install granite countertops
- Install cultured marble bathroom vanity tops

Step 37: Tile

- Install tile for kitchen backsplash
- Install tile flooring
- Install tile bathtub surround
- Install tile for walk-in shower stall

Step 38: Vinyl Floors

- Install vinyl flooring

Step 39: Final HVAC

- Replace air vents
- Replace thermostat with programmable

Step 40: Final Plumbing

- Install kitchen sink
- Install disposal
- Install kitchen faucet
- Install bathroom faucets
- Install shower and tub fixtures
- Install backflow devices at exterior hose bibs
- Install new toilets

- ▪ Replace toilet seats
- ▪ Bring existing hot water heater to code

Step 41: Final Electrical

- ▪ Install GFCI outlets
- ▪ Install new outlets
- ▪ Install new 220-volt outlets (stove, dryer, window units, etc.)
- ▪ Install new switches
- ▪ Replace electrical face plates
- ▪ Install ceiling lights
- ▪ Install wall lights
- ▪ Install assembly-required light fixtures (chandelier, etc.)
- ▪ Install recessed light fixtures
- ▪ Install ceiling fans
- ▪ Install bathroom exhaust fans
- ▪ Install smoke detectors

Step 42: Finish Wood Floors

- ▪ Refinish hardwood floors

Step 43: Lockout

- ▪ Trim interior door bottom to accommodate new carpet or tile
- ▪ Install new exterior doorknob and deadbolt combo
- ▪ Install door stops
- ▪ Install interior door knobs
- ▪ Install towel bars
- ▪ Install toilet paper holder
- ▪ Install framed mirrors

Step 44: Mirrors and Shower Doors

- ▪ Install custom vanity mirrors
- ▪ Install glass shower door

Step 45: Appliances

- Install range hood
- Install over-the-range microwave oven
- Install range
- Install dishwasher

Step 46: Carpet

- Replace carpet

Step 47: Landscaping

- Add plants and mulch
- Repair fence

Step 48: Final Cleaning and Make-Ready

- Pressure wash (sidewalks, driveway, brick, stone)
- Final cleaning

Step 49: Accessories and Décor

Step 50: Punch

- Paint touchup
- Minor drywall repairs

As always, never attempt to perform anything that a licensed professional should do.

Glossary

1031 Exchange A transaction that allows you to defer capital gains taxes on profit realized from the sale of an asset such as real estate when that profit is reinvested in a "like kind exchange": real estate for real estate. Both the old property and the new property must be held for investment purposes and not be personal residences. The tax code also states that any proceeds must be reinvested within 180 days after the sale and that the new property must be identified in 45 days.

Abandon flip What you shout when your analysis shows that a flip isn't going to generate enough profit.

Accidental landlords Landlords who never intended to own a rented property and acquired it through inheritance, because the owners couldn't sell the property, or in some other way. These owners often are motivated to sell.

Additions Adding square footage requiring both a foundation and a roof. This is a good profit strategy in neighborhoods where the average selling price per square foot is at least twice the building cost per square foot.

Advertising A lead generation strategy in which investors attract interested buyers by using signs, postcards, and other methods.

Allied resources In your network or circle of influence, the people who can and will send you investment leads.

Amenity Comfort and convenience improvements that make a house easier to live in. Amenities make a house more suitable to a person's needs, such as adding a second sink in a bathroom or putting a pantry cabinet where there once was none.

Appraisal A professional evaluation of the market value of a property. An appraisal often is used to determine if a property is sufficient collateral for a loan. It is important to remember that appraisers, in the normal course of business, estimate the value of a property "as is," which means in its current condition. You can ask an appraiser to help you estimate the future selling price by giving you an "as built" appraisal, which is an estimate of the value of a property after the improvements are made.

Backup offer A secondary offer on a property that becomes effective once a primary offer falls through. Backup offers are a good safety net and can provide an incentive for the prospective buyer not to play hardball with post-inspection repairs. However, backup offers can fall apart as easily as primary offers, so don't abandon a first offer just because you have backups.

Bandit signs Cheap signs displayed in high-traffic areas to advertise a service or business (e.g., for advertising houses). Always check the city ordinances before posting bandit signs.

Base profit A predetermined percentage (usually 10 percent) of the eventual selling price of a rehab project. By adding a base profit amount in your offer price, you're accounting for the risk associated with the eventual selling price of the house.

Basic-level finish-out Basic design is functional, with no frills. If something needs to be replaced, it's replaced with the least expensive materials available. The house looks neat and clean but plain. *Repair* is the operative word. Replace only if necessary because of safety, function, and condition but not for design purposes.

Bonded Ensures that the contractor will fully comply to the terms of the contract (he'll finish the work and do it right). A failure to perform would result in compensation by the bonding company. There are three types of bonds: bid, performance, and payment.

Buyer's agent bonus A bonus amount paid to a buyer's agent at the closing. The bonus is above and beyond the standard buyer's agent's commission and sometimes is used by sellers to entice a buyer's agent to bring qualified buyers to a property.

Buyer's market A housing market where there is an abundance of houses for sale and fewer buyers interested in them.

Buying costs The costs incurred in buying a house, such as appraisal, survey, inspection, and other miscellaneous closing costs. One of the four components of *quiet costs*.

Buying criteria The factors that determine whether a house is a good investment. These criteria include the property being in your target neighborhood, in satisfactory condition, and in your price range.

Call to action Any component of an advertising message that motivates sellers to contact you (e.g., "Can Pay Cash for Your Home. Call Today!").

Capital gains tax A tax paid on profits from the sale of an asset that was purchased at a lower price. Capital gains are either short-term (if the purchase and sale occur in one year or less) or long-term (for transactions that take longer than a year).

Closing company A generic name for either an escrow company, a title company and in some areas a law firm or attorney that settles a real estate transaction.

Comparative market analysis A report generated from an MLS database comparing properties by similarities such as size, age, layout, and neighborhood. CMAs often are run to determine the average selling prices of properties in particular neighborhoods.

Construction contingency Most general contractors will build in an additional percentage (often 5 percent) to their project costs to handle unexpected labor, fluctuations in the prices of materials, and the repairs that inevitably arise during a construction project.

Contingent upon sale A contract provision in which a buyer's offer depends on the sale of his or her existing property.

Conversion Converting a space that already has a roof and/or foundation into heated and cooled space. This is an efficient way to add square footage without the high cost of a full-fledged addition. This could be a room for special activities (media room, game room, sewing room, or exercise room) or for added convenience (extra bathroom, breakfast room, laundry room, mud room, or family room).

Core advocates The people in your network or circle of influence who are well positioned to find you investment property leads (e.g., real estate agents, other investors).

Cost of money The points, interest, and fees associated with taking a loan to pay for a home purchase and/or improvements. One of the four components of *quiet costs*.

Could-dos The things you could do to reveal the untapped potential of a house. These are the extra things that make a house a better place to live and can maximize your profits. For example, adding amenities, opening floor plans, converting existing space into heated and cooled space, building additions, and making major layout changes all have the potential to increase your profit.

Creating value Improving a house so that the increase in the selling price is more than the cost of the improvements. Along with *finding value*, it is one of the two ways to profit from a flip.

Curb appeal The impression a house gives when viewing it from the street. Good curb appeal can be achieved through landscaping, lighting, and a clean and neat appearance. Your goal as a flipper is to make sure any potential buyer will be motivated to get out of the car and take a closer look at your property.

Custom-level finish-out The top-of-the-line level. You may replace functional and even up-to-date systems and features with even more high-end brands. The house systems represent the latest technological advancements and are in perfect working order. The structure and finish-out are architecturally and creatively designed and appointed.

Designer-level finish-out A designer house is intentional with respect to design and finishes. You may replace functional systems and features solely for the sake of improving the design. Everything is in new or "like new" condition.

Duration The time it takes to complete a construction task. Duration, along with *sequence* and *lead time*, is one of three key elements in scheduling a construction project.

Earnest money A deposit of money, accompanied by a signed real estate contract, from a potential home buyer indicating that she or he is serious about purchasing the property. The earnest money is deposited in an escrow account. When the property closes, the earnest money is deducted from the buyer's closing costs.

Escrow account A bank account set up by a neutral third party to hold the earnest money or profit from a 1031 Exchange.

Escrow company A neutral third party that holds the money and manages the documents in a real estate transaction.

Eventual selling price (ESP) The price at which a house will sell quickly after it has been fixed up. The ESP is the first part of the four-part FLIP Maximum Offer Formula.

Finding value Buying a house below retail market value. Along with *creating value*, it is one of the two ways to profit from a flip.

Finish-out level The process of comparing houses on the basis of design by identifying four distinct finish-out levels. This enables you to walk through a house quickly and immediately classify the design level as basic, standard, designer, or custom.

Fixed bid A legally binding contract to perform a defined amount of work at a fixed price.

Flip and fall The unfortunate circumstance that occurs when you're about to put a flip up for sale and the housing market tumbles below anyone's expectations.

Foreclosure A legal process in which a lender takes the title or forces the sales of a property as a result of the borrower's failure to comply with the terms and conditions of the mortgage. Properties that are in preforeclosure or foreclosure typically can be purchased by investors for below market value.

FSBO (For Sale by Owner) The selling of a property without representation by a licensed real estate agent.

General contractor A construction manager who takes responsibility for an entire construction project. The contractor manages the materials, labor, budget, schedule, and outcome of the project.

General liability insurance An insurance policy that provides liability protection for a business. We recommend that you or your general contractor have coverage before any workers set foot on a worksite.

Hard money lender See *private money lender*.

Holding costs The costs incurred by an investor on a property based on the time the house is owned during the flip. Holding costs is a component of quiet costs and includes taxes, insurance, utilities, and maintenance. One of the four components of *quiet costs*.

Homesteading The real estate investing strategy of buying a house and then living in it while you renovate it. Homesteading is an economical way to start flipping, since your holding costs are offset by your not having to pay for rent or a mortgage on a separate living space. The downside is that, for the duration of your flip, your living space is a construction zone.

Improvement analysis walkthrough Going through a house and capturing the list of improvements by asking, What must I do? What should I do? and What could I do?

Improvement costs per square foot The ratio of improvement costs to the square footage of the house. This useful value is used to help (1) estimate the complexity of improvements, (2) estimate the risk associated with improvements, (3) estimate how long it will take to make improvements, and (4) decide who will manage the construction project.

Improvement plan The plan you create that incorporates your must-should-could repairs and improvements and then forms the basis for the scope of work.

Individual worker A contractor whom investors hire individually rather than as part of a company. Using individual workers for a construction project is usually less expensive but requires more management.

Institutional lenders Financial institutions whose loans are regulated by the government (banks, mortgage brokers, and credit unions). They usually offer better interest rates than do private money lenders but have more stringent personal qualification requirements.

Junk fees The lender and title company fees that typically are charged to a buyer to process paperwork. These fees often can be reduced or waived depending on the circumstances.

Layout changes Redesigning within the existing heated and cooled space to enhance navigation, flow, organization, entertaining, and the like. Examples include creating an enlarged master bathroom, moving the kitchen, and combining two small bedrooms to make a master bedroom.

Lead generation The process of searching for or attracting investment property leads by prospecting, advertising, and networking.

Lead time The amount of time it takes before a task can start. For example, some materials have to be preordered, some trades tend to be backlogged, and sometimes permits have to be filed before work can begin. Lead time, along with *sequence* and *duration*, is one of three key elements in scheduling a construction project.

Listing agreement An agreement between a real estate broker (or agent representative) and a homeowner that authorizes the real estate agent to market and sell a house within a specified period of time for a specified fee, usually a percentage of the selling price.

Loan-to-value (LTV) ratio The ratio of a loan amount to a property's value; often used in calculating a maximum loan amount to an investor. Depending on the situation, the value could be the current value or the future, after-repair value. For example, a financial investor might set a 70 percent LTV limit, which means that the investor would lend a maximum of $70,000 on a $100,000 property.

Mechanic's lien A lien filed against real property on behalf of a contractor, subcontractor, or individual worker whose work improved a property and where payment for those improvements is in dispute. As a result, the owner's title to the property is not clear until the dispute or payment is settled. Without clear title, the property owner cannot transfer ownership.

Material specifications A list of all the specific materials needed to perform each task in a construction project. Style, brand, model, color, and size are all components of material specifications.

Minimum profit The total of the base profit and the rehab risk profit. This is the minimum profit required to compensate you for the risk associated with a flip. This is the fourth part of the Flip Maximum Offer Formula.

Must-dos The problems in a property that absolutely need to be fixed and are determined in your improvement analysis walkthrough. These are things one typically sees on home inspection reports. Is it functioning? What's its condition? You're determining what's dead or alive—what works and what doesn't.

Neighborhood misfit A house that has one or more permanent characteristics that cause it to deviate too far from the typical houses in the neighborhood and that cannot be mitigated or improved easily, thus increasing the risk of not achieving a timely or profitable sale. Examples are properties nearby railroad tracks, overhead power lines, seven-foot ceilings, and an irregularly sized lot.

Network A circle of friends, family members, business associates, vendors, and peers who know that you're an investor and understand what kind of property you are looking for. Your network sends you investment property leads.

One-call wonders Trades or suppliers who provide the management, materials, and labor for a specified construction task with one phone call (e.g., flooring companies, tile companies, insulation and roofing companies). One-call wonders guarantee their work, materials, and labor and require little or no management.

Openings Widening doorways, building a kitchen pass-through or removing walls, furdowns, kitchen fluorescent light boxes, and dropped ceilings. All these are examples of improvements that can give a home a more updated look and let in more light.

Paid in full A method of paying for a house in which the buyer comes to the closing with the funds necessary to pay off the seller completely (compare with *seller financing*).

Paper flip Doing a flip deal without having to lift a hammer or do any improvements. This also is called *wholesaling*. The entire transaction is done simply by exchanging paperwork (e.g., assigning an accepted contract to another investor for profit).

Point A fee associated with obtaining a loan, equaling 1 percent of the loan amount.

Preapproval A guarantee from a lender that a buyer will be able to qualify for a loan up to a specified amount as long as the house appraises for the amount of money requested.

Preforeclosure The period between when the lender formally notifies the borrower that the property will be sold at auction and the actual auction that transfers title of the property to another party or back to the lender. Some investors prospect for preforeclosed properties.

Prepayment penalty A fee, usually assessed by a private lender, for paying off a loan prior to a specified time frame. The penalty effectively sets a minimum duration of the loan, often six months, and compensates the lender for any interest lost on the loan.

Prequalification A lender's assessment of how much a buyer can borrow. The amount is based on information the borrower submits but does not include a formal application process. Thus, it is only a rough estimate and not a guarantee that a buyer will get loan approval.

Private money lender An individual or group that lends money to real estate investors; often called hard money lenders. The decision is based primarily on the merits of the opportunity rather than the personal finances of the borrower. The interest rates and origination fees are typically higher than with institutional, long-term mortgage loans.

Prospecting The careful examination of neighborhoods, foreclosure lists, or classified ads—anything that can lead you to a potential investment house. It's done to search for investment opportunities.

Qualified house A house that meets your buying criteria.

Qualified lead A lead that has both a qualified house and a qualified seller.

Qualified seller A seller who has the ability and motivation to sell for less than retail market value.

Qualifying The process of determining that a lead is good enough to warrant further investigation of the property and its owner.

Quiet costs The less obvious expenses associated with flipping a house (including your buying costs, holding costs, cost of money, and selling costs). These often overlooked costs can quietly consume your profit if they are not accounted for when you make an offer.

Real estate contract A binding legal agreement that details the sale of a property from one person to another. Real estate contracts should meet the legal requirements specified by contract law in general and should be in writing to be enforceable.

Rehab risk profit One percent of the eventual selling price for every $5 per square foot in construction costs. This element of your minimum profit takes into consideration the risk associated with fixing the house based on the complexity of the improvements.

Remodeler's risk insurance An insurance policy purchased by an investor that provides hazard protection for a house that is being remodeled.

REO Real estate owned by institutional lenders as a result of foreclosure, usually after an unsuccessful attempt to sell the property at auction. Some investors regularly purchase REO property for below market value.

Retail market value The price a house could sell for in an acceptable condition for the neighborhood and in the typical time it takes to sell a house in the neighborhood.

Right of redemption A borrower's right to redeem property that was taken at foreclosure. The borrower has a limited amount of time to exercise the right and must make full payment of any outstanding debt including interest, fees, and any other costs.

Rough work Work that takes place behind the walls, above the ceilings, and below the floors. It typically requires extensive management, high labor costs, and permits. Examples are framing, plumbing, electrical, HVAC, and drywall.

Scope creep This is where your original scope of work expands during a construction project as a result of poor planning or lack of commitment to the improvement plan. The result is reduced profit.

Scope of work A document that details the tasks, material specifications, quantities, and costs of a construction project.

Scout A person hired by an investor to prospect for properties.

Seller financing The seller of a house lends out or finances some or all of the money needed by an investor for the sale and fix. The seller and the buyer work out the terms of the loan, including the interest rate and payment schedule (compare with *paid in full*).

Seller's disclosure A legal form in which the seller discloses any known issues with the history, function, and condition of the systems of the house that may affect its value.

Seller's market A housing market where there is an abundance of buyers looking for houses and fewer houses for sale.

Selling costs The costs associated with selling a house, including real estate agent's commissions and the closing costs. One of the four components of *quiet costs*.

Sequence The order in which construction tasks should be performed. Sequence, along with *duration* and *lead time*, is one of three key elements in scheduling a construction project. The HomeFixers Fifty Steps to Rehabbing a House provides a tested sequence for completing a rehab.

Settlement statement A document presented before closing that itemizes all the incoming and outgoing funds for both the buyer and the seller in a real estate transaction.

Should-dos The finishing touches that affect the look and feel of a house and make it more beautiful; typically are noted during a property walk-through. Examples are flooring, countertops, trim, tile, lighting, and paint. The should-dos typically are dictated by the four levels of design: basic, standard, designer, and custom. Design choices should be dictated by the neighborhood norm.

Skinny flipping A risky strategy of taking on rehabs with small profit margins. Not recommended. With no margin for error, you could lose your shirt.

Specialized trades Typically businesses (e.g., a plumbing, countertop, or roofing company) or individuals who are highly skilled at performing a specific task from start to finish.

Staging The process of adding furnishings and decorations to a house to give prospective buyers a sense of what it would be like to live in a recently rehabbed house.

Standard-level finish-out Standard design is nice but inexpensive. If something needs to be replaced, choose materials that match the rest of the house. As with basic-level finish-out, never replace just for the sake of design.

Steps A collection of "like" construction tasks that are rolled up into one of the major construction steps. Rolling up many like tasks into fewer steps makes tasks much easier to manage. Although it takes hundreds of tasks to rehab a house, it takes only about fifty steps.

Subject to inspection clause A clause in an offer contract that gives a buyer a specified amount of time to back out of a deal without losing any earnest money if something shows up during an inspection that the seller is unwilling to remedy.

Subject to marketable title clause A clause in an offer contract that gives a buyer a specified amount of time to back out of a deal without losing any earnest money if something shows up in a title search (a cloud on the title or a lien on the property) that the seller is unwilling or unable to remedy.

Survey An official drawing or diagram of a property that shows property boundaries, easements, zoning, and the location of any improvements. Traditional lenders typically require surveys to be completed and submitted as part of their due diligence in issuing a loan.

Target audience A specific demographic or geographic group of people toward which an advertising campaign is aimed.

Targeting criteria The parameters that you use to select target neighborhoods (proximity, selling prices, sales activity, ages, appeal, and safety) in which to invest.

Target neighborhoods The neighborhoods you have determined best suit your investment needs. This is where you will aim your lead generation efforts.

Task The basic unit of work activity in construction. Tasks are grouped into steps. The task encompasses the work to be performed, the materials required, the trade who will perform it, where it will be done, and the expected cost. An example would be installing one elongated white toilet in the master bathroom with the help of a plumber for $200.

Title An official document establishing the true ownership of a property.

Title company A company that performs title searches and issues title insurance policies. In some areas, a title company also acts as the escrow or closing company.

Title insurance Insurance designed to protect against loss resulting from liens, judgments, and other claims arising from a title dispute after a house is closed upon.

Title search To determine whether a title is free and clear to be assumed by a buyer, the title company or the investor searches for the property title to find out whether any liens or other claims have been filed against the property.

Trades Another name for contractors who perform the specialized work of improving a house (e.g., a mason or a plumber).

Turnkey trades Contractors who give you a price for both the materials and the labor. They're specialists at doing one thing and can give you a fast, accurate, and consistent price for doing many of the tasks (carpet, countertops, paint, tile, appliances, etc.) in a rehab project. Also called *one-call wonders* because all it takes is one call to hire and manage them.

Unique selling proposition (USP) A unique slogan and/or advertising campaign that is strong enough and memorable enough to pull customers to a product, service, or opportunity.

Wholesaling A real estate investing strategy that focuses on finding houses for other investors to fix up and sell. Wholesalers either assign an accepted offer contract to another investor or purchase the house and sell it to another investor. The purchase and sale often are done on the same day as a double close.

Index

full-time flipping, 362–363

gambling and flipping, 7
garage doors, 265
general contractors. *See* contractors
Gladwell, Malcolm, 240
glossary, 371–386
Gold Rush of 1848, 44
grading and drainage work in, 257
gutters and downspouts, 265

hard money lenders, 197. *See also* private
    lenders
Hawthorne effect, 298
hazard insurance, 228–229
heating systems. *See* HVAC work
Hill, James, 364
hiring contractors, 288–292, **288**
holding costs, 163, **163**, 169
HomeFixers, 45, 102, 151, 192, 347, 364
HomeFixers Cost Assessment Report, 109
homeowners associations (HOA) newsletters for
    advertising, 61
HomeVestors, 58
house wrap, 259–260
HVAC work, 262, 270–271

identifying target neighborhoods, 35–38, **37**
improvement centers as source of cost
    information, 148–150
improvement cost estimate, 141–158, **141**. *See*
    also cost assessment; improvement
    identification
    Basic design standards and, 111, **113–118**, 125
    budgeting for, 244–247, **245**
    closing and, 224
    complexity vs. cost in, 153, **154**
    contractors and, competitive bidding in,
      247–251, 292
    cost assessment for repairs/improvements,
      109
    cost vs. value in, 120
    Custom design standards and, 112, **113–118**,
      125
    Designer design standards and, 112, **113–118**,
      125
    do-it-yourself estimating in, 145, 147–153,
      157
    fifty steps to rehabbing a house and,
      249–250, 251–275, 299, 364
    five percent contingency addition in, 152–153
    general contractors and, 145–147
    improvement centers as source of cost
      information in, 148–150
    labor costs and, 150–151
    make-hab projects and, 154
    Marshall & Swift's Home Repair and Remodel
      Cost Guide for, 151
    maximum offer vs., 142
    offers and, 211
    one-hundred-and-one most common tasks in,
      364–370
    per-square-foot estimates in, 155–156, **156**

professional input for, 144, 145–147, 157
quiet costs in, 159–169, **159**. *See also* quiet
    costs
rehab projects and, 154–155
remodel projects and, 155
restructure projects and, 155
rules of thumb for estimating in, 145,
    153–157, **155**
scope of work and, 246
specs and materials needed for, 246
spreadsheet to track costs in, 148–150, **149**
Standard design standards and, 111–112,
    113–118, 125
steps, tasks, and who will do the work in,
    247–251, **248**
stock-keeping unit (SKU) units for tracking
    costs in, 148
thoroughness, accuracy, speed in, 143, **144**
improvements identification, 10, 101–126. *See*
    also Fix stage; improvements cost estimate
    additions in, 123
    amenities added in, 122
    Basic design standards and, 111, **113–118**, 125
    closing and, preparing for, 229–230
    contractors for, 247–251
    conversions, converting space in, 123
    cost assessment for, 109
    cost vs. value in, 120
    could-do's in, 121–125, **121, 124**, 125
    Custom design standards and, 112, **113–118**,
      125
    Designer design standards and, 112, **113–118**,
      125
    fifty steps to rehabbing a house and,
      249–250, 251–275, 299, 364
    layout changes in, 123
    must, should, could questions in deciding
      what to do in, 102–103, 142
    must-dos in, 103–109, **104–108**, 125
    one-hundred-and-one most common tasks in,
      364–370
    openings, doors, windows, etc. in, adding,
      122–123
    repair requests from buyers and, 345
    scope of work in, 246
    should-do's in, 110–121, 125
    specs and materials needed for, 246
    Standard design standards and, 111–112,
      113–118, 125
    steps, tasks, and who will do the work in,
      247–251, **248**
individual workers vs. contractors, 279–280,
    280, 286–288. *See also* contractors
inspections, 133–135, **134**, 189, 222–224
    criteria for, 133–135, **134**
    foundation, 223
    specialists/professionals for, 224
    structural engineer for, 223
    subject to inspection clause and, 215
institutional lenders, 195, 197. *See also* financing
insulation
    batt type, 264
    blown in, 269